NOTES

FROM

THE

WARSAW

GHETTO

THE JOURNAL OF Emmanuel Ringelblum

NOTES

FROM

THE

WARSAW

GHETTO

THE JOURNAL OF

Emmanuel Ringelblum

EDITED AND TRANSLATED BY

Jacob Sloan

SCHOCKEN BOOKS • NEW YORK

First SCHOCKEN PAPERBACK edition 1974

10 9 8 7 6   86 87 88

Library of Congress Cataloging in Publication Data

Ringelblum, Emmanuel.
    Notes from the Warsaw ghetto.

    Reprint of the ed. published by McGraw-Hill, New York.
    1. Jews in Warsaw. 2. World War, 1939–1945—Personal narratives, Jewish.
3. Ringelblum, Emmanuel, 1900–1945. I. Title.
[DS135.P62W333 1974]   914.38'4'06924 [B]   74-10147

ISBN 0–8052–0460–1

ACKNOWLEDGMENTS

Parts of this book originally appeared in *Midstream,* Winter, 1956. I am indebted to that periodical for permission to reprint the material.

Dr. Philip Friedman, Miss Dina Abramowicz, and Mrs. Rose Klepfisz gave me valuable advice and assistance. The archives of the YIVO Institute for Jewish Research in New York were kind enough to make available for reproduction the maps of the Warsaw Ghetto and Poland in this volume.

Jacob Sloan

This English version of *Notes from the Warsaw Ghetto* is based upon the selection printed in *Bleter Far Geszichte*, Warsaw, March, 1948, and in the volume published by the Jewish Historical Commission of Warsaw in 1952. Unfortunately, it was impossible to secure access to the full text, either the original in Warsaw or the copy in Israel.

CONTENTS

Introduction   ix

Street Map of the Ghetto   xxviii

Map of Poland   xxx

Guide to Pronunciation   6

NOTES FROM THE WARSAW GHETTO

BEFORE THE GHETTO

Editorial Comments   3

1. January, 1940   7
2. February, 1940   14
3. March, 1940   24
4. April, 1940   32
5. May, 1940   36
6. August, 1940   44
7. September, 1940   46

MOVING INTO THE GHETTO

Editorial Comments   59

8. October, 1940   61
9. November, 1940   82

INSIDE THE GHETTO

Editorial Comments   97

10. December, 1940   105
11. January, 1941   120
12. February, 1941   124
13. March, 1941   135
14. April, 1941   146
15. May, 1941   169
16. June, 1941   185
17. August, 1941   194
18. September, 1941   210
19. October, 1941   221
20. November, 1941   229
21. December, 1941   239
22. January, 1942   244
23. April, 1942   256
24. May, 1942   258
25. June, 1942   290

THE GHETTO BREAKS UP: JULY, 1942– DECEMBER, 1942

Editorial Comments   307

26. July–December, 1942   309
     Afterword   345
     Chronology   348
     Index   361

INTRODUCTION

To millions of people, the Warsaw Ghetto will remain forever a symbol of man's inhumanity to man—and of the heroic resistance of the human spirit. For within these walls, in an area of about 1,000 acres, or 100 square city blocks, some half-million Jews were methodically ground to death in the course of less than three years. Yet, at the end of that time, when more than 90 per cent of the Ghetto's residents had been sent to their fate in extermination camps, armed resistance broke out—resistance so fierce that a regular German army group was required to put it down. The German army leveled the Ghetto to the ground; nothing remained but rubble and what the Nazis could not extirpate—the memory of those dread days.

It is that memory that has been preserved in the *Notes from the Warsaw Ghetto*. These *Notes* are the day-to-day eyewitness account by the man who was the best equipped to keep that account: Emmanuel Ringelblum, the archivist of the Warsaw Ghetto.

He was a man ideally fitted for the task he set himself in November, 1939, two months after the Nazis had overrun Poland—to record the whole story of the Jewish catastrophe for posterity. Born in 1900, Ringelblum had already established himself as one of the most promising of the Young Historians group in Warsaw when World War II broke out. He had written four books and innumerable monographs. Significantly, these were all based on research into original sources—despite the difficulties Ringelblum encountered in digging up authentic records. He spent tedious hours poring over dusty court records and minutes of council meetings for his works on the role that Jews played in the Kosciusco revolt of 1794, and on the history of the Jewish Community Council in Warsaw in the eighteenth century. Everywhere he looked for the vivid, personal detail that could illuminate the human meanings of the past. For Ringelblum was a social scientist in the larger sense of the word. He had begun his studies as an economist, later turned to sociology, and finally concentrated on history, while still retaining the tools of economics and sociology. He was a social historian, rather than a political scientist; he saw history as primarily the interplay of social, economic, and institutional forces, and only secondarily as the effects of the actions of powerful individuals.

But if Ringelblum had been only a social historian, however talented, if he had not been deeply immersed in the experience of his generation, we would not have had the *Notes*. For these, as their author repeats time and again, are not the observations of a single man. They are one man's cullings from the experiences and information supplied by a large group—several dozens—of people from various backgrounds. For Ringelblum was by conviction an active practitioner of popular education, a communal worker, a political party member, a dedicated man of the people.

Emmanuel Ringelblum's personal history is instructive. At eighteen, he was living with his parents in the small town of Nowy Soncsz, at the foot of the hills in Western Galicia. He was attending a *gymnasium*, the European cross between a high school and a junior college. His family, formerly well-to-do, was now impoverished, and Ringelblum had to work his way through school. His days were full. All morning and until two in the afternoon he studied at the *gymnasium;* then he tutored other students. Of course, he had his own school work to do. But, before turning to it, he spent several hours every day at a self-education group conducted by the branch of the Labor Zionist movement he belonged to. But he was not content with self-improvement; Ringelblum's social conscience drove him to organize evening courses for working men and for the pietistic Orthodox youth, the Chasidim, whose learning was completely theological.

In the fall of 1919, Ringelblum left home and enrolled at the University of Warsaw. There he continued the same pattern—the classic pattern of the poor university student precariously earning his own keep. Again, he showed himself to be exceptionally social-minded. Evenings he taught courses subsidized by the Central Jewish School Organization of Poland (CJSO). The pay was meager; many days Ringelblum literally went hungry. But he was an idealistic teacher, and he quickly made his influence felt through sheer weight of character. Soon he became the principal of a large evening school in Warsaw; then, chairman of the educational council for all the five evening schools. He was the favorite of the many hundreds of young workers who attended these schools after working hours. In addition, he organized an extracurricular central club for all evening students, meeting Saturday afternoons and evenings when there was no class. He ran meetings, lectures, special-interest classes. His enthusiasm was infectious.

All this time, Ringelblum was attending the University of Warsaw. There, too, he involved himself in extracurricular projects. He led the fight of the General Academic Federation of Jewish Students to induce the government to reduce tuition fees. He also was active in the Federation's self-aid organization, which maintained a cooperative kitchen, free loan society, and the like. And then, from 1920 to 1927, he was on the central committee of the Labor Zionist Young Workers Federation of Poland, and published in its journals.

Most of this work was voluntary, as well as time-consuming. Ringelblum earned very little and had to supplement his teaching income with tutoring. He was forced to prolong his studies. Nevertheless, he persisted; in 1927 his doctoral dissertation on the "History of the Jews in Warsaw Up to the Expulsion of 1527" was completed. It was published in 1932 by the Warsaw section of the Polish Historical Society and won immediate recognition as an authoritative work.

Between 1927 and 1939 Ringelblum taught history in a *gymnasium* in Warsaw. Absorbed as he was in scholarly research and writing, he managed to find the time to supervise night classes for adults in 165 towns throughout Poland, and to develop sport clubs, choirs, dramatic groups, music circles, libraries, and summer camps. All the while he was a devoted member of the left wing of the Labor Zionist movement.

There is an ancedote about Ringelblum's political loyalty that illustrates his character. Though Ringelblum was very busy, he made it a point never to miss any of his party's public functions. One evening, he was detained and came late to a memorial meeting in honor of Ber Borochov, the party's brilliant theoretician. The hall was packed, and the police would not let him in. Ringelblum paced back and forth in front of the hall in the cold December air all evening. "This is my way of paying my respects to Borochov's memory," he said, "though I may catch a cold doing it!" This balance of reverence for the intellect and ironic self-deprecation is typical of the author of the *Notes*.

The last few years before the outbreak of the war, Ringelblum was on the staff of the American Joint Distribution Committee, a philanthropic Jewish organization. During these years, too, he helped set up a historical section of the Yiddish Scientific Institute (YIVO), whose headquarters were in Vilna, and became the chairman of a Young Historians Circle.

The last week of August, 1939, Ringelblum was in Geneva as a delegate to the twenty-first World Zionist Congress. Panic broke out among the Polish delegates when news came of Germany's mobilization. Some of the Polish delegates decided to go to Palestine, others to fly to Paris or London, and from there to try to emigrate to the United States. But Ringelblum, with the other delegates of his party, decided to return to Warsaw. It was a difficult and perilous journey. They traveled through Italy in sealed trains, then through Yugoslavia, through Hungary—under police supervision—and finally across the Polish border. By that time, war had broken out: Germany had invaded Poland. They journeyed to Warsaw in a blacked-out train, bombed by German planes en route. But the morning after Ringelblum arrived in Warsaw, he was at his desk in the JDC office.

The sixth day of the war, when Warsaw was seriously threatened by encircling German forces, and a mass evacuation of the city had begun, Ringelblum made the second crucial decision. He would stay and not run. There were two reasons for this decision: his relief work for the JDC and his position as one of a triumvirate representing his party.

Many JDC workers were badly wounded in the bombing of Warsaw. The building where the JDC was housed was hit; in the light of the flames Ringelblum rescued the most important documents and materials from the JDC files (a presage of his historic role as the saver of records!). The siege of Warsaw lasted longer than anyone had expected. The city held out for three weeks before it succumbed, weak from hunger and thirst. Jews played an active part in the defense of Warsaw—for patriotic reasons, and because they had special reason to fear the Nazis. Tens of thousands of Jewish workers who had lived from hand to mouth and had no reserves to fall back on began to hunger. Thousands of refugees who had fled to the safety of Warsaw from the captured provinces now found themselves trapped and helpless in the capital. It was clear to Ringelblum that the people of Warsaw could not afford to sit back and wait for the bombing to stop. With the approval of the other JDC workers, he called an urgent meeting of community leaders. They decided to set up public kitchens immediately. These were donated by the various organizations represented at the meeting—federations of professionals, labor unions, political parties, handicraftsmen's guilds, relief institutions (the Jewish community of Warsaw was highly organized). Ringelblum and the other JDC men were constituted a committee to coordinate all relief activities. Besides one hot meal a day, the refugees were provided with lodgings and clothing. Ringelblum worked twenty hours a day; he was the inspiration of the others. He could barely stand, he was so tired; yet he worked on.

After Warsaw fell, the plight of the Jews became even more difficult. The Jewish section of Warsaw (later to become the Ghetto) had been the worst-bombed section of the city. The Jews had to wear special badges of identification on their arms; thousands were forced into labor battalions or sent to labor camps. Jewish-owned factories and businesses were expropriated. Jews were put on starvation rations. Jewish children were turned out of the public schools; no Jewish schools were allowed to function. Demoralization threatened.

Ever larger numbers of the Jewish population of Warsaw urgently needed relief, but the Germans refused to permit it. Ringelblum, who spoke German fluently, made the rounds of the German occupation offices, urging in the name of the neutral JDC that the relief work not be interrupted. After one such appeal he was beaten till he bled by a brutal German officer. Still bleeding, Ringelblum returned to his office in the Central Relief Committee and went back to work.

It is at this point that the *Notes from the Warsaw Ghetto* begin.

In September, 1939, Emmanuel Ringelblum was thirty-nine years old. He was married to a school teacher from a good middle-class Warsaw family, and was the father of a seven-year-old boy, Uri, whose bright sayings the proud father was fond of quoting. The family lived in one of the apartment-house courtyards on Leszno Street that figure so frequently in the *Notes;* their apartment was large, and the Ringelblums were able to put up out-of-town visitors.

Ringelblum himself was tall for a Polish Jew, about 5 feet 10, slim, black-haired, vivacious, full of jokes, eminently gregarious—not at all the pedant in private life. If one were to look at a photograph of Ringelblum, one would experience a flash of immediate recognition: here is the face of someone we know, someone we have certainly met before. There is something very pleasant about the face of this young man —nothing strained, or disturbing. That essentially is the key to the personality of the author of the *Notes*—a relaxed relation to people and things as they are, a kind of temperamental equilibrium. But this conventional sanity, though important for a reasonable man to retain in unreasonable circumstances, was not enough to sustain a man through the accomplishment of a task that was to win him immortality. For that, something special was required—an imaginative enthusiasm that was beyond mere fanaticism. Here again, elements in Emmanuel Ringelblum's character that had been clearly adumbrated before the war were sharpened into focus by the Ghetto experience. The man had always been capable of expanding small ideas, organizing them into concrete plans, and—most important—seeing them through. "One word was enough to set him off; he would immediately begin to talk about a dozen workers, ten books, all sorts of plans," as a co-worker of Ringelblum's has put it in private conversation. There was something in the author of the *Notes* of the *Luftmensch,* the "man of air" epitomized in Jewish fiction by Sholem Aleichem as Menachem Mendel, a European parallel to Mark Twain's Colonel Sellers—the furious dreamer of grand projects. But Ringelblum, who possessed no genuis for deep and original work of his own, had a wonderful sense of balance. It was typical of him that he could understand those opposed to his own strongly held political views—an unusual phenomenon among European radical Zionists. At heart, Emmanuel Ringelblum was a pragmatist. He was the opposite of doctrinaire.

Some time at the beginning of 1943, more than three years after his first entry in the *Notes from the Warsaw Ghetto,* Emmanuel Ringelblum wrote a summary account of the underground archives with which the notes, as well as his name, are indissolubly linked. He called his report simply "The O.S." These initials, as he goes on to explain in his usual careful fashion, stand for Oneg Sabbath (Sabbath celebrants), the secret name of that "society of brothers" that he had gotten together to preserve the record of his time and people for posterity.

"I laid the cornerstone for the O.S.," says Ringelblum, "in October, 1939." At that time, the Jews of Warsaw lived in terror of raids and execution by firing squad. Fearful of being picked up on charges of sedition, they went so far as to burn any books that might be considered dangerous—and would commit nothing to writing that might be regarded as suspect if found during a raid. But Ringelblum began collecting material about the current situation practically at once. What impelled him to do so, when it was so obviously perilous an act?

First, it was a kind of reflex action. Ringelblum was a historian; written information, data, were the material of his craft. And now the long-dreaded catastrophe of war had begun. An anti-Semitic maniac had invaded Eastern Europe, an area with the largest concentration of Jews in the world. The world had to be persuaded that Hilter's threats against the Jews were more than propaganda. The United States, in particular, had to be made aware of what was happening, must be induced to intervene in the war—the United States was the only world power capable of defeating Germany. (Russia, of course, was Germany's ally; besides, her strength was untested.) By keeping records of what the Germans were doing to the Jews of Poland, Ringelblum was appealing to the conscience of humanity. Later, as the war dragged on, and it became all too clear that the Jews of Poland could be saved from physical extermination only through a miracle, the keeping of the records became meaningful as a gesture for posterity—a pure historical act. The future would avenge what the present could not prevent.

Here Ringelblum was in his element. For he was a trained and professional social historian. He knew what posterity should be told, needed to know, if it were to understand what his generation were going through in this time of catastrophe. And he knew how to go about accumulating that information. It could not be done haphazardly by individuals, however zealous, however well-informed. Like all modern scientific study, it had to be a group effort. There had to be a staff; they had to be trained in interviewing techniques; the informants had to be carefully selected on the basis of representative occupations, social status, geographic distribution, and so forth. The data had to be assembled, checked, interpreted, and written. Monographs had to be done: community histories, special subject treatments of things like health, currency, production.

But all this was in the future. Meanwhile, it was October, 1939; the Germans had just occupied Warsaw; Emmanuel Ringelblum was working twenty hours a day at relief for the JDC. He was in a key position.

> I . . . had daily lively contact with everything that was happening. . . . News came to me of every event affecting Jews in Warsaw and its suburbs. Almost every day I saw delegations from the Polish provinces.

But that was not enough. Ringelblum had a historical mission.

> At night, when my work at the committee was done, I made notes of what I had heard during the day. In time, these notes accumulated into a large volume of 100 closely written pages mirroring that period. Later, I worked the daily notes over, at first into weekly and then into monthly summaries. This I did when the Oneg Sabbath staff was quite large.

From the first, he tried to persuade people to collaborate with him. He needed a staff. It was hard finding the right people. Finally, in May, 1940, he succeeded and turned his individual note taking into a collective record keeping, an "archive." Rabbi Simon Huberband, who had originally kept notes of his own disguised as marginal comments on religious texts, became Ringelblum's right-hand man. Hirsch Wasser, a refugee from Lodz, became secretary. Like Ringelblum, Wasser had been active both politically and communally. Wasser was an invaluable acquisition: "His daily contacts with hundreds of refugee delegations from all over the country made possible hundreds of community monographs—the most important material in the O.S." Menachem Kohn became the O.S.'s financial sponsor; nor did he think himself too proud to take on onerous as well as dangerous missions, carrying written information from one part of Warsaw to another.

The Ghetto was instituted in November, 1940. After the first commotion, the Jews of Warsaw settled down into their imprisonment. They began to give and attend lectures, courses, concerts. People relaxed a bit. "Paradoxically, the establishment of the Ghetto, and with it the enclosure of Jews within walls, furnished even greater opportunity for the archives to function." The Jews felt safe behind the Ghetto walls. They were among their own. They had a two-thousand-year-old tradition of mutual aid. They set up House Committees, community kitchens, institutions for the aged, for homeless children, refugees. They talked freely, even argued politics out in the open, in coffee houses, at public meetings. They thought that the Germans weren't interested in what the Jews did behind their walls—whom could they harm? True, it was common knowledge that there were many Jews who worked as informers for the Gestapo—it was a way of making a living, albeit a despicable one. But all They were interested in was uncovering secret hoards of merchandise, gold, smuggled goods, and the like.

In this "free society of slaves" (the phrase is Ringelblum's) the O.S. archive could expand. Dozens of people joined. The material they collected grew. The difficulty was no longer one of finding capable people to help, but rather of keeping out the loose-lipped. For the work had to be kept conspiratorial. Every informant was carefully checked before he was interviewed. Journalists were kept out (they are notoriously voluble, even when honest), and anyone at all associated with the suspect Jewish Council. The O.S. could take no chances on Gestapo agents finding out about the archives.

By the beginning of 1943, so much good material had been amassed in the O.S. archive that the staff all felt "the time was ripe for some kind of larger treatment—if not a synthesis, at least several summaries of what was known about developments and important problems in the life of Polish Jewry." It was an ambitious plan that could not be realized. Life in the Ghetto was too insecure. The O.S. contributors lived in fear of their lives. The people who volunteered to write various chapters of the summaries could not finish. Many of them were seized by the vicious Jewish police and dragged off to the Umschlagplatz ("Trading Place"), the plaza separating the Ghetto from the "Aryan" part of Warsaw, for shipment to extermination camps. Others were shot to death in Warsaw itself; still others were fortunate to escape to the other side of the Wall. The O.S. editorial committee decided to divide the whole summary into four sections. Ringelblum himself undertook to do two of the sections—those dealing with cultural and literary history. Outside specialists were called in for help on specific points.

At hour-long editorial sessions we mulled over the main points in each of the themes. What we wished to do was to draw the author's attention to specific ⌐rends, and to indicate the lines along which he could develop his theme—not that we wished to force any of the authors to follow a particular line of our own. Some of the themes we worked out dealt with the Law and Order Service (Jewish police), corruption and demoralization in the Ghetto, community activity, and the educational system. We drew up special questionnaires designed to elicit information on such subjects as the relations between Jews and non-Jewish Poles, smuggling, the situation in various trades, the special problems affecting young people and women.

But at this very moment, the large-scale deportation of most of the remaining Jews in the Warsaw Ghetto began. Three hundred thousand Jews were sent to their death.

The O.S. work was interrupted. Only a handful of our friends kept pencil in hand and continued to write about what was happening in Warsaw in those calamitous days. But the work was too holy for us, it was too deep in our hearts, the O.S. was too important for the community—we could not stop.

Instead, they began to collect material about "the charnel house of European Jewry—Treblinki." They pieced together a picture of the experiences of Jews sent to Treblinki from the provinces. In December, 1943, Ringelblum was still optimistic —not about his own chances for survival, but that:

> With a little peace we may succeed in making sure that not a single fact about Jewish life at this time and place will be kept from the world.

That peace, of course, never came. In January, 1943, the first abortive uprising in the Warsaw Ghetto had taken place. Though there is no mention of this in the *Notes* (the whole underground movement had to be clandestine), Ringelblum himself was a leader of the resistance. He was smuggled out of the Ghetto just before the uprising in April, 1943. His life was too valuable to imperil. But on March 7, 1944, Emmanuel Ringelblum was executed among the ruins of Warsaw, together with his wife and twelve-year-old son, Uri.

The archives, meanwhile, together with Ringelblum's notes, had been cached deep under the ruins of the Warsaw Ghetto just before the Warsaw Uprising began in the spring of 1944. They were buried in two sections. The first section was located in September, 1946; the second, at the beginning of December, 1950. Ringelblum's notes were found sealed in a rubberized milk can.

The archives had survived the archivist, and the archivist's personal *Notes from the Warsaw Ghetto* with them.

"Everyone wrote," Ringelblum says:

> . . . journalists and writers, of course, but also teachers, public men, young people—even children. Most of them kept diaries where the tragic events of the day were reflected through the prism of personal experience. A tremendous amount was writ-

ten; but the vast majority of the writings was destroyed with the annihilation of Warsaw Jewry during the resettlement days. All that has remained is the material we have preserved in our Ghetto archive. . . .

And then there were my own notes. . . . They are particularly important for the first year of the war, when other people were not keeping diaries. My weekly and monthly reports not only give the facts about the most important happenings of the time—they also offer an evaluation of them. Because I was active in the community, these evaluations of mine are important as expressions of what the surviving remnant of the Jewish community have thought about their everyday problems.

Thus, briefly, Ringelblum characterizes his notes, placing them against the background of the universal mania for keeping diaries, and assessing their historical significance as representative of the mood of his time—and not, by inference, of his own personality.

Both points are well taken and do honor to the precise objectivity Ringelblum aimed for at all times.

For the very first thing to understand about *Notes from the Warsaw Ghetto* is that they really are notes toward a history of the times, and nothing else. They are arranged in chronological order, and were written by a single individual, but they are not a diary. Diaries usually restrict themselves to the lived experience of the diarist; they reflect his feelings and thinking; they are personal outpourings, confessions of a sort. *Notes from the Warsaw Ghetto* is nothing like that. Much of the material Ringelblum recorded he heard or saw himself; but he rarely describes how he felt about it. A great deal of the material came to him from outside sources: refugees he interviewed during the day's work; superintendents of the public kitchens; House Committee workers; people in the street he spoke to; smugglers; employees of the Jewish Council; friends, of course; even the universally detested Jewish policemen. Then, too, he jotted down information from the O.S. archives: about incidents that took place in the provinces, about the cost of living and the rate of currency exchange (there was a complete monograph on the subject); about personal experiences (like the first-person story told by a woman who spent a harrowing night in a provincial railroad-station waiting room, with its surprise ending).

The scope of these notes is very wide. Ringelblum tries to encompass all of life within the Ghetto, and as much as he can of what was happening in the rest of Poland—the rise, spread, and decline of typhus; night clubs; informing; clandestine religious education; the techniques of beggars; the attitudes of German soldiers recuperating in military hospitals in the Ghetto, of Polish tax collectors. He tries to be as comprehensive as the O.S. archives, which contained "a photographic reproduction . . . the same event . . . described by a number of different persons from different vantage points."

Whereas in the diary the diarist is usually the hero, in the *Notes* it is the Ghetto that is the hero, and not Emmanuel Ringelblum. He does not try to conceal his feelings (how could he?), but he makes every effort to be objective ("the whole truth . . . however bitter . . . our photographs are true, not retouched"). He enjoins his colleagues in the O.S. to avoid preconceptions, even about the abominable enemy. Only so can they keep the human touch, the common passion —and the *Notes*, for all their terseness, are full of passion. The tone must be one of "epic calm . . . the calm of the graveyard."

The final injunction that the author of the *Notes* seems to have addressed to himself is one that he never explicitly declares—yet it is striking in every line: Keep your head out of the center of the picture; remain only an eye and an ear: the eye that looks at the shed in the graveyard where the corpses are heaped, the ear into which a respectable merchant can confide that "if it were not for smuggling, we should all die of hunger." This withdrawal from the center of the stage is not false modesty on Ringelblum's part. It is simply that *he* does not matter. The *Notes* are not about him—they are about the Ghetto. So when he is informed on and thrown into jail for a while, he only comments on what a disgusting thing that was, informing on Muni (his name for himself). And later he mentions some information he received "when I was in jail." Emmanuel Ringelblum may be all in all to himself, but to the Ghetto, no man is terribly important.

In the *Notes* Ringelblum functions as a mirror where the Ghetto reveals itself—in snatches, flashes, odds and ends of events, ideas, experiences, suffering, heroism. The *Notes* cannot be complete; they cannot attempt to make a coherent whole out of these fragments, because they are, after all, only notes toward a history of the time, not the history itself.

Some of the notes are perfectly clear. "A decree was published stating. . . ." The context is one of discriminatory laws directed against the Jews of Warsaw or other parts of the Government General of Poland by the representatives of the German occupation. There are many such decrees sprinkled through the book; they must be related to the time when they were published and to the specific situation at that time. Sometimes the relationship is made perfectly clear: A decree making leaving the Ghetto without authorization punishable by death is preceded and followed by cases of persons leaving the Ghetto without authorization and being executed as a result. But in other instances, the connection between one note and another—often the very next one—is less direct, or the all-important context is not provided. One has to guess. For example:

Extraordinary slackening of kinship ties. There are frequent cases where They come and search behind one particular picture, because They know there is foreign currency or gold hidden there.

We know from the very first page of the notes who the cryptic "They" refers to. "They" are the Germans. It is not a good idea to mention Their real name too often; the notes may be confiscated by Them. For the same reason, the notes have many phrases and passages in pidgin Hebrew. "They" can easily understand Yiddish, the language of the notes, Yiddish being basically a medieval variant of German. But "They" would have more trouble decoding the Hebrew.

But what is the link between the evaluative statement that kinship ties have slackened and the fact that "They" know just where to look for concealed valuables? The answer is clear: because people no longer protect even their own relatives, they are willing to inform on members of their families, and lead the Germans to the family treasure!

Then there are notes so cryptic, or where the references are so personal, that one cannot even guess at their meaning. "Heard from someone that Jews may not address police chiefs by title. Heard about that, and about the beard."

We cannot even hazard a guess about the beard story.

Another characteristic of the notes is the variety of tone. The author is marking down not only the bare facts of Ghetto life—the people, the places, the institutions—but also how people felt about those facts. Life was grim, and, on the whole, this is a grim record—of panic, suffering, demoralization, cruelty, and death, relieved only by the occasional humane actions of exceptional individuals. The style matches the information: These things are told plainly, in concrete detail. The over-all style is one of controlled understatement. For the author was consciously trying to communicate "what the common man experienced, thought, and suffered." So he shuns the subtle ratiocinations of the intellectual, or the imaginative passion of the artist—though these too are reported, in their place. But, generally, things are said straight out, without embellishment—and, thus nakedly stated, they stand forth in larger-than-life size. There was no need to add dramatic quality to the Ghetto: it had its own rising and falling, its own tension. Incidents and characters were all at hand; nothing needed to be invented. The catastrophe followed its own inexorable movement. No pace had to be introduced.

> The war transformed Jewish life in the cities of Poland with tremendous speed. Each day differed from its predecessor. It was like a motion picture, in which a series of still shots are run together in rapid sequence. . . . It has been important to seize each day's development while it . . . was still fresh and pulsing —because each day was like a decade in ordinary times.

Most of the notes are overpoweringly sober. But the common man in the Ghetto had his own way of relieving tension— by making up and telling jokes. The *Notes* tell dozens of these jokes—sardonic, bitter, violent, wishful. Why did Hitler put on brown drawers when he invaded Russia? What did the newborn baby say to its mother? How did the rabbi of Ger answer Churchill when that great statesman came to him for advice? And that man who was buried up to his neck in the sand—what did *he* say when "They" let him go, laughing that it was "only a joke." These jokes have a desperate quality; they are all the stronger for being part of a tradition of wit that Jews share with Negroes and other people who have a long history of oppression behind them. In *Notes from the Warsaw Ghetto* humor is a brilliant counterpoint to the dominant note of repressed anguish. The author himself, for all his dedication to inconspicuousness, cannot resist: "In the liberated Poland of the future they shall have to put up a monument to the smugglers."

Finally, the anonymity of style, the awkward prosiness, is not to be regarded simply as a failure of esthetic taste. These are jottings, deliberately left lean for the future historian to put the meat of interpretation on them. A fuller style would have hindered the work of analysis. And they were part of the character of the Ghetto; that was not the time and place for gracious ornamentality. Besides, this was a highly moral man with a strong sense that his time was running out, and he had a destiny to fulfill. That destiny was not his own; these notes were not his private creation, where he might display his own sensibility. He was acting as the mouthpiece of his time and place and people. These notes were to serve mankind —as a warning of how men consume one another, and yet can love one another. Service, as he put it, was the motto of the group he represented.

The O.S. was a brotherhood. ". . . truly an order of brothers; on our banner we have inscribed the motto: 'Be ready to sacrifice. Be loyal to one another. And serve society.' "

JACOB SLOAN

May, 1958

HAGSTROM CO., N.Y.

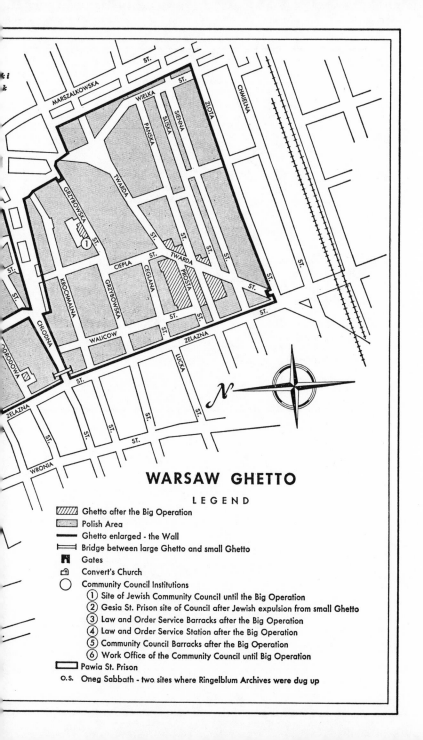

WARSAW GHETTO

LEGEND

- ▨ Ghetto after the Big Operation
- ▨ Polish Area
- ── Ghetto enlarged - the Wall
- ⊨ Bridge between large Ghetto and small Ghetto
- ⬛ Gates
- 🏛 Convert's Church
- ◯ Community Council Institutions
  - ① Site of Jewish Community Council until the Big Operation
  - ② Gesia St. Prison site of Council after Jewish expulsion from small Ghetto
  - ③ Law and Order Service Barracks after the Big Operation
  - ④ Law and Order Service Station after the Big Operation
  - ⑤ Community Council Barracks after the Big Operation
  - ⑥ Work Office of the Community Council until Big Operation
- ▭ Pawia St. Prison
- O.S. Oneg Sabbath - two sites where Ringelblum Archives were dug up

Baltic Sea

POLAND

- Boundaries of Poland 1943
- Boundaries of Poland 1939
- ■ Labor Camps
- O Extermination Camps
- ++++ Railroads

Szczecin
Slupca
Gdynia
Gdansk
Tczew
Starogrod
Grodzisk
Bydgoszcz
Olsztyn
Lomza
Torun
Bialystok
Vistula
Poznan
Wloclawek
Kutno
Lowicz
R.
Treblinki
Warsaw
Siedlce
Zielona Gora
Chelno
Bzura
Skierniewice
Pruszkow
Kalisz
Zgierz
Zyrardow
Glowno
Lodz
Pabianice
Lignica
Wroclaw
Piotrkow
Tomaszow-Mazowieck
Radom
Lublin
Chelm
Majdanek
Nysa
Opole
Czestochowa
Kielce
Ostrowiec
Bedzin
Vistula
Sosnowiec
Belzec
Zabrze
Katowice
Oswiecim
Cracow
Tarnow
Przemysl
Lwow
Kavnas
Vilna

BEFORE THE | GHETTO

Editorial comment

Emmanuel Ringelblum's Notes from the War-
saw Ghetto *begin in January, 1940, three months after the
occupation of Warsaw by the German army. In September,
1939, the Germans found some 360,000 Jews living in Warsaw.
The Jews had fought desperately with the Polish army
against the overwhelming Nazi blitzkrieg; Ringelblum notes
several instances of individual bravery. They had formed a
special Jewish Committee to aid in the defense of Warsaw
during the three-week siege. No one could have anticipated
the genocide that was to annihilate the mass of European
Jewry during World War II. But the experiences of German
Jewry under Nazism had made it quite plain that Polish Jews
could expect nothing but evil from a Nazi occupation of their
country. It would be some time before Hitler was to try to
fulfill his promise to extirpate all of Jewry from the conti-
nent of Europe. Soon after the occupation of Warsaw, however, a series of special decrees were directed against Warsaw
Jewry. The economic, political, and social ruination of the
Jews was intended—with their physical "liquidation" as the
inevitable result. The property of the Jews was registered,
their bank accounts frozen, their factories and businesses expropriated, making it almost impossible for them to earn a
living. The Jewish quarter of Warsaw was termed a quarantine area, and the refugees who poured into Warsaw from the*

3

provinces—both Jewish and Christian, either voluntarily, or deported—were forced to live in that area. Jews were further set off from the rest of the city's population by having to wear a special arm band—a white brassard 10 centimeters wide with a six-pointed Jewish star. They were forced into labor brigades and put on very meager rations.

It was the Nazi practice to force the Jews themselves to administer the discriminatory decrees that produced their suffering. A veteran Jewish community leader, Adam Czerniakow, was called to the Gestapo on October 4, 1939, and ordered to appoint a new Jewish Council to supplant the old, limited Jewish Community Council of Warsaw. (Until modern times, Community Councils had been autonomous self-regulating bodies, accepted by the Jewish communities in Eastern Europe as the local authority in Jewish religious life. But since the emancipation of Polish Jewry and the rise of a secular society, they had lost their original representative function.) The new Jewish Council was to be a government-in-miniature, but without a trace of independence. It was the Council's duty to furnish the work battalion demanded by the Occupying force; to maintain peace and order (through an Ordnungsdienst, or Law and Order Service, consisting of Jewish policemen); to train skilled workers; to attend to sanitation and medical needs—particularly to combat epidemics. For these purposes they could levy taxes (Ringelblum has many harsh words about the inequities of the tax system). Later, after the Ghetto was set up, the Council also organized a workshop where raw materials allotted by the Germans were finished by Ghetto workmen and artisans for the Wehrmacht. The Jewish Council was from the first in an unenviable position. Its members could satisfy neither their despotic Nazi masters, whose demands were impossible, nor the Jewry of Warsaw, who viewed them as a thinly disguised German agency, and, as such, necessarily evil.

It was a year before the Ghetto was set up. In November, 1939, one had been projected, but the Warsaw Jews had succeeded in averting it by paying a huge sum of money. Meanwhile, the "Jewish quarter of Warsaw" was at the mercy of Nazi soldiers, abetted by their Lett and Lithuanian auxiliaries and the riffraff of the city. The notes for this period are full of incidents of individual, casual brutality—the usual random violence of an occupying army, in this case intensified by the conviction of the conquerors that they had at their mercy a species of submen.

There was as yet no organized armed resistance—the situation was still too fluid, too novel, not sufficiently desperate. Warsaw Jewry was in a state of shock after the bombings of their homes, the loss of their livelihoods, the dislocations and stresses of readjustment to living on the edge of catastrophe. Everything was still in a state of emergency; the city teemed with strangers—German soldiers, refugees from the provinces, foreign civilian administrators. Indeed, the whole country was in a state of upheaval. The Germans and Russians had divided Poland between them: Germany taking a large western third for itself to be reincorporated into the Third Reich; Russia annexing an eastern third; and a buffer state, the Government General of Poland, being set up between the two armies, as an "unincorporated territory." The new Government General lay in the region between the Vistula and Bug rivers, and was ruled by a German Governor General, one Hans Frank, whose seat was in Cracow, not the former capital, Warsaw. Reports of disaster streamed into the city. People held their breath, waiting for the worst to happen.

At the end of April, 1940, the first ghetto was established in Lodz, the foremost industrial city of Poland. Now the picture began to become clearer. The Middle Ages were returning.

GUIDE TO PRONUNCIATION OF POLISH NAMES

POLISH VOWEL	ENGLISH EQUIVALENT
a	a, as in *arm*
e	e, as in *bed*
i	ee, as in *bee*
o	o, as in *honey*, or u, as in *but*
u	oo, as in *school*

POLISH CONSONANT	
c	ts, as in *Tsar*
j	y, as in *young*
w	v, as in *vice*
cz	ch, as in *charm*
rz	French j, as in *jeune*, or English *garage*
sz	sh, as in *shape*
ch	ch, as in Scottish *loch*

1/JANUARY, 1940

Dear Father,*

What happened in Wower, outside Warsaw, has been cleared up slightly. It was this way: Some Poles were sitting in a restaurant. Two German policemen came in (one of them a captain of the watch) and began to shout at the Poles. The latter took out revolvers (apparently there was only one) and shot the Germans. Some of the Germans shot were bandits. Nevertheless, They are demanding that the murderers be handed over. Meanwhile, They've ordered the body of the restaurant owner to be exhumed and hanged. He is to hang for all to see for seven days.

The consternation of Friday, December 30, was, it is now said, unfounded. Not a single German was killed. Word has it that this time it was thieves' work. Still another rumor is that a German soldier got into a fist fight at night on Towarowa Street and was knocked out.

The mortality among the Jews in Warsaw is dreadful. There

* The salutation at the head of certain notes was intended as camouflage. Ringelblum was not addressing anyone in particular, but, in the event the notes were discovered, the pretense that they were letters might save them—and their author—from destruction.

are fifty to seventy deaths daily. Before the war, the rate used to be ten. The burial tax rate has been fixed at 50 zlotys in Warsaw proper, and 100 zlotys in the suburb of Praga. In Radom the synagogue was burned down, as was the Jewish Council building. The same in Torun, where there were 1,000 people deported from Lodz. In Rajsze there are about 6,000–7,000 refuges from Kalisz, Lodz, Upper Silesia. The *lords and masters** not too bad. If you grease the right palms, you can get along. In Torun, Polish soldiers were shot, the Jews ordered to bury them. No Jews are taken on any jobs. Two Jews were standing on . . . , two *lords and masters* sprang out of a passing auto, dragged one of the Jews into the car, shouting, "You bandit!" What happened to the Jew unknown. Tonight Dr. Cooperman was shot for being out after eight o'clock. He had a pass. A Jewish worker who belonged to the labor battalion was killed in Praga.

The public announcement page in the *Lodz News* looks like a graveyard. Full of notices put in by the ethnic German trustees of Jewish firms calling on the firms' debtors to report the debts to the new trustees.

Many of the deportees die afterward as a result of the terrible experience. An elderly woman from Posen, who had walked 70 kilometers from Lewartow to Ostrow, died in Warsaw. The Jewish shopkeepers no longer keep their cash in drawers, in the usual way, but conceal it somewhere in the building—in chests, vessels, glasses, pots, or the like.

A sign on the main registry office at 26 Dluga Street: Eintritt Fuer Deutsche Soldaten Verboten [Out of Bounds for German Soldiers]. Because of the great dread of epidemics. A whole row of streets—Sliska, Rivna, and others—sealed off

---

* Italics are used to indicate Hebrew words and phrases in the notes. Since the Germans could understand Yiddish, Ringelblum used Hebrew either to conceal particularly damaging information, or for the purposes of irony— as in this instance. Brackets [ ] indicate an editorial insertion, to supply missing material.

with barbed wire. Today saw a house on Grzybowska Street that is under quarantine. Two hospitals for communicable diseases have been quarantined; the doctors and nurses can't leave. The Jewish Council of Warsaw ran a collection of sheets and pillows for the hospitals. There are cases of packages having been left outside an apartment when the porter found out there was (supposedly) typhus in that household.

From some time in October until about six weeks ago, the Swedish consulate accepted messages for transmittal to America. Lately, many people have received questionnaires from America asking how they were; you could send a personal reply of up to twenty-five words. Communicating with one's relatives abroad is enormously important. There are thousands on thousands of families here that used to be supported by their relatives abroad. But now all foreign contacts have been broken. The despair of people.

Community activity has completely ceased. Everyone looks after himself, first and foremost. We're afraid to walk in the street, for fear a press gang might pick us up for forced labor. That saying of someone's [Hitler] that the next world war . . . would see an end to the Jewish people is frequently quoted. Those words of prophecy seem about to be fulfilled, particularly since no one sees any prospect for improvement. The hope placed in battalions of . . . petitions has passed.

My dear,

The economic situation is very hard, no basis for a normal economic existence. Raw supplies are being removed on a large scale and sources are cut off. The Jewish merchants from Lodz are importing certain items of merchandise from Lodz here, where they are sold at three times their value, because the prices in Lodz are prewar. They have to pay 40 to 60 per cent of the merchandise's value to have it transported. The goods are sold by street peddlers, and in private homes, behind locked doors. The calculation is that this will all stop in a month or two, because the merchants are robbing their own shelves in Lodz. The stuff is moved by smugglers, who carry it away on their backs.—Today, the 4th of January, I heard of cases where Jews have been warned: "They are going to search your place today." The messages were passed along by women, who are said to belong to a certain political group. The warnings have turned out to be justified.—The doctors' situation has taken a turn for the worse. There were doctors who used to earn 1,000 zlotys a day. Not nowadays. People simply haven't the money to be cured.—The teachers are so bad off that some of them are going into glass blowing and are willing to take any kind of menial job, janitor or a domestic servant or the like. In Lublin a Polish policeman called Lewandowski informed on seven Polish university students who had installed an illegal radio transmitter. Shot. . . . The woman principal of a Polish public school paid 10 zlotys for not wearing a Jewish badge. In Kalisz all who remain are the few hundred Jewish patients in the hospital. The rest of the Jews have fled. The retirement pensions of Jews insured with the Social Security Agency are not being redeemed, though the Jews have to continue to pay premiums. Neither are 100-mark bills from American funds being honored, because the Government General of Poland is still considered abroad in respect to the Reich. So it's necessary to get permission from America to pay in another currency.—There was talk today about a conference among neutral governments—Switzerland, Turkey, Italy, and Belgium—under the aegis of the Allies.—Yesterday heard about a concert that Paderewski gave in London, after which the King pressed Paderewski's hands warmly. The Polish Christian refugees are dispersed into the countryside. Every farm family that has more than 10 morgs of land has to take in a refugee family.—Decree (2d of January): ban on posting obituary bills. Punishment for printing them: culprit to be handed over to the authorities. Attitude no good, not even at the nearby madhouse. Every few days another decree, one confiscating furniture, another kitchen utensils, etc.—In Naleczow the madmen were sent out of the city institution, children thrown into wagons, driven off . . . in a lamentable state.—Today, the 5th, a decree appeared to the effect that Jews may not move out of their residences except with permission of the authorities. Nor may they walk about the streets between 9 P.M. and 5 A.M. . . .

This incident took place yesterday in Warsaw: In a restaurant on the street where Szymek lives—Leszno Street—one of the diners asked that the band play the Jewish National Anthem, *Hatikvah*. Everyone stood up. [I?] Got the first slap. A sign in the main dining room: Poles and Jews Forbidden.— In Posen the streets very empty. In Torun only a few people on the streets during the day.—During the famous killing in Ostrow, a woman offered 25,000 zlotys if They would let her child live. Refused.—A Jewish tailor had a suit that a Christian had given him to work on taken away from him. The Christian now threatens the tailor with the Gestapo, if he doesn't return it in a week.

Change de profession: Zama,* director of the former Vilna theater group, is now distributing lunches to residents of apartments. A teacher registers refugees; same for an ex-university tutor. Orleska, star of the Vilna troupe, is a bus girl; teachers are janitors, glaziers, and the like. . . .

Yesterday, the 5th of January, an ordinance restricting street selling was published. Jews can only sell on the Ghetto streets, beginning with Cracow, Przedmieszcie, Karowa, Kro-

* The name was really Maza. Sometimes this transposition of letters in a name is accidental, simply a typographical error. In other cases, where the same name is transposed several times, it seems to be a deliberate attempt at concealment.

lewska, Sienna, etc. You have to have a special commercial card. The decree limiting the right of Jews to resettle is being interpreted as aimed against Jewish trade, smuggling, the immigration to Warsaw. Those who declare that they wish to resettle in areas closer to Russia are not subject to these restrictions.

On Franciszkanska Street there is a whole row of houses that have been isolated—Zalman the Bourgeois's house revived again. *How was this accomplished?* The problem of how to protect the big book collections. The Socialist-Zionist Hashomer Hatzair's books are being used by the refugees to stoke ovens at 6 Leszno Street. At Kasawalackie Street there are 1,300 refugees from Kalisz, Wyszkow, Staczszek, Czyzew. Three have died. There are people who are making thousands, first by informing the authorities about hidden goods, then, when the goods are confiscated, getting them back to their original owner for a consideration. The question of the new-made rich from different cities.—Some of the Jews from Posen are now in Wloszczowa (200). . . .—The picture that was printed in the Berlin *Illustrated Daily* was staged: They imported five Jews who had been picked up elsewhere and photographed them being caught in a raid. . . . The decree requiring all Jewish residents of Warsaw to report their debts includes a clause making it compulsory to report within twenty-four hours after arrival in Warsaw. A Jew who had a house in Bydogoszcz worth 100,000 zlotys, and houses in other cities as well, has been left without a groschen.—Marpa, the madhouse in Otwock, hung out a sign that it is a hospital for infectious diseases. *The intent is clear.*—A rumor has spread that the Finns have crossed the Russian border, and have even occupied Leningrad,* and that Hungary and

* The Soviet Union had invaded Finland on Nov. 30, 1940, bombing Helsinki. Perhaps this rumor had its source in the Finnish destruction of the Russian 44th division in the "waistline" of Finland.

Rumania have appealed to Italy to accept a protectorate over them. The 53 Nalewki Street Jews [who were executed in November, 1939, because a Polish policeman had been shot there] included two men from Posen—who had escaped a similar fate at the Astoria restaurant in Lodz. . . . How you can get your money out of Gruber's Postal Savings Bank: One of Mendelssohn's boys—a German—says I owe him money. So I am allowed to withdraw it. I get half; Mendelssohn's boy gets half.—Three "Skulls" from the Totenkopf company came to an apartment on Wloclaweka Street, with *spitters,* sawed-off shotguns, in their *hands,* took all the money there was. Four of the usual company—Wehrmacht, Skulls, ethnic Germans, and Poles—went through the neighboring apartments and collected *to the sum of 500 zlotys.* A sufficiently varied crew.

With affectionate greetings,
Yours—Fayvel.*

* An alias, to conceal the identity of the writer, and to make it appear that the notes are a letter. Actually Ringelblum calls himself Muni in the *Notes.*

2/FEBRUARY, 1940

My dear parents:

Today, heard this story about Rzeszow. The relations there between Germans and Jews are good . . . but the week in question the Jews didn't meet the quota—instead of 120 workers, they presented only 110. So They took the Jewish elders and shot them down in the middle of the market place. The officers were angry at the soldiers for doing it. This ambivalence noticeable in many aspects of Jewish life in Poland. According to the Lodz newspaper, the Jewish Council of that city is responsible for "transportation"—i.e., deporting Jews from Lodz. The populace of Warsaw is absorbed in registering for employment again. They're comparing it to Pathom and Rameses in the Egypt of the Bible. People would travel miles to see the immense works the Jews had built. Jews are to build a Baltic Canal—the Black Sea. The Polish policemen are accepting only "noodles" [dollars] now. . . . Recently, their value has gone up again. The price of "liberation" [from work or imprisonment] has gone up too: used to be 2,000, now is 5 and more. . . .

There are only two "liberators," so their demands are very high. One of them is from Vienna, wears civilian dress. The liberating "hero" explained the cost to me as the result of the prison officials' refusal to permit the papers containing the charges against the arrestees to be looked through. Just getting permission to see the papers costs 500 gold pieces. It is said that those recently imprisoned were sent to Modlin. "A dark life," a Jew told me on Karmelicka Street, for there were no lights there until today. In general, the Jewish streets are very dark. They let us in through the kitchen door; that's the symbol of our present status.—The rumor spread that matzoh meal had arrived from America. There were attacks on Jews at various points; on Chlodna and on Zelazna Streets. Violence in connection with robbery.

Work camps again the order of the day. By now there are yellow cards marked with a large *Jude* to be used for registration purposes. Officially they cost 5 groschen; they're sold on the street for 10. According to [my son] Uri, the children tell one another: "The old people will be shot, the middle-aged will be sent to the camps, and the children will be baptized and passed out among Christian families." There are various ways of getting out of Warsaw. Some people plan to leave Warsaw for one of the cities in the Reich itself, where there are no work camps. Others are planning not to report for registration. Still others believe that matters are not so tragic.

The 2d of February, a decree requiring Jews to declare their possessions was published. This is viewed as a new attempt to take away the rest of our possessions. My meeting at Szymek's with the Christian doctor who talks Yiddish and a little Hebrew ("There is nothing new under the sun"). Learned it during the last war from his Jewish barber. When Minkowski* answered his toast of "Your health" with "Your health," he directed M.'s attention to the fact that the proper

* Should be Milajkowski.

response should be "Your good health and peace." An elegant man of pleasure, jolly, full of life.

Lassalle (*Historical Writings,* "Works," see part II, chap. 3, p. 735) writing of the Damascus pogrom said: "Sometimes the worm turns. But you [Jews] only grovel deeper."

The Warsaw Jews answer the Christian hoodlums in the Jewish streets with blows, although the example of what happened at 9 Nalewki Street shows that touching a Christian can lead to serious consequences. News about an armistice in the Cap area. *They killed the heads of the Asch factory, and everybody who came there was arrested.*—A few weeks ago the members of the Jewish Council were placed under the obligation of reporting.

Gertner's restaurant has been done away with. The waiters had to carry out the cutlery, furnishings, and so forth. In the morning you can see Jewish divisions marching to work under the eye of a Jewish police officer. Everyone out of step or lagging behind gets a blow. Incessant shouting. No talking, just shouting. This is a kind of system. It's said that these blows and shouts are meant to impress the Others, too.

Dear father:

7th of February. Entry to Krasinski Place at a certain point near the courts is forbidden to Jews. Jews may not visit the public libraries which were built through Jewish philanthropy. Special wagons introduced for Jews. Queueing up for a delousing certificate. . . . Jews must present it when traveling by train, good for ten days. . . . *A payment of 7,000 because* Jews living in a certain house didn't want to go to the disinfection place. Horrible scenes in the children's kitchens. They cut off their hair. *It is said that many hundreds of madmen have been killed.*—In Lodz, at the beginning of the war, bonds were issued for. . . . Jews were ordered to cover the whole issue, so many people who had money deposited in the bank withdrew it. (Analogy between the Jewish Community Councils of the old days and the Jewish Councils of today.) The duty to report for registration, the obligation of Jews to report their possessions by March 1 has evoked consternation among the Jewish populace. In Wloclawek and other provincial cities there was a trend at first to try to get rid of possessions, of shops. There was a demand for buyers. *It is said that there are people who go on sit down strikes, in private apartments, refusing to move until they are paid off.* Both yesterday and today women were seized for labor. And, it just so happened, women in fur coats. They're ordered to wash the pavement with their panties, then put them on again wet. Several Jews were pressed into pulling an auto that was stuck and then ordered to march in line, saying: "Good luck." They were forbidden to turn around. They walked and walked for a long time, unaware that no one was following them. In times of destruction one thinks of constructive aid; one does not wish to live off alms. There are proposals for the refugees to learn trades. But They compare the Jews to a plant, a parasitic plant that lives off other plants—that's what England and the Jews are like, They say.

Best regards,
Faybush

A new decree today, the 8th, in the *Warsaw News:* Jews may not travel by train because of the danger of smuggling and epidemic. A special permit from the authorities is necessary. They seized a Jewish woman who was an American citizen, sent her to work in her fur coat, ordered her to wash the pavement. She handed over her watch and 10,000 zlotys to the *lords and masters.* Today Polish hoodlums attacked Jews in the street again. Also today someone proposed that every Jew contribute 5 grams of gold for a *citizens' representation to secure exemption from compulsory labor.*

My dear:
9th of February. In Lowicz Jewish craftsmen have recently been put to compulsory labor—shoemakers, tailors, etc. The rumor has spread that there will soon be registration for compulsory labor of women between the ages of twelve and forty-five. Mothers of children under twelve are to be exempt.—In every street you see furniture being removed from Jewish apartments, from all apartments where Jewish lawyers live, for instance. First They come and requisition it, afterwards remove it. Cases where They took doctors' instruments from them. Of late, Christians have been standing around near isolated courtyard gates. They wait for a likely Jewish candidate to come along. When they catch one, they take him aside into the courtyard; the Jew emerges with empty pockets.—The news about the Lodz Ghetto being instituted has made a great impression. They're allowed to take with them into the Ghetto only as much as they can carry. There's talk again about a Ghetto in Warsaw; it's supposed to include the suburb of Praga and a few Jewish districts.—A short time ago They published a decree granting government offices and institutions the right to requisition Jewish apartments. People are fined for wearing a dirty or wrinkled arm band. A lawyer covered his arm band with his briefcase. They put his fur coat on him backwards and commanded him to walk the streets that way.—The madwoman of Marszalkowska Street is loose again. She beats Jews with a stone she wears in her glove. Before the war she was active in anti-Semitic agitation, her story being that the Jews had killed her brother in Grodno. Never had a brother.—Some of the refugees who had come to Warsaw have fled back to

the provinces in fear of the compulsory labor registration. Polish unemployed are being called up for compulsory labor. They are sent away to Germany. The frost has created a dearth of fats and potatoes. Despite the restrictions, the prices of these items haven't fallen.—Many released prisoners of war are arriving. Commissions charged for merchandise have risen steeply. The merchandise passes through many hands. A doctor who pushed his Red Cross band over the Jewish arm band was beaten and fined. . . .

12th of February. Special papers are forged, identifying the bearer as a Christian. Women have been seized for compulsory labor every day of late. They found a louse on a nurse's jacket in a hospital, so They have ordered all hospital nurses to be deloused. Pegner* is getting out 1,000 gold pieces from his fortune. The number of male Jews registered for compulsory labor totals 120,000.—The Poles are dissatisfied because so many Poles have lately fallen on the French front. Great hopes for the coming spring. Important things will happen. Bombs to fall; it doesn't matter so long as this all ends.—A Jew who had angina pectoris died after having been beaten up by hoodlums. The bacillus-carriers may not ride in trains.

Here's a game they play at the garages in the Dinance Park. The workers are ordered to beat one another with their galoshes. A Jew who was taken to the garages wearing phylacteries for prayer was forced to work all day in them. A rabbi was ordered to shit in his pants. They divide the workers into groups, and have the groups fight one another. They take away the workers' coats, so that they have to come back to work the next day. I have seen people badly injured in these games. Christians are pressed into working there too.

* Should be Gepner. *See* footnote p. 11.

There's a society organizing illegal flights to Palestine. The relatives of the emigrants pay 100 dollars abroad.

The madwoman, today the 13th, loose again, annoys people who don't wear arm bands.

Today, the 14th, *I heard that seventy people were killed. It is not known whether forty of them were Christians. Their faces were* covered with newspapers.—A commissar in disguise came to a frontier city, registered 40-odd Jews; the next day they were all killed.—A Jew who lived at 6 and 15 Franciszkanska street froze to death in his apartment.

A few weeks ago I heard a story about a *head man* who gave money to a Jewish child selling in the street and told him to go home.—In the street nowadays they're selling hot bagels, cigarettes, and "What'll you exchange?" The cost of exchanging "big" Polish banknotes has fallen from 20–25 to 12.—There have been houses where they've asked the doorkeepers whether there are any Jewish lawyers living there; twelve-year-olds are taken and forced to carry off the furniture.

Best regards.

Yours,

Fayvel

Feb. 21

My dear:

The Others threw a woman out of a moving streetcar. There have been cases of Jews seized off the streetcars for compulsory labor. Took women from a number of cafés (incl. the Polonia), no one knows where to; it is said that about a hundred came back a few days later, some of them infected.

At Hirshfeld's three days in a row. The first time, They searched everyone; the second time, They took away their papers; the third time, They imprisoned them. Took away their jewelry, watches. Polish women were taken and made to search the Jewish women.—The artist Adam Herrschaft's studio burned down during the war; rare aquarelles were lost. Many houses on Nowolipki Street searched. Again, furniture removed.—Polish professors Kastaniecki, Rzhanowski died in camp.—A few weeks ago the Jewish Council ordered all Houses of Study and Pietists' schoolrooms closed. A rumor that Kot* broadcast from France. Melancholy news about what happened during the "resettlement" in the Lodz Ghetto; 3,000 people stood outdoors all day in the bitter cold. Those who loaded their things on to carts to pull along after them into the Ghetto were arrested. Access to the Batuly suburb cut off with barbed wire; a special intervention necessary to have the barbed wire opened. Fearful crowding in Batuly. Several families living together in one small room. A wave of optimism among the Poles. Have to stick it out; that's why the leaders of the intelligentsia have remained. At the same time, terrible fear. The attitude of the Polish intelligentsia to the Jews has markedly improved. Saw a soldier ordering Christians standing around to take away . . . from a Jewish tinsmith. Insecurity significantly less [among Poles?]. Number of Jewish shopkeepers and street vendors used to be large, now is very small—mostly goods in baskets, but very little.— The value of the dollar has gone down to 140–150. The reason being that those who bought dollars when exchanging larger bills for small are now selling the dollars because they need bills for everyday use.—Noticeable increase in the number of madmen. Heard about a good-looking ten-year-old boy beaten on the head who went mad.—Forced labor already instituted in Lublin. Jewish artisans must work for the army,

* Leader of an underground resistance group.

but can't work at home, rather at larger outside shops. All they get for their work is meager meals. The 23d of Feb. a decree was published ordering a second registration for work of those between 14 and 60, in two stages: the first, on the 1st of March, for those between 16 and 25; all the rest to register on 2d of March. They have to supply their own implements. The elders of the Jewish community responsible for this provision. *It is related that in one place during the work registration those Jews who said they were sickly were killed.*

Feb. 23

It is related that a Jew was killed on Banna Street for coming half an hour late to a business that had been taken from him.—The work battalions in Germany are supposed to sing: "Sweet Hitler, beloved Hitler, we had no work in Poland."

Nalewki Street looks like Hollywood nowadays—wherever you go you see a star! [The Jewish star on the arm band that Jews had to wear.]

Jews get smaller rations than Christians: Christians get 50 sugar, Jews 30. If there's no influx to Warsaw of Jews from the provinces, the rations for Jews will be cut in half. When the authorities decided that Jews would be permitted to buy only in Jewish stores, a number of Christians opposed this measure, arguing they would lose all their business.—In Wloclawek, the enemy of the Jews is a former German, a man who was an instructor in the Maccabee sports organization, lived off Jews all his life.—The Eleventh Commandment: *Thou shalt convert thy grandmother and thy grandfather.* The Jews are suffering now because they did not keep the Eleventh Commandment. Mimicry: People fasten visors to their hats, which they wear pulled down over their foreheads. Boots, or high shoes with high stockings. A lot of sport shoes—all to look more Gentile. Women wearing lipstick and smartly dressed have become a rarity. Also warm coats and garments. The thoroughly assimilated intelligentsia is joining us . . . the head of the public library.

A large concentration of Jews has begun in Lublin. Homes there are becoming more crowded every day. Recently, 1,500 Jews from Szczecin arrived in Lublin. Further transports from the Reich are expected.—*I have heard that in the [building of the] Council of the Four Lands* in Warsaw [?] two men do the killing, one shoots through the head, the other through the heart. Jews are forced to bury the bodies quickly. Four Jews carry off each corpse, by the arms and the legs. And a great many Gentiles have been settled in our city. At one house in Koszkowa Street there are daily arrivals of prisoners of war returning from Germany; they were well treated in the Austrian cities. Many of them died in time of frost. One of their leaders stated that 10 per cent died. The farmers who journey there are living under very bad circumstances. In a railroad station one man heard the cry, Woe! . . . They travel in trucks.* There was a notice in the Lodz newspaper that the Lenczic synagogue had been burned down. The *Warsaw Courier* published an inflammatory article attacking the Jewish administrators.

* National coordinating body of Jewish Community Councils in Poland during seventeenth century.

3/MARCH, 1940

My dear:

Today, the 6th of March, heard this story: Rabbi Vel-vele was taken to the Dinance Park garages to work there. "You're not human, you're not animal, you're Jew." He was beaten because they ordered him to throw down his fountain pen, later took it away—but ordered him to look for it. Lay sick in bed for several weeks.

At 2 Tlomackie Place three *lords and masters* ravished some women; screams resounded through the house. The Gestapo are concerned over the racial degradation—Aryans consorting with non-Aryans—but are afraid to report it. At the sight of Itzik and Knefel's sign,* They mutter, "Jewish swindle." They came to a hospital to remove the beds, but couldn't, because of the JDC.—Jews may not ride in any streetcar in Lodz. In Cracow, according to the *Warsaw Courier,* only on the rear platform.—More than a thousand people from Lodz were banished to Piotrkow.—900 Poles and 600 Jews. The Poles are offered jobs and then taken there. The rumor is that

* Isaac Giterman and Knefel (Guzik) were the representatives of the American Jewish Joint Distribution Committee (JDC).

Poles are putting on Jewish arm bands both in Warsaw and Cracow. During compulsory labor round-ups, Poles thought Jews sent to camps in Poland had it easier than Christians, sent abroad to the Reich.

The tragedy of the prisoners of war from Wartegoj. A transport of over 600 was sent out. In Lublin, the Jewish Council couldn't accept them; it had no civilian clothing for them. Were sent on, toward Parczew; those who tried to escape en route were shot at. Wore wooden shoes that fell off. Many of the wounded were shot. Later, took them into two barns, and more than 200 of them, taken out of the barns in groups of twenty, were killed. Of 627, only 387 were left alive. Some 20-odd managed to escape. *Three men* killed with one bullet. In Parczew many of them wanted to commit suicide. *Thought of rebelling during the trek, because there were only 13 guards, but They said to them that would be a great catastrophe for all the Jews of Poland. The cruelest of the guards wantonly killed people walking along the road. Promised they would give Them money, and so managed to save those left. The head said he was doing this* [killing the 200] *because they were trying to escape. When the blackguards arrived at Biala, someone asked, 'Where are the others?' and They pretended not to know. I heard that two soldiers came to a home and took away some things: one a Jew, one a Pole.*

Two hundred children died in the Warsaw foundling home. —*In the village of Nagoszow four farmers were killed for going off to the forest to cut trees.*—A fine of 500 zlotys levied in the same village for not having a wagon and horses ready.—Three janitors along with a Christian came to a Jewish apartment in Warsaw and demanded that the resident give them a place to live, or else they would inform on him to the Others.—The Jewish Council takes 60 zlotys as a kickback for each job clearing snow for five or six days. *From the funds that were* *in the bank Felix Friedman used, They took 200,000. Of this sum, the Warsaw Jewish Council got 400. From the fund for migration to Palestine belonging to the Council, the grave-diggers took 110,000, because they said the Council had no use for the money.* Jewish Council employees have been caught clearing off the snow, beside their other work.* Jews from abroad do not have to wear the arm band.—There are plenty of dollars about. What is lacking is Polish money to exchange for dollars.

28th. Many Poles were seized, at home, in the street, in cafés. . . . Melancholy news from Lodz. Rumkowski is throwing poor families out of their apartments, and giving them to the rich. Nevertheless, whole families are returning to Lodz from Warsaw; they would rather die at home than in a strange place. Jews are transferred from Lodz to Warsaw, permitted to take only 10 marks with them.—Thousand of Jewish prisoners of war arrive in Warsaw daily. The problem of clothing for them. They are forbidden to wear military clothing and have no civilian ones.—The interesting story about the artist Eljowicz. He was seized for work at the armory. Did a good job stoking the oven. They asked him, "How is it you're so good at it?" "I'm an artist," he said. Asked him to paint. He's now working on his sixth portrait and keeps getting a higher rank for a subject with each portrait. Gets a fee of 150 per portrait, with the agreement that the artist's name appear on each one. Well received.

The decree ordering women to register for compulsory labor published on 26th of February. *Rumors about the cruelties practiced in the Polish Council*—the Sejm building — . . . . *They beat people about the ear and head. Two men*

* To make extra money. There was a great deal of competition for snow removal jobs.

do the beating. People come out of there half-mad, work there two weeks. When Jews are being beaten, the other workers turn their heads to the wall. The rabbi excommunicated Christians. The fear They suffer from of being good to Jews. A man will be speaking decently to a Jew—then, seeing someone approach, will mutter, "Get out of here!" and add a curse.—The price of gold fallen from 80 to 40. The dollar 100. The Polish lawyers who have Jewish wives or clerks are expunged from the bar rolls . . . , only a couple of hundred of Polish lawyers left. One lawyer, a perfect Aryan specimen, formerly an anti-Semitic National Democrat, now is proud of the fact that he was expunged from the rolls for having a Jewish law clerk. Took 200 Christian women out of cafés, *afterward came violation. I have heard that this same thing happened many times in the streets of Warsaw.* Marszalkowska Street is half-empty at night. In the morning Jewish streets look like a Jewish small town. Jewish compulsory labor divisions under the supervision of the Council going to work. Faces horribly emaciated from hunger; earn half a zloty a day.

End of March

My dear:

They write in the newspapers about the "excellent order" in Warsaw—actually, disorder is rampant wherever you look. If we had the 1914 German organization here now, given the present ideology, there'd be not the vestige of a Jew left. Many laws are completely ignored, such as the one permitting Jews to carry no more than 2,000 zlotys about their person. The rest is supposed to be deposited in the bank and withdrawn at the rate of no more than 500 guilden a week. And the law setting maximum prices [at prewar levels]. The only way Jews can live these days is to break the law. No possibility of living within the law. *When they were in Cracow for the talks,** *said to them: "I know the situation of the Jewish communities. How long will you be able to exist? What did the rich Jews do for their worker comrades? Didn't they give them help before the war—hospitals, homes, built by rich Jews?"* Lately, the spectacle at the former Sejm building has stopped as well as the goings on at Obozhna Street, the Dinance Park garages. It is also said that fewer people are being impressed to work. Whether this is a psychological illusion, a supposed consequence of the Cracow talks, or an actual fact, is hard to evaluate.—The inefficiency of the Council tax department. Five Jews were having a game of bridge. One described how he had given 60 zlotys to the tax department when he could and should have given 4,000; the others could have given 6,000, but were asked for nothing.—Every Jew, even the poorest one, must before he leaves town pay an "emigration tax" of 200 zlotys—to the Jewish Council of Warsaw. Someone suggested to a Council department head that he free a poor seamstress of the need to pay this tax by charging to her account the 200 zlotys due her from the social-welfare department of the Council. Replied *that he was afraid of the spies from the Gestapo.*—"The Leviathan would be too small to accomplish the work Thou hast performed up to now," said Mr. Isaac Giterman, on returning from there—a concentration camp. Wooden fences are being set up at nine points in the city, particularly at Krochmalna Street. The health authority says that Krochmalna Street is the chief source of infection for the whole city. If they could, they would burn it down. In Krasznik, They walled up a whole street, immuring the healthy with the sick. The only way to get food in to them is to pass it through a single opening. Excrement all around.—Heard today that the opinion in Polish

---

* A delegation from the Warsaw Jewish Council went to Cracow and appealed to Governor General Hans Frank to halt the persecution of the Jews.

intellectual circles is that the Jews have had a talk with the Others and the result has been the mass arrests of Christians. —Count Ronikier, in Cracow during the developments, transmitted a memo in the name of the *RNA* [Polish Central Welfare Council], whose chairman he is, stating that excesses had taken place, that they had been filmed (he did not state by whom), and that the security police had done nothing to halt these developments. The memo evoked great interest in Cracow. Orally, he confirmed the facts. In Cracow, it is said, Czerniakow, head of the Jewish Council in Warsaw, gave a well-drawn picture of a day in the Council, describing how people come with sad news from every quarter, about someone being shot at work at this place, and someone else being impressed to work at that place. But in the course of the discussion he faltered; talking about the Jewish arm bands (incidentally, this was made out to be the chief problem—unnecessarily, in the opinion of some of the other delegates), he said that one can buy oneself off from wearing an arm band for 500 zlotys. But he could not prove this with any particular instance, so They lost confidence in everything he said.— Levin had been in hiding all the time since the German occupation. But since the Others have come looking for him [at home], he has decided to go out into the street. At 2 Tlomackie Place *men of valor* took away furniture and all, ordered an invalid woman to leave her bed, and removed it together with the bedding. One person had his bureau taken away so quickly that he didn't manage to get out the paper exempting him from just such a requisition. Something has altered, it is said, on Okencia Street, where the Jewish workers were formerly given nothing to eat for their forced labor. The last few days they've been getting a soldier's midday meal of hot bread and bacon. The story about the head of the Jewish work battalion goes this way: When his barbed whip was broken in the course of beating Jews who came late to forced labor, he ordered it given to a leather worker to be fixed and to be brought back to the bureau office by nine o'clock.—The dollar rose considerably, to 150 zlotys, in connection with the decree published today—March 17—authorizing the exchange of all Bank of Poland banknotes for the notes of the newly created Bank of Remittances. The forecast is that the cost of living will rise steeply.—These days people arrested in November in the mass arrests were set free. Only Jews, it is said. There is talk of Partisan battles, and individual attacks on Others in the Kielce area.—In Anin, a week ago, *two Germans were killed, and 100 Poles killed* [in retaliation]. It is said that during the anti-Jewish excesses, a Jewish delegation visited Archbishop Gall, who refused to intervene with the Polish populace.—There is talk about a rebellion in a regiment stationed in Skierniewice, where every twentieth soldier was executed. In Wlodawa there was supposed to have been a battle between the Others and the Russians. In Chelm and Wlodawa the question of what to do with madmen was solved in a radical manner through euthanasia. In a number of provincial cities the local city councils issued edicts banning Christian doctors from treating Jewish patients. Since those places have no Jewish doctors, the Jews are without medical care. The situation of the doctors in Warsaw is bad. At first typhus had an easy course; now, in March, it's "tough." They closed a number of Polish bookstores and took away Polish and German books. In Cracow a decree was received ordering Jewish Councils to be the sole agents for Jewish compulsory labor. The registration of all Jewish handicraftsmen was to be completed by the 5th of August. Actually a small part of the Jews in this category have registered. Sumner Welles is supposed, in a conversation with Ribbentrop, to have touched on the situation of the Jews in Poland.*—*Gattenhafen*† is now

---

* Welles, United States Undersecretary of State, was in Berlin on March 1.
† The German name for the Polish port of Gdynia.

called "Totenhafen" [Death Harbor]. It is so quiet there now-adays; there's no ship movement at all. There's said to be panic in Danzig. They're sitting around, all packed, ready to leave. When the question of deportation was mentioned in the Cracow meeting (of March 27), it was explained that suspension of the deportations depended on Berlin. They propose the creation of a Jewish trustee organization to take over the liquidation of Jewish possessions on the Other Side. A man wanted to hold a birthday party. Since any meeting of more than ten people has to be reported, he went to the Gestapo and left the list of his guests. The next day he was told they would not bother to send one of their men to the party; there were already three of them among the twenty-odd guests.

4/APRIL, 1940

April 26–27

Heard an interesting characterization of "King" Merin, administrator of ghettos in Zeglembia and Upper Silesia. Before the war, he had been pretty much on the decline. Politically kept changing sides. . . . Always was a political middleman. Played cards and lost a lot of money, divorced his wife; just before the war began a comeback.—The day the Germans came to Sosnowiec, the 14th of September, all Jewish males over fourteen were packed into a cellar behind the City Hall. The crowding was awful, they sweated buckets. If it had lasted another half hour, everyone would have choked to death. They were ready to tear out the water pipes and drown. Finally, They let them out and took them over to the market place. There, They lined the Jews up six in a row, and said that the Jews had shot at the Germans from windows when They entered town. Shaved off their beards and ear locks. Sent eight barbers for their instruments and threatened to shoot the seven Jewish professionals, whom They stood against a wall, if the barbers did not come back in fifteen minutes; finally, They were bargained down to a half-hour deadline. The seven had already made their last testament, the Others were loading their guns, when, at the last minute, the barbers came running, the sweat rolling down their faces. Stayed in camp another few days, then gradually were set free, first the artisans, then the rest, who lost in those three or four days over 10 kilos, looked half-dead. There *They killed 300 Jews.* In Sosnowiec no one knows whose idea it was to have a gold and silver contribution. It's suspected that the idea came from the King [Merin]. The Poles don't consider it proper, but the Jews think it should protect them from persecution. Entering this kind of tax on the books is a problem. In Bedzin, it's entered as a normal tax. The King has a warm Jewish heart. Is very well received in Merysz-Ostrow and Prog, where he managed to free the Jews of Merysz-Ostrow from the camp in Nisko. They needed the place for another purpose; hence agreed to let the Jews leave the camp. Luck has played into his hands in many instances. Still, it is maintained that he will wager everything on emigration [of Jews from Poland], and will stop at nothing. Has recently been working for some grant of authority from the Warsaw communal leaders; probably needs it because the German Jews ask him skeptically—in Biblical diction—"What is thy name?" Recently has compromised himself by promising 20,000 [emigration permits]. Nothing came of it. This has seriously weakened his position. Still, he managed to delay the deportation from Silesia for a few months. Today, the 26th of April, Jews are expected to be deported from Rivnik, as well as from Oderberg and other cities in the east into Socha, Czebynya, Zawierczie. Thousands of Jews will have to abandon their homes. King M. now wants to remove to Cracow and there become the king of the whole province, and of the old Reich, together with the protectorate, in general. The Poles have expressed their antagonism to him and his system in flyers. In a train met a woman who talked about the "King" as though he were a redeeming angel. Anyone who has ever been in the four-day camp in Sosnowiec feels like a worm squirming under a boot, pressed down into the mud, about to choke. After a while, the boot is lifted; but in a second, the game begins all over again. In the camp there in S. are special chambers that are surrounded by barbed wire, where every untoward movement brings you into contact with barbed wire. For punishment, they hang you on it [the barbed wire].—The Jews of the place live off currency dealing. They travel to Myszkow, near the border between the Reich and the Government General of Poland. They buy up Polish money; they buy permits for raw material. . . . A few Jewish businesses work openly, particularly small shops. In the camp near S. They ordered a party of prisoners to clean the toilets with their bare hands.—The last few days there's been a new rash of impressing people for work in Warsaw. The work battalions aren't meeting their quota. A few days ago petty police officers accompanied by soldiers seized people in the street. There's a new method. A motorcyclist drives ahead, shouting: "Stop, Jews!" Those who stop are arrested and loaded on to a police wagon.

Today, the 24th of April, soldiers stood in pairs at Zamenhofa Street before a courtyard gate for perhaps an hour detaining Jews. The seizing of people for compulsory labor has assumed frightful proportions. A month ago they came to Reb Mendel from Leszno Street, asked him, "Where is your money?" They searched until They found it. . . .

There was a soldier who went from house to house in the Jewish quarter forcing men to have sexual relations with women in his presence. After a while, he was put in prison.— The House Committee* people have come to the fore.

They hope for a change in Poland because of what has hap-

* A House Committee was a voluntary organization of all the houses in a courtyard for social-welfare activity.

pened in Norway.*—Mietek Zucker from Lodz, who defended his father from an attack by soldiers, is in the Otwock madhouse. They beat him on the head until he went mad. Many of the madmen were shot without their trousers [which were stolen from them].—The building of thick gates on the corner of Pruzhany and Zlota Streets and elsewhere is costing the Council a quarter of a million zlotys.—The shock of the bombardments had a beneficial effect on the madmen. The insulin cure [has been] made more difficult, because it is expensive. —The Jewish work battalion busy at the Okencia airport loading and sorting metals.—Indelmann tells how, in the camp he was in, he was given a plate of hot soup but no spoon, had to pluck out the steaming potatoes with his fingers. Was allowed a couple of minutes to do it in.—On Leszno Street crowds of Jewish workers from the labor battalions stand around unoccupied while They're impressing people off the street.—If you pay the Germans 2,000, the house can be exempt from the disinfection steam baths. The doctor gets 220 zlotys a month. Everything is destroyed during the bath. They take the clean linen, too. It is said that, to prevent epidemic, walls will be put up on Zholibozh and Soska Streets—i.e., a strategic fortress. . . .

There's street selling of summer things at Nalewki Street. The Jewish . . . itself.† They live off what they smuggle through. The streets are fearfully dirty now.

* On April 9, 1940, Germany invaded Norway and Denmark. The British came to the rescue.
† The sentence is illegible.

5 / MAY, 1940

2d of May. Yesterday—the hunt.—The shoemaker from Smocza Street; the storekeeper from Nowolipki Street.—The legend about the fifty who were freed.* An auto [?] drove up on the pavement. . . . Sand and water on the roofs—apothecaries—took out a thousand—streets were dead empty. Night before last took away the Unknown Soldier—nobody laid flowers on [Mickie]wicz's† grave.—People voluntarily take on a Polish commissar, rather than be given one of the Other kind. Under the commissar's direction, they hang out signs only in German, to curry favor with Them. The pensions are down almost 75 per cent from prewar days. . . . Nowodworski and other anti-Semitic lawyers are in prison because of the Jews. They were called in and asked what their attitude was toward the Jews. Replied that the question was no longer a current issue. Every lawyer, before every court transaction, has to declare that he is not of non-Aryan origin. Plawski, rector of Cracow, showed the door to Studenicki, who wished to form

* Fifty prisoners were rescued from the Pawia Street prison by Poles disguised as S.S. men.
† A famous Polish poet.

a collaborationist Polish government.—King Christian of Denmark stands side by side with the Jews, himself wearing a snow-white badge in sympathy.—From which I learn that They are in Denmark.

May 4

Misery over the defeat in Norway. Our spirits have fallen. In Zgierz They ordered the Jewish Council to pay for the benzine They used to set fire to the synagogue.—52 Leszno has turned obstinate; we refuse to contribute money for disinfection steam baths.—Enormous sums paid to avoid steam baths. 23 Nalewki is paying 7,000 zlotys. Law and life.— There's a ban on selling bread, but bread is displayed in every store window at 23 zlotys. The same goes for fixed prices, which are not observed.

May 6

The petty officer who had presented thirty-eight Jewish workers instead of the fifty-two that were the quota, and had gotten a receipt for the whole number, was ordered to appear with fifteen men and to bring two whips along with him.

Complaints because only poor Jews are doing compulsory labor; the rich twist out of it.

In Cracow Jewish women may not have hair-do's, wear short sleeves or high heels. A decree by the authorities.—The Jewish members of the Council were beaten.

In Lublin there have been sessions attended by more than 2,000 people.—On the 3d of May, 300 were killed.—"Jew, come to work; work makes life sweet!" "I don't have a sweet tooth."

They took all the Jews out of Gertners' restaurant for compulsory labor. Didn't bother anybody in the street; surrounded Kercelak's Trading Place and took everybody there for work. The same thing happened in streetcars. They took a couple of kilos of cheese from the Christians. Milk and cheese, though concealed in every possible manner, confiscated all the same.—Heard that the Poles are putting together lists of persons who collaborate with and serve Them.

May 7

Commissars imprisoned. Young Poles between ages of fifteen and twenty-five are hiding at home. In Cracow more terror than in Warsaw. People are afraid to utter a word.—Café Gertner is now Aryan. Only Jews go there. The Jewish waitresses must try to pretend to be Polish. Didn't answer me when I asked a question in Yiddish.

May 8

Horrifying day. At twilight, Poles were seized in every street. Jews had their papers checked to make sure they weren't Christians. Stopped streetcars, dragged everyone in them off to the Pawia Street prison; from there, it is said, they are sent to Prussia. Dozens of autos drove off toward Dzielna Street and the Pawia Street prison. All the Jewish barbers were picked up, ordered to cut the hair of those being deported. Seized not only young people, but older people as well, over forty.

May 9

During the round-up of Poles (there was one again today, on Nowy Swiat Street), seventy-two Jews were detained. Imprisoned in the Pawia Street prison at Dzielna Street. The Polish guards take 5 groschen per egg from the street-corner peddlers, because they have to live too (an egg costs 70 groschen).—In Lublin the Jews have to take their hats off to the German guards. A witty letter describing the situation in Vienna: "A shame you're not here, you'd be convinced the House of Detention is true."*—Nobody can understand why walls have been put up in the middle of the Ghetto. People are afraid that the Germans will set fire to the Ghetto when they leave. It has been proposed by the magistrate that the walls be moved to Rymarska Street, as the merchants prefer, for a bribe.— *I heard that a German went to a Jew in Lodz. He woke the Jew up and said, "Come, let's set fire to the House of Study in Lodz." They went there, but*† it was forbidden to approach it. Heard that when They were seizing Poles for forced labor, a number of Jews with an Aryan appearance were ordered to speak Yiddish as proof that they were Jewish. —In a refugee center an eight-year-old child went mad. Screamed, "I want to steal, I want to rob, I want to eat, I want to be a German." In his hunger he hated being Jewish.—Heard that the Germans went into the baptized Jews' church on Grzybowska Street. The priest tried to calm the congregation, but there was a fearful panic. The same thing happened a few days ago in the Church of the Three Crosses, from which people were seized for compulsory labor. In a synagogue on Powszechna Street all the children were taken and forced to give blood.—Heard that the Germans are preparing for the future in Germany: They get certificates stating that They treated prisoners of war well, and have them sewed into military coats.

* That is, "You'd be in prison, too, if you were here."

† In November 1939, the Nazis set fire to a synagogue in Lodz, and attributed the act to Polish patriots resentful of Jewish desecration of a memorial to Kosciusco. This act of provocation was obviously designed to create bad feelings between the Jews and Poles.

May 13

Heard that in the Theater Plaza, Marszalkowska Street, etc., They ordered Jews to dance. The Poles standing around who joined in the laughter were beaten as well.—A new fashion nowadays. They order Jews to take their hats off, then throw them away.—Heard that the walls ("Frank's Line")* are being put up on Nowy Swiat Street as well. Their reputed purpose is to serve the Jews as a protection [behind which to fall] in the case of street attack.

Horowitz [Hitler] comes to the Other World. Sees Jesus in Paradise. "Hey, what's a Jew doing without an arm band?" "Let him be," answers Saint Peter. "He's the boss's son."

May 16

The [German] victories on the Western front have made a powerful impression.† The populace is enveloped in deep melancholy. I know one doctor who has a vial of poison prepared to take in case of complete German victory. People attribute the victory to German airplanes that convert into tanks when set down. Another explanation is that the Germans shoot a heavy-air bomb which surrounds the parachutes with an impregnable nimbus, rendering the paratroopers like angels whom no bullet can touch. Heard about a *strong man* in Wlodawa who levies on those Jews who have 20,000 guilden a tax of 1,000 guilden a month, and those who do not obey are thrown into prison. When asked what a person is to do who can't pay the tax, he answers, "He'll get relief from us."—Heard that in Radom the Jewish Council has organized an arbitration court that Jews apply to, rather than to the government courts. The Jewish elders may be the members

* After Hans Frank, the Governor General of Poland.
† On May 10, 1940, Germany invaded Holland, Belgium, and Luxembourg. On May 15, the Dutch army, and on May 27, the Belgian army, capitulated. On May 28, the British evacuated Dunkirk.

of the court; the secretary of the court, its head. Expenses are met by income from the cases, as well as from a fixed amount from the Council. Heard that Polish landed gentry have applied for working hands; this is an important problem, because if Jews go to work on the gentry's estates more Poles —whom the Jews will replace on the estates—will be sent to work in Prussia.

Contents of a code letter: "Father *Meat* doesn't visit us. The same with neighbor *Butter*." ... The labor office demands that Jewish businesses in Warsaw fire Jewish employees and take Germans or Poles in their place.

May 26

The melancholy news has arrived that the Jews of Cracow were ordered to leave the city by August 15. Those who leave the city voluntarily will be able to take everything with them. About 5,000 have to leave each month. Only 10,000 can remain. News arrived from Silesia that the deportation of 140,-000 Jews is on the agenda again.—The administrator of the work battalion, Advocate Goldfajl, was given twenty lashes in the Jewish Council last week for failing to meet his quota of workers.—Heard that two Jews came to the Council and showed the black and blue marks on their bodies where they had been beaten working in the Dinance Park garages.— There's talk in the Council of imposing a tax of 2 zlotys for bread ration cards. This will affect the poorest people most seriously, for they won't be able to buy the ration cards. Recently, the bread ration for Jews was cut in half, from 500 to 200 grams, while Christians receive 570 grams. The Jews don't get sugar at all. The Christians do.—The value of the dollar has fallen lately; it's 90 zlotys.—In Tomoszow-Mazowiecki Jews are allowed to be out in the street only between eight and twelve o'clock in the morning. The reason, so that Ger-

man soldiers going to the front won't be forced to see Jews.—
In Czestochowa thousands of Jews are working outside the
city. They're allowed into the city only once a week, to rest;
they get food for their work.—The walling up of Przejazd-
Nowolipie Streets created an impossible situation on Karmelicka Street. It's fearfully crowded there, tremendous
movement back and forth.—The farm at Czestochowa was
taken over and converted into a sports place.—Heard of a
Jewess who, when a German soldier stole goods from her, ran
after him, shouting, "Thief!"—Heard about a boy who, in the
same situation, grabbed hold of the thief's hand and yelled.—
One of Them stuck two lamps in his pocket. The Jewish shopkeeper put her hands in his pocket, saying, "Where I come
from people don't steal. Things are different in our country."
—Heard that in Cracow the Jewish Council has been bargaining with Them, and that They have agreed that 30,000 Jews
may remain. It is said that the Council is itself responsible for
the deportation because they kept on saying there were too
many refugees in Cracow.—Jews are being impressed to work
in Malkin digging trenches.

May 27

Today . . . heard this story: A wall was supposed to be put
up on Swientojerska Street, so [the Jews of that street] offered
a bribe. The deadline was postponed to the 13th. Again they
offered a bribe; again the deadline was postponed. The same
procedure was then followed in other neighborhoods, such as
Nalewki Street, Nowolipki Street, where there are no walls to
this day. All because they offered bribes.—There are fifteen
cases of typhus in one house on Muranow Street. The house
has not been quarantined, because the doctor is getting 800
zlotys a day. If the war were to last as long as the Jews can

hold out, that would be bad, because the Jews can hold out longer than the war can last.

May 28

Heard very sad news about Lodz, where they're living on a diet of bread and water. No one is allowed to leave. There's the threat of capital punishment for leaving the Ghetto. The seventh- and eighth-grade children in Rumkowski's gymnasium were taken out of school for forced work.—On Gesia Street an ethnic German was beaten up, some dozen Jews thrown into prison.—In Lodz people smuggled themselves out of the city in coffins. Jews are allowed to accompany coffins to the gates of the Ghetto.—Horrible conditions in Lodz. Long lines at the toilets, crowding, no packages are allowed in, only letters. Smuggling people out [of Lodz, to Warsaw] costs 1,000 zlotys and more per person. Sixty Jews die every day. There are still 200,000 left in Lodz.—There are still Jews left in Kalisz, those who have remained in the market.

6/AUGUST, 1940

Aug. 25

Two transformations. . . . A man became an anti-Semite in Vienna because he bought two motion picture machines on the installment plan, and then lost them during the crisis of 1923 when he couldn't meet the installments. The manufacturer was Jewish. His family went hungry. He used to hide the bread on a very high shelf. But one day one of his boys miraculously climbed the shelf and took the bread. He couldn't forgive the Jews for that. At that time he joined the anti-Semitic party. But recently he has become acquainted with the chalutz farm in Grochaw, outside Warsaw, and has come to know Jews personally. He is full of enthusiasm for the work.* There is where he feels good. It's the only place he gets any gratification. He knows everybody at the farm by name.

Schraempf, health officer for Warsaw, came to Grochaw. He and the Jewish doctor he is traveling with sit separately. He does not speak to Jews, but points with his fingers to have the pot lifted in order to see whether the bottom is clean.

From Lodz got the news that King Merin is to become the supreme master of the Lodz Ghetto.—Heard that in Cracow

* Preparing young people for life on collective settlements in Palestine.

people can buy their way out of deportation. They pay many thousands to the Jewish Council. Whoremongers and the like remain, but not artisans, etc.—An illegal National Democrat anti-Semitic paper wrote that Jews were privileged. True, they were beaten; but Poles were shot. True, Jews are impressed into work; but Poles are sent out of the country to work. "We congratulate you on your latest contact." (Jews were deported from Cracow in the course of several weeks, Poles in a few hours.)

Heard that, when Posen was taken and the Jews evicted, the Polish populace accompanied them, particularly the old folks, with tears in their eyes. In Lodz, on the other hand, there was no evidence of any sympathy from the Polish populace when Jews were driven into the Ghetto. An increase in the number of beatings for failure to remove one's hat in the presence of a man in uniform. At the Blank Palace Jews are halted and ordered to do a couple of dozen push-ups; one person was order to jump over the gym horse a hundred times.

During the last few days (August 28), expulsions inside a half hour from streets with a large Polish population (Wielcza, Karolkowa, etc.).—Yesterday, the droshky drivers had their licenses taken from them.—Announcement by the Jewish Council that all persons from eighteen to thirty-five must be ready to go to the work camps; any moment they might receive an order to report. Prospective workers are examined by doctors' commissions. From Sochaszew, 143 Jews were called up, but only 100 were accepted; the rest were too weak.—The mother of someone killed in January hit a German in the street, then took poison. . . . 40,000 Jews are said to be working in war factories. Jews may buy between four and five o'clock. An important publicity man [Josef Goebbels] is supposed to have said that if the Others win the war, the Jewish question will be solved in three months; if They lose, in an hour.

7/SEPTEMBER, 1940

Sept. 6–9

Heard during September instances of "God's people" refusing to bend. The Jews hold on to their positions. On Wielopole Street permission was granted to both Jewish and Christian shopkeepers to set up the market again. But the Christians weren't satisfied, because some of the Jewish shops were in the front. So they pushed the Jews to the back of the market. Quickly, however, all the business moved to the back, and 120 Christians shops had to close down. The Others began to take revenge. But the Jews solved that too. They hired a German watchman, who gets a fee of 150 zlotys and comes twice a day. At last, there's peace and quiet.

How Jews do business in manufactured goods: The store is half empty; two partners stand side by side, holding goods under the coats. When a customer approaches, one of them goes over to him.

The Jewish populace is now working at home. They produce less, but they earn more. For example, they earn something like 30 zlotys per sweater. Peoples' spirits have improved. The Jewish populace believes the war will end in two or three months because of the recent bombardments [of Berlin].* They keep repeating stories about new peace proposals offered through the mediation of the Swedes, the Pope, and so on.

It's possible to buy one's way out of serving in a forced work camp officially by contributing 10–25 zlotys for clothing the poor. The fact is, only poor people go to the camps. If you contact an "operator," it's said you can get out of it cheaper. Melancholy news from the camps, worst of all from Belzec. Physiological needs are regulated by the clock. Twelve men can go every hour. There have been cases where weak people were shot to death. Happened to an old man of over sixty. Of 600 campers in Josefow, 400 became sick with bleeding diarrhea. They were dispatched while still sick. Young boys thirteen to fourteen years old are sent back without papers, without a railroad ticket for the trip. They walk on foot to the nearest community. There are not enough bakeries. Cooking utensils are missing; they get to eat very late, because the mess line is long. The food is cold by then, and not everybody gets some. The German guards are prospering, because they get paid for their work. The terrible news from the camps has led many of those called up not to report. As a result, there's been a case where thirty-six Jews were seized for work in the Praga suburb, only thirteen of whom were accepted as fit by the medical commission. The first few days only single men were taken, so there have been a lot of weddings of late.

Recently heard that there are more than 600 [?] prayer quorums in the courtyards.—Today, the 6th of September, there arrived from Lodz, Chaim, or, as he is called, "King Chaim," Rumkowski, an old man of seventy, extraordinarily ambitious and pretty nutty. He recited the marvels of his Ghetto. He has a Jewish kingdom there, with 400 policemen,

* The first British bombs fell on Berlin the night of August 25–26, 1940.

three jails. He has a foreign ministry, and all the other ministries, too. When asked why, if things were so good there, the mortality is so high, he did not answer. He considers himself God's anointed.

Heard about the infamous Schultz, at the Dinance Park garages. Ordered a Jew to pick one of the sticks hanging there, and then he beat the Jew—not with that stick but with a heavier one. They clean autos there and transport benzine; he rides around in an open car, grabs two Jews at the same time, honors each of them with a blow. When the Jewish Council offered to supply him with workers daily, he replied that he didn't care for their tattered Jews, he's looking for the well-dressed kind. Besides, he can't deprive himself of the pleasure of picking up his own Jews. In Otwock Jews were impressed for the work camps, a large number escaped, more than ten paid with their lives.—There's been an increase in the practice of turning Jews out of their apartments in individual houses. They're given half an hour to carry their things out. In one house they were ordered to change the linen instead of packing in that last half hour. Occasionally, the furniture and bedding have to be left behind.—While They're at it—moving Jews out of the Christian quarter— They have made a racket out of coming to the Jewish quarter and pretending to order people to move out of their apartments. They allow you to stay, for a consideration. Jews sit around waiting, all packed. This makes for a terrible mood in the street.—Heard that in one city They assembled all the rabbis *and they were killed*. Fewer and fewer Jews wear the frock coats of the pious.—There are more scoundrels about nowadays. Some of Them came to a merchant, put him in prison; a few days later Jewish middlemen appeared and had him set free, for a few thousand zlotys.

The 1st of September* passed calmly. The Poles published

* The first anniversary of the German invasion of Poland.

illegal appeals. PPS [Polish Workers Party] called for a home sit-down strike. Practically nobody was in the streets in the Polish quarter. Little movement about the streets in the Jewish quarter. A few dozen young Poles went through Leszno Street, wearing in their lapels a badge red and white on one side, the slogan "Long Live Poland!" on the other. When an auto passed, they lifted up their collars and covered their lapels.

The work-camp situation has become clearer. It turns out that the German firm that has undertaken to do the work gets 2 zlotys a day per worker, and only has to supply 1.08 zlotys worth of food per worker per day.

The Jewish Council has already received more than 200,000 zlotys from people who pay not to go to the work camps, and it uses the money to provide the campers with clothing, army blankets, and the like. Another problem is that people are impressed to work in Warsaw, and then put in the Pawia Street prison over night. The explanation for this is that, according to the latest decree, Jews may not be employed at compulsory labor. But the law does not say that prisoners may not be so employed. In Pawia Street 1,200 tailors are now imprisoned, at work during the day. This subterfuge is practiced by the Gestapo, S.S., and the like, who have no respect for the Government General's decrees.—A joke is making the rounds: Thousands of hammers from America have arrived. Their purpose: to drive dreams of London [winning the war soon] out of people's heads.—In Otwock the week Jews were impressed for the work camps, Jews escaped in a few villas; six were killed, eighteen wounded. One in the shed, near the wall.—Heard from someone who came here from Bzszesziny that in that town all Jews from eighteen to sixty were impressed for work.—Interesting fact about how the Polish commissariats administer some houses. Some of them use all the rent money to remodel apartments unnecessarily, so as not to have to turn the money into the German treasury. For patriotic reasons. Other commissariats try to ruin the Jews. So they don't pay taxes, or make mortgage payments to the banks—all to embarrass the Jews. But this has its bright side. The Jewish tenants don't pay rent. Skilled Jewish laborers not permitted to work in these houses; the same true of Jewish real-estate agents.

Heard from someone who was in Lodz at the beginning of July that they've removed the signs with the names of the streets in the Ghetto. All that remain are numbers, so as to give it more of the appearance of a regimented camp. The post was abolished, for this reason: Many packages containing means of subsistence arrived. King Chaim Rumkowski used to take some of them away for the hospital, kindergartens, and other public institutions. The postal officials imitated him. They were caught at it and shot. And then They abolished the post altogether. This is a general calamity. Rumkowski figured out that too much money was spent on newspapers, so, out of sheer miserliness, he forbade the sale of newspapers. So, for a smuggled paper they're paying 3 marks instead of 30 pfennig. The gold banknotes, nicknamed "Chayims" [after Rumkowski], were his brainchild—they bore R.'s signature. He has two beribboned German bodyguards around him all the time, so hated is he. . . .

Sept. 9

My dear friend:

Most of the madmen are mad for political reasons. Know a case involving Dr. Berlinski from Lodz. One day the Germans took the Jews from the courtyard where he lived for forced work. At work They lectured the Jews about the virtue of That One [Hitler] and maintained that the Jews didn't want to work. Later he, Berlinski, was taken to the medical office, where he declared that That One is the savior of the world. On that ground he was declared mad and sent off to the Zofjowka madhouse. While he was there, he heard various patients singing and crying the praises of That One. It seems that almost all of them have the same obsession, constantly mentioning his name. They give one another the [Nazi] salute. They're a dangerous problem because of their aggressive behavior toward the Others. But there are frequent cases of patients having to be sent home because they don't have money for maintenance. A few days back (before the 9th of September) Jewish Council officials were seized and kept busy day and night. Put into the Pawia Street prison.

Illustrative of the economic ruination of the Jews of Warsaw: Out of every 1,000 Jewish shoe shops, 12 received concessions enabling them to stay open.—The change in the attitude of the health authorities after becoming directly acquainted with Jewish institutions and houses. They became convinced that the stories of Jewish filthiness were true.— People picked up the last few days have been sent to Falenti Street, the S.S. domain. They spend the night in the Pawia Street prison. Get fed well. Very characteristic, this competition and wrangling among different parts [of the Nazi apparatus]. Competitive warfare.—It's been a week since Jews have been forbidden to walk on Saxon Place. Name changed to A.[dolf] H.[itler] Place.

On the one hand, there are many signs of anti-Semitism. For example, there are the commissariats that administer houses owned by Jews who have been dispossessed. Unemployed Polish judges and lawyers are the managers. But, on the other hand, one hears constantly about a new attitude on the part of the tax offices—they spread the taxes over longer payment periods, advise Jews how to take full advantage of exemptions, and one hears of good relations in the police commissariat, and the like.—Heard that there are signs in both Yiddish and German in Lublin. Requests from Jews to the German authorities must be written in German.—At 30 Franciszkanska Street, a few days ago a cellar was uncovered where a store of leather was walled in; it had been ruined by the dampness.—A few weeks ago, during the registration of Polish army officers, Jewish officers were ordered to stand, while Christian ones were given seats.—There are also reports that some house commissars are being liberal about the earlier debts of the Jewish tenants.—Success achieved today in a big matter: Packages can now be sent to those who work in the Falenti Street headquarters of the S.S.—Frequent cases of Poles voluntarily taxing themselves for Jewish causes.— Rabbi Asher wrote from Switzerland: "Hitler is having a bad time."—Many Jews give their things to Christians to hide for them, but frequently the people they give them to don't wish to return them. The same thing has happened to goods in Lodz.—The collaborationist *Jew. Gaz.*[ette] printed an article describing the humane character of the deportations from Cracow. . . . It's known that an old Jewish journalist with a reputation, P. Rosen, refused to work for the newspaper. He didn't want to sully his name in his old age.

At the funeral for the small children from the Wolska Street orphanage, the children from the home placed a wreath at the monument with the inscription: "To the Children Who Have Died from Hunger—From the Children Who Are Hungry."

Some of the courtyards are open, because the wooden gates leading to them have been torn down.

Sept. 24–29

. . . . the game. In a certain building where Jews are working They look through the telephone book for addresses of

Jewish professionals. Finding a professional, they enter his apartment, keep him there all day, and leave at night. All this to terrorize them. They beat up people for saluting Them ("I'm no friend of yours"). And they beat up people for not saluting them. Sometimes both things happen to the same person.—The pious Jews believe that the war will end this month. The measure of suffering is full. They resort to various cabalistic calculations to prove this.

Today, the 24th of September, the rumor of an armistice being declared spread through the city, in connection with Ribbentrop's visit to Rome.* On the other hand, other gossip has Horowitz [Hitler] leaving for Spain and a surrogate standing in for him. In a word, fantasy is at work.—Heard about something that happened a few weeks back on Karmelicka Street: An auto drove down the street, a *fine fellow* jumped out, seized a Jew by the hair, dragged him into the car, where three men brutally beat him and threw him out into the street again. Only one thing helps on such occasions: a general outcry. Since the 23d of September, Jews have been prevented from riding in the No. 9 streetcar. Probably the reason is that many soldiers are riding in it.

Rumkowski came to fetch Jewish doctors for Lodz. There's a dearth of them there. They have 30 in all, when some 200 are needed. They make a fortune.

Heard that the president of the Jewish Council of Warsaw, Adam Czerniakow, was kept standing in a German office for eight hours and not offered a chair. There are some who consider him a martyr who is honestly fulfilling his duty. "He is picking up the smell of the Gestapo," said an elderly community worker. The influence of environment.

There's a great deal of talk about education. A project's

---

*Joachim von Ribbentrop, German Minister of State, visited Rome on September 19, 1940; on October 4, Hitler and Mussolini met at the Brenner Pass; Ribbentrop was present.

afoot that would have all tuition fees flow into one fund from which it would be apportioned equally among all the teachers.

On Sliska Street Jewish furniture was drenched with water, ruining it. On the same street, water was poured on beds at night.—They took Dr. Gellmann, a hunchback, to work in the Auersdow hospital. They struck him so severe a blow that he went flying all the way to the door.

There's a project to set up a Ghetto in the Pawia Street prison, so as to concentrate the Jews in one place.—A decree published on the 24th of September, ordering Jews to travel in separate cars.—All Warsaw was seething yesterday with talk of an armistice. Cynics say: "What happened is this. They are taking the gates down at Nowolipki Street. Jews were impressed to do the work. The Jews bribed the guards, who stopped impressing people, and went into a Jewish bar to celebrate. There's the armistice for you!"—Twin babies were born in Germany, one called Horowitz [Hitler], the other Moses Ber [Mussolini]. They were bathed, and then got mixed up; no one knew which was Horowitz, which Moses Ber. They asked a Jewish passer-by to tell. He answered, "The one who makes in his pants first is Moses Ber. . . ."

Today, the 25th of September, widespread rumors about a Ghetto is to be smaller, i.e., Zlota, sienna, Chmielna, as well Jewish populace. There have been further evictions of Jews from houses outside the quarantined epidemic area. Sometimes people are given fifteen minutes to take their things out.

Moses [Mussolini] asked the Jews to help him—to tell him how to get out of Egypt. . . .*

* On September 22, four Egyptian ministers resigned in protest against the failure of the government to declare war on Italy.

Today, the 26th of September, people paid 10 groschen extra for German newspapers showing pictures of the destruction of German cities by Allied bombing. Heard about this game: One Jew was ordered to play General Rydz, [head of the Polish Army], another Mosciecki [head of the Polish state], other Jews had to applaud. The general and statesman were forced to quarrel and then come to blows.

. . . . A huge operation emptying Jewish apartments in Warsaw of furniture and other objects is under way.

Horowitz [Hitler] asked the local Governor General [Hans Frank] what he has been doing to the Jews. The Governor mentioned a number of calamities, but none of them sufficed for Horowitz. Finally, the Governor mentioned ten points. He began: "I have set up a Jewish Social Self-Aid Organization." "That's enough; you need go no further!"

It is said that the rabbi from Kozienice, when They were beating him, remarked that when the ram's horn was blown at the end of the world, the Germans would turn into geese. The rabbi asked, "Are there any Jews in Holland?" He was told there were, and in Denmark, France, and Norway as well. "If that is so," he said, "the German is the prisoner of the Jews!"

Today, the 27th of September, a rumor has spread that the Ghetto is to be smaller, i.e., Zlota, Sienna, Chmielna, as well as Leszno, Elektoralna, and Ogrodowa Streets. The Poles have addressed themselves to Zlota Street, claiming it should be theirs, because the Jews are in the minority there.—Heard today that Jews are returning to Cracow. They journey by ship, sailing the Vistula to Cracow, where they rent lodgings. —Jews were forbidden to do business in the countryside along the line running from Warsaw to Otwock.—A Ghetto is imminent.—Heard about a man who wouldn't open the door;

They chopped it down with a hatchet and threw him out of his apartment in his pajamas, flinging his pants out the window after him.—From tomorrow on, Jews will be allowed to ride in certain streetcars, but there's not a single streetcar on Zholibozh Street that Jews can ride. In the cooperative apartment house on the same street, the law forbids Jewish cooperators forced to leave their apartments to be paid back their share. Read an issue of the Zionist Young Guard paper *Flame* which justifiably decries the tendency among some of the young people to envy the Others, who are strong, firm, proud, enjoy the good things of life. There's a tendency for some of the young people to imitate Them.—The insecurity about apartments. The constant danger of being driven out of one's apartment is leading some people to wish there might be a Ghetto where the Others would not be able to enter.

Today, the 29th of September, got a blow in the mouth for not saluting a German. Today Jewish streetcars appeared, painted yellow, bearing a Jewish star on each side, and the sign: For Jews Only. A Christian hoodlum ran into one of the streetcars and tried to pass out free calendars, making anti-Semitic remarks. No one took his calendars, and one person ordered him to get off the streetcar at once.—A rabbi predicted that something would happen on the 27th of September and the Jews would be really and truly saved: Japan signed the treaty.*—One of the streets threatened with being kept out of the Ghetto is Zlota, where a short time ago a large number of Jews, and very recently Jews from the south, settled and bought apartments for a couple of thousand Zlotys.—In Otwock a decree has already been published stating which streets Jews may live in.

* On September 27, 1940, a ten-year pact between Germany, Italy, and Japan was signed in Berlin. It involved mutual recognition of a New Order and war in common against any intervening power.

MOVING INTO THE GHETTO

The building of the Warsaw Ghetto took the better part of 1940. At first the "Jewish quarter" was marked off as a quarantine area by barbed wire and fences. But by September, a wall 8 feet high began to take shape around the Jewish quarter. (It was not completed until the summer of 1941.) It eventually formed an oblong, about a mile and a half long, and it enclosed, besides the medieval ghetto, the long, straight streets of the industrial quarter running north of the railroad station. The northwest corner of the wall nearly touched the Vistula River, and it was bisected by the main line to Posen and Berlin. The Ghetto originally contained 1,500 buildings in an area of about 100 square city blocks, or 1,000 acres. In October, 1940, the 80,000 Christians living in the quarantine area were given two weeks to move out; their homes were to be taken by some 140,000 Jews living outside the area.

Though anticipated, the move into the Ghetto was a dread event. People feared to be cut off from the sources of their old occupations. (About a half of Warsaw Jewry were handicraftsmen, a fourth engaged in commerce, another

59

fourth professionals, and some 5 per cent industrial workers.) How were they to live? Their only hope was that the Ghetto would be open—that is, that the Ghetto residents would be able freely to come and go to other sections of the city through the twenty-two entrances. But that hope was soon dashed. On November 15, 1940, the Warsaw Ghetto was sealed off. Guards were stationed at both sides of the Wall—Jewish policemen on the inside, Polish and German militia on the outside. Only those who could prove the absolute necessity of their leaving could receive special permits. (Ringelblum notes the difficulties that doctors encountered in receiving permission to leave the Ghetto to work in the Jewish hospital on the Other Side of Warsaw.)

Meanwhile, the brief military stalemate that had followed the invasion of Poland had been disastrously broken. Germany had set forth to conquer the world. Holland, Belgium, and France rapidly fell before the German army. The British were lucky to be able to evacuate Dunkirk. Western Europe was at the mercy of the Third Reich and ruled by puppet governments that readily acquiesced in German demands for persecution of their Jewish citizens. The massacres in Eastern Europe had begun on the day Germany invaded Poland. Now it was Western Europe's turn. The Vichy government deprived refugee Jews of their civil rights; anti-Semitic measures were put into practice in Holland. German troops arrived in Rumania, and the Balkans began to totter. Wherever the Germans conquered, the Jewish badge, forced labor, Jewish quarters and ghettos, and finally, deportation and death were to be the pattern. As the Jews of Warsaw moved into the Ghetto, the situation seemed hopeless. They knew, as Ringelblum says time and again, that "only a miracle can save us—the war's speedy end." A few optimists prophesied such an ending. The rest dug in for a long stay.

8/OCTOBER, 1940

My dear:

This Rosh Hashana eve (2d of October) was a very sad one. Furniture was removed from the houses at 4, 6, and 8 Leszno Street. Besides, there was an order to clear out the apartments at Brami Zelazna Place 8, in the Wall. Tomorrow, Rosh Hashana, some of the prayer quorums will begin services at six in the morning. Placards with the traditional appeal to worshipers to come to the synagogue "to hearken unto the joy" have been put up in a number of courtyards in the Jewish neighborhood. In a word, business as usual among the pious.—Heard many favorable comments about the behavior of the Cracow Jews to those deported from Lodz (came from the camp at Radogoszcze). Arrived at Cracow at 9:30 P.M.; within half an hour they were all settled in lodgings. They rode before that for three days in the train with nothing to eat or drink.

Today began the removal of Poles from certain streets in the south of Warsaw: Poznanska, Vospulna. As for the Jews, for a few coins, they're allowed to stay a while longer and to take everything out.—The Jewish populace is terribly uneasy; no one knows whether he'll be sleeping in his own bed tomorrow. People in the south of town sit at home all day waiting for the hour when They will come and drive the Jews out. This is the system for removing furniture and household things: In the morning, the courtyard gates of the house involved are closed, and no one is allowed to leave.—The story is that King Chaim Rumkowski used to address Them in the following words: "May a Jew speak?"

Today, the 3d of October, the first day of Rosh Hashana, the mood was terrible, the Jews from the house at 31 Dzielna Street were ordered to leave within a short period. People paid the janitor 10 zlotys for leave to take out a valise full of things. The Polish guards were in business, too. Jews threw their things over the fence.—The story about Brami Zelazna Place 8 was a hoax. It ended with the payment of 150–200 zlotys.

Scenes in the streetcar: A Jew wearing a visor and with a red kerchief at his throat cries at a Jewish woman who is speaking Polish to him: "In the Jewish streetcar one must speak Yiddish!" Someone else shouts: "And Hebrew, Hebrew too!"—An old Jew gets off the streetcar and says to the passengers, "Good day, Jews." In a word: People feel perfectly at home. The only trouble is it is just a mite too crowded.— The conductors are also doing business at the Jews' expense: They don't hand out tickets when you get on, but collect the money. Getting off, one has to pay again. The price lists in the Jewish restaurants have to be in Yiddish. A foreign citizen not wearing an arm band wanted to get into a Jewish streetcar, but the conductor wouldn't let him.

The hoggishness of the rich Warsaw Jews. A year ago, when a Ghetto was imminent, and it was agreed that a contribution of 300,000 zlotys was necessary as a bribe to prevent the Ghetto's introduction, Uncle—the American Joint Distribution Committee—had to give over 100,000, the Warsaw millionaires 20,000 zlotys each.—Now in October it is said that the military and the health authority are against a Ghetto.— There are 350,000 Jews living in the quarantined epidemic area; the density there is nine times what it is outside.— Clearance sales are the most important source of income for thousands of Jews.

The joke is that there is a Government General [of Poland] and a Bombardment General [Europe] (the rest is Germany).*—Hundreds of Christians are making pilgrimages to the graveyard in Praga to visit the grave of the mother and seven children who fell during the bombing. The husband and father, who has returned from Russia, had a tombstone made in their memory, with an engraved representation of himself mourning his wife and children.

Heard today about the deportation (4th of October) of Jews from Zgierz. The Jews are allowed to live in the neighboring villages, but the peasants are not permitted to sell any Jew more than 1 kilo of potatoes. The Jews were also driven out of Rajsze.—Heard about a Polish professor, deported from Cracow to Oranienburg, who has been mild as an angel all his life but now maintains that *there is no other recourse for the new generation of Germans but complete extermination.* A simple Jew from a small town who went through fearful persecutions said there must be schools for torture in Germany. Otherwise, he could not understand where people could have learned such novel forms of torture.

* The Battle of Britain had begun July 10, 1940. The British Royal Air Force began bombing Berlin the night of September 23–24, 1940.

—Three days after the anticipated death (on September 27)*
of a famous villain in Germany [Hitler], when their expecta-
tion was not fulfilled, a man called Fridlajn committed suicide
with his wife.—A few days ago (the eve of Rosh Hashana)
pious Jews who recite prayers for the dead at the graveyard
were impressed into work.—A Christian tries to get on a Jewish streetcar. They stop her. She shouts: "See that! Even the
streetcars are for Jews only!"—An elderly Jewish lady wearing
the traditional headgear addresses Jewish children: "You
might speak Yiddish."—Yesterday the Jewish streetcar was
stopped and Jews were taken off for forced work. The conductor is subject to a fine of 1 zloty for letting a Christian on
the Jewish streetcar. There have been cases of Christians
insisting on riding in the Jewish streetcar. "I'm no anti-Semite!" one of them cries out. Some of the Jews say, "Well, we've
finally achieved a streetcar with a Jewish star." Others joke,
". . . and with a *mezuzah*, too!" In the Kutno Ghetto, memorial days in honor of Herzl† as well as Jabotinsky† were held
with the consent of the authorities.

Lately, only Germans are being engaged to remove the
furniture from Jewish apartments; They don't trust Jews to
do it, because they used to carry the goods down and then
up again.

Today, the 5th of October, more than one hundred Lodz
Jews were put in prison. Some say because they left the
Ghetto; others because they smuggled merchandise or got
their goods out with the help of Germans, who later informed
on them. Besides, They put old folks in prison, even Jews

* September 27, 1940, was the day on which, according to a nameless
rabbi's prediction, "something would happen and the Jews would be really
and truly saved." It was the date of the signing of the New Order pact. (*See
above*, p. 56).

† Founders of political and revisionist Zionism, respectively.

over sixty, because their children did not present themselves to register for the work camps. Also took tenants who concealed boarders.

A decree published stating that Jews may move about the Ghetto from seven in the morning to nine at night, outside the Ghetto from eight to seven, Poles until eleven.—A Jewess enters the Jewish streetcar: "I wish you all luck with your new streetcar!"

On Rosh Hashana people were taken to work on Rokowiecko Street. Many elderly Jews with gray hair.—Frank* or Leist† said he couldn't work fast enough to keep up with the things Jews think of (Ghetto, and so forth). When the question of a Ghetto was in the air, the Christian artisans from the quarantined epidemic areas appealed to the authorities: The resettlement would cost them their Jewish clients, with whom they've established close contacts.—Gallows humor: "Why should the Germans bomb London and the English Berlin? All that flying back and forth is a waste of gas. The Germans ought to bomb Berlin, the English London."—Any number of Christians may enter the main post office, Jews only ten at a time; hence the long line outside, mostly of women. The Jews wanted the war; the Jews are responsible for the war. That's the slogan repeated by the Others, even the best of them, in every conversation. . . . The "pure Jewish" streetcars—i.e., a single streetcar for Jews has a yellow placard; when there are two cars in a train, one of the cars is for Jews, the other for Christians (the Jewish one in the rear), and the placard is half-yellow.—Many firms, such as Wedel, have taken down the sign reading: Jews Not Wanted.

Characteristic that there's a Jews Not Wanted sign at the Jewish firm of Plutos. . . . I know a firm where the Jewish workers were forced to come in, though they had been dis-

* Governor General of Poland.
† Administrator of Jewish Quarter (Ghetto) of Warsaw.

charged, because the Others had not yet mastered the work. The Jews were threatened with the Gestapo if they did not report. In some of the district offices Jews are greeted, "Stay away, stay away!"—and They motion them off with Their hands. The "dirty" Jews are not to come too close.—*"Machen Sie dass Sie verschwinden!"* [See to it that you disappear!], a Jewess was told in a district office. She replied: "I am not air to disappear."—Heard of a big shot who made sure of his future by being pleasant to a Jew who came. Perhaps Germany might lose the war and having been kind to Jews might redound to his benefit.

A Jew of over sixty worked hard on Rosh Hashana, begged the Others for water, was told that a Jew could die but he would not get any water.—On Nalewki Street the Christians warn the Jews of a press gang approaching by shouting the air-raid warning signals: "Air raid over Warsaw, danger, still danger, danger approaches, danger over." Very interesting, the help from the Christians. Everybody who appears in the street is warned that They are seizing Jews in such and such a place. Christians pass the word along to Jews that They are beating Jews and ordering them to take off their hats when they don't salute.—The Fuehrer principle attracts some Jews. Saw the director of six handicrafts who strides about in boots and talks in the self-assured tone of an absolute ruler. He repeats the word "I" exactly as though he was one of God's anointed.—The reason why Jews can't go out until seven o'clock in the morning is an economic one. They don't want Jews going out early in the morning to the villages and buying up the produce of the peasants.—A Jew prayed poorly on Rosh Hashana. When asked why, he replied, "The praying matches the year."

The rabbi from Kozienice, speaking of the "slaver camps," said that he had news from them today. The best were in Tisovec and Siedlce.

The Jewish Council of Warsaw shows the least interest in its people. The best of the Councils is that of Radom, which often provides Jews in the forced-labor gangs with bread, medicine, and so forth. But in Warsaw there are sick Jews working who have not been relieved. And Zabludowski [of the Warsaw Jewish Council] says that everything is *all right.**
A Jew in Tisovec has undertaken to feed the campers there for 65 groschen a day.—Read a letter from Belzec a few weeks back: "Rather than go to a camp, jump into the Vistula." Yet the Poles are convinced that the Jews are better off than they!—Heard of a number of instances of Polish customers sending packages with means of subsistence to the Jewish merchants they used to deal with who are now in the Lodz Ghetto. The packages are in payment of the debts they owe the merchants. Heard moving stories in this connection.

Regrettably, the Jewish streetcar is dirtier than the non-Jewish one. Who is responsible? Both the streetcar management, which does little to keep them clean, and the Jewish passengers, who feel far too much at home there.—Today, on Marszalkowska Street, a Jewish streetcar was stopped. The Jews were ordered to get out; the placard turned to white; the sign "For Jews Only" thrown over the bridge; and *men of valor*† got a ride.—There have been cases recently of Jews from the south of Warsaw exchanging apartments with Christians from the north side. The south Warsaw Jews sit around on their valises waiting to be ordered to get out.—German Gestapo agents (they tell me they're called "candidates") receive no pay; consequently, they must find their own living for the three-year term of their candidacy. They were back of the Brami Zelazna Place 8 incident, where people were able to buy off the purported evacuation with 100–200 zlotys per apartment.—The populace is waiting for

* In English.
† Soldiers.

America to enter the war, but at the same time they're afraid of what's going to happen to the Jews. Even the most optimistic are beginning to entertain doubts about living through the war themselves—though they believe in Germany's ultimate downfall. Actually, it's hard to see what they pin their hopes on and how they imagine things will end.—It's said that appeals to stop fighting have been circulated among the German soldiers, but this report has not been confirmed. Meanwhile, the soldiers are imposing in their gloves and shiny boots, smooth-shaven, well-fed, wearing elegant uniforms of the best material.—There's a joke about a Jew riding in a streetcar. When he comes to the Hitler Platz,* he cries, "Amen!" The declaration in *Der Stuermer* that the moment America enters the war They'll put an end to the "Jewish question" in Europe has made a terrifying impression here. —Frank, it is said, made a speech full of hatred for the Jews. . . .

The news that the Jews could stay outside the walls of the Ghetto only for a certain time turned out to be incorrect. Apparently, the limitation was only for the duration of Frank's stay in Warsaw.—Saw this scene today: Students from Konarski's high school are beating Jews on the street. A few Christians stand up against them, and a crowd gathers. These are very frequent occurrences, where Christians take the side of Jews against attacks by hoodlums. That wasn't so before the war.—Frank telegraphed Czerniakow of the Warsaw Jewish Council that the Jews were not to produce so many decrees, because he (Frank) wasn't in the position to carry them out. —The Christians from the Old City of Warsaw, with Count Tarnowski at the head, began a movement to exclude the Old City from the Ghetto.—How was the law setting up a Ghetto in Warsaw voided last year? Count Ronikier appealed to the authority in Cracow (a man called Kundt, from what was

* Platz (plaza) also means "burst" in both German and Yiddish.

formerly Czechoslovakia). There were four armchairs in the room. Kundt was highly annoyed at the Graf for daring to intervene on behalf of the Jews. At a crucial moment, a yawn was heard. It came from a huge dog. The dog yawned again, the tension that filled the great hall was broken, and the Ghetto decree was called off.—Today a decree was published permitting Jews outside the Ghetto from eight in the morning to seven at night; also, Jews have to yield the right of way to soldiers, by getting off the sidewalk when they meet. This evening, at Zamenhofa Street, saw someone having a good time. The Jews say that doesn't bother them at all; when they see something like that, they hide behind the gate.

Jewish bakers are forbidden to bake white bread. This is a hard blow for the whole trade.—Jewish artisans who are not using their machines have to share them.—The *Warsaw News* published an item about a conference of doctors who declared there was a pressing need to isolate the Jews from the rest of the populace in a Ghetto for health reasons.

Today the rumor is spreading that a decree has been issued ordering Jewish men to wear satin caps; Jewish women, kerchiefs.—Today Jews and Poles were thrown out of the poorer houses on Powiszla Street; the deadline [for leaving] is three days.—Heard today that most of the porters* from Nalewki Street are informers; they follow merchants carrying bundles, and then inform on them. The porters who don't inform die of hunger. There was this case: They took 100 zlotys for not informing, and in an hour came along in an auto and took all the goods.—Tonight heard about this scene: At three o'clock in the morning *captains of valor* beat a Jew, shouting: "You said he has diamonds—where are they?"—Many people from south Warsaw have two apartments, one in the south of town, and one in the north [the Christian neighborhood]. Dr. Isaac

* Porters carried large loads commercially.

[Schipper]* was saved from being conscripted for labor by paying a petty police officer 20 zlotys.—A year ago, at the Feast of Tabernacles, there were long lines waiting to buy citrons for the holiday. Not knowing what it was all about, Christians got on line too.

Jews are volunteering to work in the villages to escape being conscripted for the work camps.—Heard about Gryce, where a group of young people are working as volunteers at the estate of a German magnate.—A mob of Jews originally from Cracow have gone back home [although] there they have to report for temporary residence permits, won't receive rations cards, and the like.—According to a decree issued by the Occupying Power, Jews have until the end of October to apply for permission to employ Aryan servants, or to discharge them.—Heard about a family of converts† that was given eight months in prison for not wearing the badge of shame.—Heard about a German who, seeing a Jew get off the pavement when he approached on Hoza Street, asked him why he did it, took him by the hand, and escorted him home. Another German waved his hand at a Jew from a distance, warning him off the sidewalk. This forces the Jews to zigzag across the street in the neighborhoods frequented by Germans.

[The entry that follows is a specimen of a first draft of notes hastily jotted down.]

Oct. 10

Whether or not the opposition to the Germans is greater than it used to be.—The Madagascar plan.—Attitude to Jewish emigration.—Of the ill.[egal?] leadership in the party.— 50,000 German Jews in work service; 100,000 Jews in Ger-

* A historian and the chairman of the Jewish District Aid Committee.
† Baptized Jews.

many. Of them, half more than fifty-five years old. Forced labor for women up to thirty-five, men to fifty-five, to seventy for those who are on relief. Yellow arm bands with a Jewish star.—72 pfennig an hour.—One psychological blow sufficient to break [the German Jews?]. The impression made by the occupation of France, the armistice [there]*—Slovakia: [Jews] locked out of schools. Set fire to the schools.—Vichy removes Jews from official positions; foreign Jews interned. Prominent Jews confiscated for 825 mill.[ion francs] Bank Marian closed; the governor of Madagascar, Abraham Shramek [?], arrested. September 4th: anti-Semitic excesses in Marseilles and the Riviera. . . . Thirty thousand Jews in concentration camps, among them 3,500 from Belgium and 1,500 from Alsace. Those who fled to Vichy can't go back again. Altogether, 100,000 helpless.—Unoccupied France: The Jewish stores designated. Yellow arm bands. In Bordeaux and Ar. . . papers with a special designation, mashinations of Jewish firms. Ritual slaughter forbidden. The schools in Strasbourg destroyed. . . .

Oct. 12–13

My dear:

Heard today of two tendencies in the PPS [Polish Workers Party] one to the right to Witos,† the other to the left. The second group is called Spartacus. There are guesses that some of the political groups are managed by the Gestapo. It's said that some of the political publications are put out by Them. They even receive food allowances; the goal of the Gestapo is to find out what's happening among the Poles. It's under That influence. Naturally, there's no proof.

* On June 22, 1940, France signed an armistice with Germany; on June 24, with Italy.
† Head of the Polish Peasant Party.

Today, Saturday the 12th of October, was dreadful. The loud-speaker announced the division of the city into three parts: a German quarter, encompassing midtown and Nowy Swiat Street; a Polish quarter; and a Jewish quarter. By the end of October, everyone but the Germans has to move over into the quarter assigned them, without taking their furniture. Black melancholy reigned in our courtyard. The mistress of the house had been living there some thirty-seven years, and now has to leave her furniture behind. Thousands of Christians businesses are going to be ruined.—Heard about a police chief who jumped out of a streetcar at the sight of students from Konarski's school attacking Jews, ran after them, and fired in the air. Don't know how it ended.

There are 140,000 Poles living in the quarter assigned to Jews; 60,000 Jews outside that quarter. Heard from some Poles of a sentence executed on Poles in Torun: The prisoners were bound to a motorcycle, their hands and feet were tied, [and the motorcycle was driven] until they breathed their last.—Gradually, a Ghetto is being established. All telegrams have to be dispatched through the Jewish Council; they handle train tickets, too.—The Jews have received a bitter "gift" this Yom Kippur. Some people maintain that it is even worse for the Poles, who have a great many business undertakings in the Ghetto.—On Walowa Street the Jewish merchants have solved the security problem by a very simple method: There's a German in uniform sitting in a café. He gets 100 zlotys a day; his duty is to come to the aid of any merchant on the street threatened with robbery.*—The fact that Jews of Praga may not go out of the Ghetto after seven o'clock at night is a great [economic] blow to the Jewish populace.

* The same was true of the merchants on Wielopole Street. (*See above*, p. 46.)

Today, Sunday, the 13th of October, left a peculiar impression. It's become clear that 140,000 Jews from the south of Warsaw and the Praga suburb will have to leave their homes and move into the Ghetto. All the suburbs have been emptied of Jews, and 140,000 Christians will have to leave the Ghetto quarter. The question of what's to happen to the Christian businesses has not yet been clarified. All day people were moving furniture. The Jewish Council was besieged by hundreds of people wanting to know what streets were included in the Ghetto.—A group of assimilated teachers are said to have gone to the Polish [school] inspectors for support against the Jews who wished to introduce the teaching of Yiddish in the folk schools.

The porters take advantage of every opportunity to make money. When the house at 31 Dzielna Street was closed down, They threw the things in the house over a fence. The porters locked the gates and demanded 2–3 zlotys per package retrieved.—The removal of the Jews from the suburbs as well as from poverty-stricken Praga signifies their complete ruination; they will not even have the money to resettle.— Some people are having terrible trouble with their Christian servants. . . . They can't be laid off without the permission of the labor exchange, so they do whatever they want. There have been cases of servants putting on their mistresses' things. —The Christians who live on the banks of the Vistula and work the sand banks say they won't move, though threatened with bloodshed.—Today was a terrifying day; the sight of Jews moving their old rags and bedding made a horrible impression. Though forbidden to remove their furniture, some Jews did it. There were cases of vehicles containing furniture being stopped and taken away.—This is what happened in Wartegoj last year. A congregation of Jews were ordered to bury the president of the Jewish Council, or maybe it was the rabbi of the town. They had reached his throat before the Others explained that it was only a joke. The Jew shook the dirt off and said: "The earth take *them!*"—Heard that the Others have threatened that if typhus should spread the Ghetto will be closed.—The Jewish Council announced the recruitment of 1,000 Jewish policemen, honorary at first.—The complete impotence of the Council. Two weeks back, the city fathers congratulated Adam Czerniakow on his victory: He had staved off a Ghetto. As late as Friday, i.e., a day before the decree, the Council announced that no Ghetto was in prospect.—Some Christian landlords in Praga will not permit anything to be removed from the apartments until rent is paid for October. Others will allow nothing to be removed.— "Happy Corner." That's what the Jews call the newspaper page that tells about "marmalade"—the German casualty lists. —S.S. men were removing furniture from a house on Ciepla Street. Across the way, a Jewish troupe was singing and playing music. The S.S. men ordered the troupe to play a waltz and dance in the middle of the street. The well-dressed Jews who came along were ordered to give 5 zlotys for the entertainment; poorly dressed Jews, 10 groschen and more.— They seized several women, took them into a cellar. There forced them to pluck feathers. After the women had finished, They stripped them naked and gave each of them thirty blows.—According to the new law promulgated by Dr. Fischer, governor of the Warsaw district, Poles may remain living in the German quarter of the city, but they may not move into it. It is feared that the Poles will refuse to move out of the new Jewish quarter. Moving out of the Polish quarter is attended with great difficulty. Some Christians say they will not move out. They'd rather burn their houses down.—Jews were driven out of Czestochowa into a neighborhood near the graveyard, where only very few of them can live.—In Otwock the introduction of a Ghetto has been deferred temporarily.

Today the rumor spread that there would be no sick fund. There is talk of a public-morals police force in Warsaw. The city is placarded with white cards advertising apartments for exchange between Jews and Christians. The whole wall near the apartment office of the Jewish Council is white. The Poles are up to all kinds of tricks to increase the number of houses in the Polish quarter. For example, they wall up the gates of houses facing on Jewish neighborhoods; the gates facing Polish neighborhoods of the very same houses are left open. The rumor is rife among Polish *hoi polloi* that the Jews have collected 5 million zlotys and given it to the Others so as to be given the larger plazas, wider streets, and so forth. The Jews in the German section of Warsaw are particularly unfortunate, because they have no chance of exchanging apartments. Some Poles pick the Jewish apartments they want and appear with requisition orders from the magistracy. This tactic deprives Jews of the right to exchange apartments with Christians.—A Ghetto was instituted in Pruszkow.— Some Jews don't open up when the Others come. One man was praying, and in the middle of the Eighteen Benedictions, which he didn't want to interrupt. So, unable to wait any longer, They left. About Brenner:* What did Hitler and Mussolini talk about? "Benito zebito, O Adolfo, we need helpo, O sweet Duce, we are kaputshee. Heil Hitler I am looking for a middlemaner. If so, Mussolini, you are a swiney. If you have to complaino, go to Ciano, It was R . . . b . . . p [Ribbentrop] who did this to me, the goddamn s.o.b."

Oct. 20

. . . how the Jewish police have taken over the police service. They direct traffic in the street. They've put things straight on Karmelicka Street. They're already sitting around

* The meeting between Hitler and Mussolini at Brenner Pass on October 4.

in the commissariats, though the Polish police are still in charge. On the 31st the Poles are due to leave.—It's reported that a large transport of sugar was moved through Chlodna Street. Each of the guards got *five thousand*. Though Germans have to have passes to enter the Ghetto, a number of streets were robbed today again and bedding and the like taken away. Long lines standing in front of the drug stores, which are being simply sold out. The courtyards too are buying large amounts. . . . The dearth of medications in the Lodz Ghetto, where a spoonful of castor oil was worth a fortune during the dysentery attack.

The people who have come here from Lodz, experienced in Ghetto life, have concentrated on buying up large quantities of produce. They also buy big amounts of wood, rather than coal.

Today there was a vicious article in the Polish rag [*New Warsaw Courier*] about the Sabbath Gentiles who serve as the Jews' catspaws, bringing produce into the Ghetto. A series of such articles is being published—with photographs of the persons involved.

Heard that the group that was impressed to work in Polaw under Jewish supervision have found good conditions there. They earn 3 zlotys 20, of which 1 and 20 goes toward maintenance. The rest is for the family. They live in stone barracks; the place is kept warm; on arrival they received breakfast. The Jews from Henrikow and neighboring towns were sent into the countryside; the same in the area around Radomsk. People prefer to work in Okencia. On the way back from work, they buy a couple of breads and make some money selling the bread in the Ghetto. The *righteous Gentile* cursed out the Polish police chief of Grochow for putting the *chalutzim* in prison; made him personally responsible if a hair of their heads was touched. Bought a Dutch cow for them. Has great feeling for Jews who work on the land.

The Jewish Council is maneuvering so as not to have to create a food-supply office itself for the Ghetto, but to have the city magistracy continue to handle this function. The Poles are in accord with this; one of their head officials in the magistracy has promised to help in this matter.—Janusz Korcszak arrested for not wearing an arm band.—Today the Germans declared that no potatoes would be allowed to enter the Ghetto, because the Jews have large hoards of them. We are to receive potatoes later.

Today, the 23d of October, another announcement over the loud-speaker that Walicow and Zeglana Streets have been excluded from the Ghetto. At the same time, news that the deadline for moving into the Ghetto has been postponed until after the 31st of October, i.e., until the 15th of November. People are walking around crazy with anxiety because they don't know where to move to. Not a single street is sure of being assigned to the Ghetto, but every street has something that puts it in jeopardy. On Zeglana Street it was Ulrich's factory that decided for its exclusion from the Ghetto. The head of the resettlement office is said to be the same Sh.[Shea Braude] infamous for having organized the Lodz Ghetto. People are fearful lest the Lodz experience be repeated in Warsaw.—Today the orphanage at 6 Wolska Street sent its children, thinly dressed and barefoot, to the Society for Self-Aid offices at 5 Tlomackie Place. This was intended as a demonstration against the Jewish Council, but the children were driven away, so they overturned a few wagons.—A fearful uncertainty has seized everyone. No one knows what the next day will offer. A few days ago hoodlums broke into 93 Zelazna Street and forcibly occupied some Jewish apartments. They hung up a cross and said, "Dare to touch this!"— When, a few days ago, it became known that Zelazna and all the

neighboring streets (Lucka, Wronia, the end of Sliska, Panska, etc.) had been excluded from the Ghetto, the anguish
was indescribable. There were Jews who said they'd rather be
poisoned with gas than tortured so. More than 7,000 Jews
from the neighborhood had moved into those particular
streets, as well as Jews from Praga. The Jews from Praga had
exchanged their large apartments for small ones in the Zelazna
neighborhood. Christians who moved into apartments in the
south of Warsaw exchanged for larger ones; Jews moving
north, on the contrary, always exchanged for smaller apartments. At 9 Warecka there was a German stationed to ex-
amine what the Jews were taking out with them, each piece
separately. At the same address, a Jew who worked for the
Jewish Council fetched a German from the Gestapo. For
pointing out forty Jewish apartments with furniture, he got
an apartment free for himself, and besides his furniture was
removed by car.—Some rich Jews have lost all their money.
For example, diamonds bought for 100,000 zlotys are now
worth 5,000. Dollars bought at 250 now worth 30.—Haberbusz, the big brewer, is said to have received flowers in grati-
tude from the Christians for having saved some of the streets
for them to live in. He is said to have intervened on their behalf in Berlin.—A few days back a project was proposed for
occupying Mylna Street, and thus having access to the Evangelical Hospital. A lightning count was taken of Jews living on
the street. Numbers 1 and 3 Elektoralna Street have been excluded from the Ghetto. The exit on Elektoralna [fronting on
the Ghetto] was walled up by the Christians in the house;
the gate facing on Przejazd Street left open. Przejazd is outside the Ghetto.—The Jewish populace was more taken aback
by the news about Zelazna being outside the Ghetto (30,000
Jews involved) than they were by the news of the Ghetto itself, because they were already used to the idea. The houses
on Graniczna Street have been walled up on our side, the

exit on Skuzana Street left open; but this saved those houses for the Ghetto.—The Jewish streetcars are fearfully crowded, and not particularly clean. Riding in them is simply revolting. —Priests are out in every street, collecting signatures for petitions that "mixed streets," where both Jews and Christians live, be excluded from the Ghetto. They even demand that Nowolipki Street, which is purely Jewish, be excluded from the Ghetto because of the church there.

A friend of mine saw some twenty Jews standing with hands raised on Muranowska Street. Those murderers were holding them up. Yesterday, the 22d of October, a Pole or group of bandits shot a Jew to death on Nowolipie Street.— Found out that in Praga in January . . . Friedman . . . stood up for the rabbi when the latter was being impressed for work and beaten. Friedman was shot on the spot.

At 2 Przebieg Street two soldiers demanded 50 zlotys from a friend of mine to let him alone. He didn't have it, so they took him a few kilometers outside the city and took his coat away from him.—A Jew alternately laughs and yells in his sleep. His wife wakes him up. He is mad at her. "I was dreaming someone had scribbled on a wall: 'Beat the Jews! Down with ritual slaughter!'" "So what were you so happy about?" "Don't you understand? That means the good old days have come back! The Poles are running things again!"

Two lawyers, Koral and Tykoczynski, have committed suicide because of the resettlement decree. K. was the legal counsel of the French Embassy.

The Jewish Council's registration of apartments has broken the black-market speculation in them. People are looking for relatives and friends to share their apartments, out of fear lest the Council put strangers in to board with them.—It is said that the Lodz Ghetto is about to be declared open.* The Ghetto in Kutno is open already.—Instead of the prewar slogan of "Jews—Go Back to Palestine!" today we've a Jewish star in Poland, and Poles in Palestine.†

Swientojerska Street was saved for the Ghetto, thanks to H. Zuckerman, who stood on guard and allowed no Jews to move—or the game would have been up. Usually, the last count [of Christians and Jews] on the last day—before the deadline for moving—is decisive.

On Smocza Street there's Pfeiffer's [tannery]; on Nowolipke, a church; Mylna has a hospital; Heneberg's factory is on Chlodna—so the Christians claim that all these streets should be outside the Ghetto.

The finest public institutions in Warsaw have been ruined: Korcszak's [children's home] at Krochmalna. The old folks' home.—Eight hundred Torah scrolls desecrated.

A world of beggars and tramps in the streetcar. All merchandise transported via streetcar. Rumors that produce will have to be paid for in gold and foreign currency in the Ghetto.

Today, the 24th of October, Ceglana Street was returned to the Ghetto. So this back and forth dance goes on, and no one knows how it will all end.—There was this case: A man exchanged his apartment on Marszalkowska Street for one on Wronia. In the meantime it become known that the Zelazna Street neighborhood was to be excluded from the Ghetto. So he was left standing outside his old apartment, without a new one. Meanwhile, his things were stolen from him.—In many cases the Christians are demanding—and receiving—moving money. For the time being, the Jewish Hospital has been

---

* An open ghetto was one whose residents might leave it at stated intervals. A closed ghetto (like that of Warsaw) could be left only by persons with special permits.

† Polish soldiers fighting with the British in the Middle East.

left outside the Ghetto. At first, They wanted the hospital administration to leave the wonderful equipment behind and remove the patients. Fear has been expressed that, when spotted (exanthematic) typhus breaks out, as it inevitably must under the newly created circumstances, the Ghetto will be closed.—The Jewish Council is accused of not doing anything. They are completely uninformed about what is happening. They found out about the Zelazna Street neighborhood exclusion from the Ghetto through the loud-speaker. —The converts who must move into the Ghetto are in a desperate situation.

9/NOVEMBER, 1940

Nov. 8

My dear:

There's been the growth of a strong sense of historical consciousness recently. We tie in fact after fact from our daily experience with the events of history. We are returning to the Middle Ages.—Spoke to a Jewish scholar. The Jews created another world for themselves in the past, living in it forgot the troubles around them, allowed no one from the outside to come in. As for parallels: The present explusion is one of the worst in Jewish history, because in the past there were always cities of refuge. Someone said to me: "It's bad to read Jewish history, because you see that the good years were few and far between. There were always troubles and pogroms." A memento left over from history is this plague of informers we are suffering from so badly. Take the incident of Sachsenhaus who was supported for three months in the apartment of a Jewish communal figure, Nergep.* Imbibed their culture and from being a decent human being became a slippery one.

* Another code name for Gepner.

The Sachsenhaus incident [see below] reminds you of the proverb: "You beat my Jew, and I'll beat your Jew."

Often, police chiefs appear at the office of the Jewish Council and demand money for Jewish workers. The "amulet" on the door stating that everything must go through Leist* has been of no avail.—People think nothing of having their things taken away, because they have faith in better times coming. Their only hope is to survive the present.—The fact that the Jews have many artisans evokes the amazement of the Others. —The ragmen in the Lodz Ghetto, as well as the scrap collectors, live outside the Ghetto. They have the right to travel by train. The janitors are exploiting the situation of the last few days and the setting up of the Ghetto in Warsaw. They have become the middlemen for apartments. They are doing business in produce.—The increase in typhus a result of the growing density of the Jewish population.—Customary thing in official documents, the appelation "Jude," occasionally "Herr," but very seldom.—I marvel at the pious Jews who sacrifice themselves by wearing beards and the traditional frock coats. They are subjected to physical abuse.—Saw traces in the Jewish Council office of Advocate Popower's blood. It was he who issued the verdict against Sachsenhaus for requisitioning a Jewish apartment. Sachsenhaus made a speech to the Others about the necessity of introducing order in the Jewish Council. Recently the number of typhus cases has increased (35). Heard about someone who moved seven times because the Ghetto boundaries kept shifting. Another person, four times— turned out of Hoza Street, Freta Street, 68 Grzybowska Street, and another place.—The long wall at Wielopole Street looks like a prison wall.—It has been taking an hour and more to get to the office lately. You have to wait at the courtyard gate a long time before the danger of seizure is past. When people are seized for forced work on Leszno Street, it is known im-

* Commissar of Warsaw.

mediately at Muranowska Street.—Heard from someone that there was nothing to eat in the Lodz Ghetto, so that a man who was very rich a short time ago asked a friend for the potato leavings.—A waiter in the Lodz self-maintenance kitchen called Kaminski used to be a well-known manufacturer.

Today, the 8th of November, rumors again that the Ghetto would be postponed until April.—At Falenti Street Jews who are exempt from forced labor because of their age or occupation are ordered to exchange shoes or other articles of clothing with those who remain behind. In the same place they ordered a young man with a beard to announce to all the Jewish work gangs that he was twenty years old, and then to scream *"Ohne Beruf"*—*"No Occupation"*—louder and louder. Finally, a Jew had to shave the young man's beard off.—Every German institution has its Jew, who is well-treated though other Jews are mistreated. For example, there's a man they call "Moses" in the Dinance Park garages. He has been able to get a number of Jews exempted from work.

Today the Jewish Council received a written notice that the Jews must move out by the 15th of November. This puts an end to all the rumors about the postponing or enlarging of the Ghetto. There's a growing fear of the prospect of a closed Ghetto, especially since the Polish police were said to have been ordered out of the Ghetto today.—Everyone who can is hoarding as much as possible.—The commandant of the Falenti work camp takes produce from the peasants "for my Jews."

A police chief came to the apartment of a Jewish family, wanted to take some things away. The woman cried that she was a widow with a child. The chief said he'd take nothing if she could guess which one of his eyes was the artificial one. She guessed the left eye. She was asked how she knew. "Because that one," she answered, "has a human look."

There was said to have been an announcement over the

loud-speaker yesterday that it was forbidden to speak of the "Jewish Ghetto"; the proper term was "Jewish quarter," like the German and the Polish quarters.—Today a Jewish tailor on Orla Street had goods taken away from him. There was a Jew in the crowd who ripped the collars off fur coats and hid them in his breast.—PCH ("Pay Conductor Half") is what they call the Jewish streetcars nowadays; they're half empty. A Jew was ordered to take off his fur coat. He answered: "I'd gladly give it to you, but I've just come out of the hospital. I had the typhus." That scared Them off.—Heard that some 200 persons have died of natural causes or been killed in the work camps: In Belzec alone 80 people have died of dysentery, and an equal number have been killed at work.

The news that apartments are to be requisitioned has started people looking for cheap boarders, to fill up the apartments.—Those who turn informer get 10 per cent of the spoils. Four of them accompanied a police chief (who happened to be an honest man) to a Jewish business on Nalewki Street. They grabbed linen and other things, which they stuck into their trousers, and came out bulging like bears.—*Heute Tag Ohne Ausweisen*—"No Work Certificates Today." The joke is that that means They're seizing people for work today even if they have certificates exempting them. That's what some of the press gangers say.—Often, when Jews salute the Others, They gesture "It isn't necessary." Most of Them pass by as though the salute had nothing to do with them. The worst thing is when two or three Jews come along in a group, and only one of them salutes. Very often courteous Germans reply to the salute.

The Ghetto is much more painful now than it was in the Middle Ages, because we that were so high and mighty are now fallen so low. The appeal to develop high standards in the Ghetto: to work for leveling of, for example, taxes on silk, clothing, weddings; for mutual-aid institutions, for a rich community life.—Walls are being put up around the Ghetto at a feverish pace. It's hard to walk from Leszno Street to Grzybowska Street. The crowds on Solna and Ciepla Streets, making it impossible to get through.

Nov. 19

My dear:

The Saturday the Ghetto was introduced (16th of November) was terrible. People in the street didn't know it was to be a closed Ghetto, so it came like a thunderbolt. Details of German, Polish, and Jewish guards stood at every street corner searching passers-by to decide whether or not they had the right to pass. Jewish women found the markets outside the Ghetto closed to them. There was an immediate shortage of bread and other produce. There's been a real orgy of high prices ever since. There are long queues in front of every food store, and everything is being bought up. Many items have suddenly disappeared from the shops.—There's no connection between Twarda and Leszno Streets. You have to go by way of Zelazna Street.—Jewish businesses in the Aryan part of the city have been shut tight, to prevent pilfering.— Neither Saturday nor Sunday did the Jewish doctors get passes. The Jewish Council levies a tax of 5 zlotys per pass. —Saturday Jewish workers were not allowed to leave the city on their outside work details. On the first day after the Ghetto was closed, many Christians brought bread for their Jewish acquaintances and friends. This was a mass phenomenon. Meanwhile, Christian friends are helping Jews bring produce into the Ghetto.

At the corner of Chlodna and Zelazna Streets, those who are slow to take their hats off to Germans are forced to do calisthenics using paving stones or tiles as weights. Elderly Jews, too, are ordered to do push-ups. They tear paper up small, scatter the pieces in the mud, and order people to pick them up, beating them as they stoop over. In the Polish quarter Jews are ordered to lie on the ground and They walk over them. On Leszno Street a soldier came through in a wagon and stopped to beat a Jewish pedestrian. Ordered him to lie down in the mud and kiss the pavement.—A wave of evil rolled over the whole city, as if in response to a nod from above. At the same time there are still official optimists who believe that there will be no Ghetto, or it will not be a closed one.—The Jewish Law and Order Service (which appeared on the 16th of November) was ordered to dance on one foot around a group of Jews performing calisthenics in the street. The Jewish Council is said to be preparing a plan for a post office, food-supply service, and Jewish currency.—Because of the closing of the Ghetto and the feverish buying up of everything, all the Jewish streets are full of people milling about. It's simply impossible to pass through. Pedestrians overflow the sidewalk, spill over on the street.—Friday night, Jews were arrested in Praga and driven by car to Muranowska and other streets in the Ghetto, and there deposited. They spent the night on the stoops and in the courtyard gateways. Took nothing with them except hand baggage.—Saturday saw groups of Jews being driven from Praga into the Ghetto. Under guard they were settled down in houses and schools, dance halls, etc. The Jewish Council is requisitioning single rooms for them from Jews who have large apartments.—A scene: At the corner of Chlodna and Zelazna Streets, a Jewish family says its farewells to a Polish one. They kiss, shake hands, invite one another to "come visit us next week."—At the end of Tlomackie Place and Bielanska Street—the borderline between the Ghetto and the Other Side—stand a long line of streetcars being searched for Jews trying to smuggle themselves out of the Ghetto. Everybody is ordered out of the streetcar and their papers examined. It looks like a border point between two countries. Sometimes a streetcar stands there for as long as ten–fifteen minutes.—"Greco banditto, toto ferditto, popo babitto, Benito." A telegram from Mussolini to Hitler after the Greeks had defeated the Italian army.*—Was told about a group of workers from a work camp. Shadows of human beings, shoeless, feet wrapped in rags.—The furniture requisitioned from Jewish apartments is taken to the Splendide movie house (the Sphinx), and can be bought back there a little at a time. *Our brethren the children of Israel* are helpful in this business.—The revolting informing on Muni.†—One of the sad developments of the resettlement has been the the large number of beggars that have turned up (Jews from the suburbs).—A group of Jewish workers together with their foreman had to do calisthenics at the corner of Leszno and Zelazna Streets.—The doctors who rode the streetcar to the hospital at Czista Street on Sunday were taken off the car and made to do calisthenics for an hour. An elderly Jew passed the guards on Twarda Street and did not—for reasons of piety—take off his hat in salute although the Jewish guards warned him. So They tortured him a long time. An hour later, he acted the same way. "They can go to hell."

Many Jews make their living outside the Ghetto, and now they're cut off from it. Firms that are administered by the city commissariat, it is said, will have to move to the Other Side —i.e., the Jews who make part of their living out of these firms will lose that part, too.—It is said that the Ghetto will be half open until the 25th of November, afterward. . . .

A big man‡ came to Adam,§ kissed him, cried, and said that he did not agree with the idea of having a Ghetto. People are

* On October 28, 1940, Greece rejected an Italian ultimatum. The Italian army crossed the Greek frontier. On November 19, the Greeks announced that the Italians had been driven back.

† Emmanuel Ringelblum himself.

‡ A German officer.

§ Adam Czerniakow, the head of the Jewish Council of Warsaw.

paying 2,500 zlotys moving money for the administration that handles the Jewish houses; the same amount for concessions in monopoly items. There's also talk in the courtyards about having all the neighbors in the courtyard cook collectively, because of the shortage of wood and coal. The same thing happened in Lodz, where as early as the third day [after the Ghetto was introduced] they even had a common pot to brew coffee in.—Heard today how King Chaim Rumkowski rooted out the bribe-takers from the Law and Order Service men [Jewish police] of his Lodz Ghetto. Went into the room and tore badges off the first ten Law and Order men he saw, saying he didn't have time to investigate. The resettlement was handled very well in Lodz. They had German guards to help them in cases where Christians put up opposition. The first night of the Lodz resettlement there were 7 deaths, the second night 70, and the third night 133. A total of 300 were killed.

A Christian was killed today, the 19th of November, for throwing a sack of bread over the Wall.—The rabbi of Wengrow was stabbed last year. The blood flowed from his wound, but he kept working for four hours until he fainted.—Many Jews of means who until now never gave a groschen for relief have suddenly begun to give large sums to the Self-Aid Society, so that it can purchase produce for the winter for the poor people in the courtyards. The Ghetto game is continuing. It is said that the electricity has been turned off in the Lodz Ghetto. Jews have to sit in the dark there. The rumor has spread that electricity will cost four times as much for Jews as for Christians. One of those good ideas of ours that the Nazis are happy to adopt!

Today, the 20th of November, a rumor that the Ghetto will be open for five days, and afterwards (after the 25th) will be hermetically sealed. A rumor that They will supply the Ghetto with food on condition that payment be in gold and foreign currency.—The Lodz Ghetto said to have been opened.—The Gehenna at the corner of Chlodna and Zelazna Streets goes on. They order groups of pedestrians to walk past very fast, all at once. They drive them on like dogs. People are even pulled out of droshkies. A company of Jewish Law and Order Service men were forced to do their exercises at the Theater Plaza: Fifty of them had to be carried off afterward.—It is said that the authorities have already begun taking away the merchandise of Jewish businesses situated outside the Ghetto, a little at a time.

Often, Jews recommended by the Gestapo get apartments through Their requisitions. Two [?] Jews stayed in Zholibozh at the homes of Christian neighbors . . . not ordered to move out . . . came with letters of recommendation from the Gestapo for monopoly licenses.

Nov. 21

Two Ghettos were introduced in Otwock: one, a Sick Ghetto; the other, a Residential Ghetto. From eight o'clock Saturday to eight o'clock Monday, one may not go out into the street. The rest of the week one can go out of the Ghetto from 10 A.M. to 6 P.M.—The Jewish dealers are transporting produce, fowl, and like items from the Vistula line to Warsaw. Payment is by the wagon load. The first costs 250 zlotys, says the conductor; the second, 300 zlotys. The health authority made a check. They found that half of the passengers were driving with "Linarski's tickets."* Both doors of the train car were closed, and no one allowed in. [The food smugglers] also bribed a German with 40 zlotys per load.—Some Warsaw

---

* I.e., without tickets, but with banknotes with which they bribed the conductors. Linarski's signature was on the banknotes.

Jews have fled to the provinces.—Christian acquaintances send flowers to people moving into the Ghetto. Never were so many flowers sold before. At the beginning of the war, or before the occupation of Warsaw by the Germans, or during the first weeks of the occupation—whenever an individual Jewish businessman may have liquidated his business—the Jewish bosses gave their Christian employees a lot of money as severance pay. Etingon in Lodz gave his employees a year's pay; other Jewish businessmen gave six months' pay. Still others offered their Christian employees merchandise, but they refused it. . . . Praga refugees moved themselves into the Ghetto this way: They loaded wagons with bedding, and sat down on top of it.

The guards of the Warsaw Ghetto are from Lodz. They are old hands at the job. Today, the slogan is: "Go slow, don't run like yesterday." A Jew was ordered to kneel, and They urinated on him. They beat women, too, at Chlodna Street. The Ghetto has evoked considerable unrest among the Poles, who are fearful that They will get after them next: Trustees will be appointed—to take over Polish property, as they did Jewish property—their furniture will be removed, and the like. Today the rumor circulated that the English and Soviet radios announced every half hour: "Half a million Jews are being immured in a Ghetto."—What's the point of using tiles in the calisthenics at Chlodna Street? They give them two tiles to exercise with, one heavier than the other. You can't keep your balance when you bend over holding the tiles in your hands. To avoid the Zelazna–Chlodna corner you have to go way down Chlodna, then through 29 Chlodna Street into Krochmalna Street. But They found out about this bypass and walled up the passageway through the 29 Chlodna courtyard.

The work camp transports: Some of Those who returned came back in their underwear. Yesterday, the 20th of November, more than 800 Jews were routed from their beds for the forced work camps, invalids, too, never sent to the medical commission [for certification as fit for work].—Heard of two instances where women stepped off the street to allow soldiers to pass. The latter marveled and said they knew of no such decree.—Streets fearfully full of movement again. The populace races about terror-stricken, but the young folks are strolling down Leszno Street, as usual.

One hundred fifty Jews from Berlin are supposed to have arrived at the Zofjowka madhouse. In general, there has been no connection between the Jews from Poland and those from other countries that are now part of the Reich. Besides, Jewish prisoners of war from Poland rarely came into contact with the Jews of the cities where they were stationed.

Nov. 29

Prices keep going up daily. Now, two days before the closing of the Ghetto, potatoes cost 95 zlotys per kilo. They used to cost 30 zlotys. Bread is not to be gotten, costs 4 zlotys per kilo; the same high prices for flour and other items. All the stores are bought out.

The Master of the Universe sent an angel down to earth to see what was happening. He came back and reported: "In Germany, Italy, and Japan everyone is in uniform and talking about peace. In England everyone is in civilian clothes and talking about war. In Poland everyone is barefoot and confident of victory." (The Jews of Poland are sure that better times are coming.)

"Caterpillar Tanks" is what the Jews call people who have to pass through Zelazna Street with their things.—They have to crawl.

No Christians were allowed into the Ghetto with produce today, the reason being . . . from the Poles that everything is being transported from there—the Other Side—here.—There is talk of building two suspension bridges (viaducts), one connecting Solna and Ciepla Streets, the other Bonifraterska and Przebieg Streets.

Of the 800 Jews in the S.S. employ, They have released only some 50, despite the Poles' energetic appeals that They employ only Christians—and They have not taken any Christians to fill the Jews' place.—A man who visited the Other Side tells of the great difference. There movement is free. People can walk about as they wish, well dressed. The cafés are full of people, the streets empty. Not overcrowded, as in the Ghetto. Those who read horoscopes for the Jews say they are bad.

INSIDE THE | GHETTO

In a way, being inside the Ghetto was at first a relief. For one thing, the uncertainty was over. The Ghetto was terribly crowded (between February and April, 1941, 72,-000 Jews were deported to the Ghetto from the rest of the Government General of Poland). The rations were not enough to live on. Forced labor battalions were a constant peril—who was to take care of the family of the man in the labor camp while he was away? But, for the time being, survival seemed possible. The Jewish Council's police force kept law and order. There were no S.S., Storm Troopers, or other detachments billeted in the Ghetto, and German uniforms were a rare sight. There were only a few conducted tours for German soldiers and civilians, who seemed to regard the torment of the Jews as a form of recreation.

The Ghetto flung itself feverishly into the business of keeping alive—illegally, since it was impossible to do so on the official rations. (The average food ration contained some 800 calories. It consisted of bread, potatoes, and ersatz fat only.) The only economic activity allowed the Ghetto was importing small quantities of food and raw materials. These *were worked over in the Ghetto's shops and then exported as finished products—via the Umschlagplatz, or exchange place, an immense station set up near one of the gates. (The Umschlagplatz was later to be the terrible site of the deportations to death.) Most of this work was supplied by men like Walter Toebbens, a German whose textile factories and tanneries employed thousands of workers. Workers in such factories were sure of a fixed income, extra food, and exemption from forced labor.*

But the vast majority of the Ghetto had to find other, "illegal" ways of keeping alive. One way was exchanging jewels, currency, utensils, and other valuable objects that the Jews of Warsaw had managed to save. There were also some hidden stores of raw materials, rare commodities with a high value outside the Ghetto, to which they could be exported through friendly (and interested) intermediaries.

And then the Ghetto had a large number of enterprising and experienced manufacturers, engineers, and chemists, who developed new industries: they produced food (canned fish, horsemeat, preserves); they set up and ran tanneries, dye works, and even luxury factories—chocolate, cigarettes, watches. For a time, Jewish traders were able to export these items, doing their business by telephone.

Smuggling

When telephone and postal connections with the outside world were cut off, the Ghetto's smugglers took over. They were an absolute economic necessity. They smuggled money and products out, provisions in. (At one point, Ringelblum comments, there was actually a shortage of bread on the Other Side—so much had been smuggled into the Ghetto!) The smugglers were of all ages, sizes, and descriptions—from the small children crawling through the sewers or chinks in the wall, through the nasty porters who carried huge loads on their backs, to the big manufacturers who worked hand in glove with the German or Ukrainian guards at the Wall gates. The chief contraband imports were flour and potatoes. There were dozens of secret mills in Ghetto cellars and attics. The big smugglers were an important group in the Ghetto. Ringelblum was fascinated by their methods of operation and mores. (The Ringelblum Archives contain a special study of the smugglers.) He describes how they looked after one another in trouble and their "eat, drink, and be merry" philosophy, noting, parenthetically, that they even had an insurance firm —one that covered them only up to a certain point past the Wall. (The guards at the gates were bribed, but it was impossible to insure against random attacks by unbribed policemen.)

The Germans were aware of the extent of the smuggling and determined to extirpate it. The Jewish Council could achieve nothing with its appeals to collective morality. So the Gestapo appointed a special economic police force, directly responsible to itself, whose duty was to discover and confiscate the smuggled merchandise. Their headquarters were at 13 Leszno Street, and they were known in the Ghetto as "the Thirteen." Their leader was Chaim Gancwajch, a shady character who exploited his position to make all sorts of deals, shaking down the smugglers and the recipients of smuggled goods, in exchange for protection. (Ringelblum cites a fascinating illustration of how "the Thirteen's" police force worked.)

Gancwajch also tried to play a significant role in the Ghetto as a competitor of the Jewish Council. He set up an ambulance Special Service and dressed the members in expensive uniforms. At one point, he started a soup kitchen of his own; another time he tried to do "cultural work." But "the Thirteen" gang was distrusted by honest people, and eventually it was broken up—in May, 1942—presumably by a section of the Ge-

stapo feuding with the section they were agents for. Ringelblum devotes a great many notes to a description of Gancwajch, whom he characterizes as "75 per cent scoundrel, 25 per cent romantic." Apparently, despite (or perhaps because of) Ringelblum's strong social sense, the combination of scoundrel and romantic fascinated him.

KOHN AND HELLER

Kohn and Heller—the names of these two men are almost always bracketed together—were businessmen completely. They were "big-time operators"; but there was nothing romantic about them. Before the war, they had managed a trading house that maintained many connections with Germany. Now they used these connections to become millionaires. Their influence came from their access to the office of Auerswald, the German Commissioner of the Warsaw Ghetto. On the surface they were reputable businessmen, with various concessions. Their horse-drawn streetcars were known as Kohn-Hellers (or Uncle Kohn's Cabin, in scoffing allusion to their filthy condition). Kohn and Heller also had a large retail food shop. Essentially, however, they were informers for the Germans, and they used their privileged position to blackmail the Ghetto residents. (Ringelblum comments ironically that Kohn and Heller had a reputation for being solid men: If they promised to get you out of jail for a consideration and couldn't do it, they gave you your money back!) They were the biggest importers in the Ghetto, specializing in food and medicine, the most lucrative items. But they were not above dealing in human beings; for a large price, Ringelblum relates, they smuggled relatives from other ghettos into the Warsaw Ghetto. Ringelblum also blames them for betraying the printers and distributors of the Ghetto's undercover press, and being responsible for the massacre of Bloody Friday, April

18, 1942. When their streetcar service was abolished in October, 1941, Kohn and Heller's career began to come to an end.

It would be a mistake, however, to imagine that only the scum rose to the surface of the Warsaw Ghetto. The terrible living conditions, the chronic anxiety connected with frantic struggle for physical survival, provided a fertile field for anti-social elements. Ringelblum's most frequently used term to describe the psychological state of the Ghetto's inhabitants is "demoralization." To a highly moral man, this was the worst opprobrium.

But not everyone was demoralized. There were many who, imbued with the best tradition of Jewish altruism, retained their humanity. Soon after the Ghetto was established, these people, Ringelblum among them, organized House Committees. Each committee consisted of from five to twelve members elected by the residents of the house. These were not, of course, one or two-family dwellings; throughout the Notes from the Warsaw Ghetto, "house" refers to an apartment building. (Courtyards, incidentally, were U-shaped or semi-circular groups of houses, all entered by one gate, largely housing developments.) The committees tried to support the impoverished residents, particularly the children, with food and clothing. Soon there was a whole chain of House Committees, and they joined into regional committees; the regional committees sent delegates to a central commission. This activity was all outside the Jewish Council, and the Council, as Ringelblum records, tried unsuccessfully on many occasions to take over, or subvert, the House Committees as a rival authority. All sorts of people worked in the House Committees —people of all ages, classes, and occupations. Ringelblum notes how important the women were in these committees, particularly in 1942, when the men were exhausted.

Then there were welfare groups that tried to help the

refugees by setting up refugee centers where they might live and by feeding them at soup kitchens. The refugees, strangers in a large, heartless city, suffered worst of anyone from hunger and sickness and were the first to die. They were continually being exploited and always in need of help. Ringelblum tells a heartwarming story about one social worker who stayed awake all night at a disinfection center to prevent some refugees from having their last few rags stolen by the corrupt guards.

There were even attempts to grow food for the Ghetto. Zionist youth organizations, which would later furnish the fighters for the Ghetto resistance, tried to cultivate tiny patches of land in the Ghetto. An organization called Toporol planted small gardens on the sites of gutted houses (the Ghetto had been the hardest hit section of Warsaw during the German bombardment). Vegetables were cultivated on balconies and even on roofs. A few groups of Zionist chalutzim, passionately preparing themselves for emigration to Palestine after the war, cultivated collective fields outside the Ghetto, in the village of Grochow.

The élite dedicated themselves to preserving the Ghetto's spirit. It was forbidden to have schools for children, but they existed surreptitiously on a large scale and at all levels. There were homes for orphan children—the name of Janusz Korczak, the idealistic director of one such home, recurs time and again. (It was he who earned immortality when the Ghetto broke up by accompanying the children of his home to the deportation trains for the extermination camps.) There were classes for adults, too, for medical students (taught by world-famous scientists like Professor Hirszfeld, the bacteriologist) and laboratories, as well. The Ghetto scientists conducted research into the etiology of hunger (they had a fertile field). There were several theaters that performed up to the end. So power-

ful was the cultural drive in the Ghetto that even the venal "operators"—men like Gancwajch and Kohn and Heller—supported artists, musicians, and writers.

But it was no use. The Ghetto was actually a milder form of, an adumbration of, a concentration camp. The Jews had developed a special technique for dealing with hostile authorities over the centuries—bribing them, making themselves economically indispensable to them, even imitating them (it was the mode to dress like the Germans). For a long time, the Jewish will to live supported them psychologically (Ringelblum supplies statistics about the low rate of suicides to prove this). But the Nazis, though human and hence corruptible, were not to be conciliated in the long run. They were not interested in the Ghetto's usefulness to their military economy. Ruefully, Ringelblum remarks, as the Ghetto is breaking up, that the Germans could easily supply their manpower needs from the rest of conquered Europe. They could do without Jewish labor.

During this period, while the Jews were clinging precariously to life in the Warsaw Ghetto, the German Army had conquered all of Europe—the Balkans and Scandinavian countries, as well as the Western countries. They had attacked the Soviet Union and were softening England for an invasion. And the entry of the United States into the war after Pearl Harbor in December, 1941, only fulfilled the German prediction: Nothing now would prevent the complete annihilation of European Jewry. From the summer of 1941 on, the massacres—through pogroms, mass executions, and finally, "rationalized" gas chambers—were part of an over-all plan. Nor were the Jews residing in ghettos spared. With the completion of deportations from Lodz, the next largest Ghetto to Warsaw, in November, 1941, Warsaw's fate was sealed. The Ghetto was slowly strangled. In December, 1941, the residents were forbidden to receive food packages, and communications through the mail with the outside world were completely cut off. In April and May of 1942 the Ghetto "operators" were eliminated. An extermination brigade arrived. News came of the massacres throughout the Government General of Poland. The Ghetto's dissolution was at hand.

10/DECEMBER, 1940

Today, the 7th of December, I heard that 2,000 men were driven out of Radom and sent to the small towns surrounding the city.—Baruch was arrested for not wearing an arm band. He declared that he would not wear an arm band, and he had never worn one, because he considered it an insult. He was sent to Oswiecim, where he died. The families of a great many persons sent there have received orders to appear at a central office and remove the ashes of their dead. —The Jewish delegation from Warsaw that visited Cracow* told about the calisthenics Jews were forced to perform in the street. [The German authority] asked, "How many Jews?" When he found out that only some 20 per cent were involved, he declared that Jews must become accustomed to discipline. When told that Christian servants had no passes, he was enraged at our people for keeping servants who made pogroms on Jews a few years ago. Typhus is widespread in the Aryan part of Warsaw, so They checked all Jewish apartments for any concealed cases; not a single such was discovered.—Heard that the converts are to have a ghetto of their

* See above, p. 28.

own within the larger Ghetto.—In Rypin the tombstones were removed and the graves were dug up.—Yesterday, Jewish workers coming back to the Ghetto from their work on the Other Side with more than two loaves of bread had the extra loaves taken from them; the bread was thrown over the Wall to the Poles.—The innumerable confectionery stores that have sprung up lately, in lieu of factories, give a distorted picture of the Ghetto.—It is said that after the 15th of December no newspapers will be allowed in the Ghetto.—In Cracow Jews are being turned out of the city in large numbers.—There was supposed to be a Ghetto in Sosnowiec, but the decree was revoked.—In Kutno there is an open Ghetto. The guards were armed [?], and the people were allowed to go out of the Ghetto. [In the Warsaw Ghetto] packages can be delivered via mail from the Other Side, so a Pole can send a package from Bielanska Street on the Other Side to Tlomackie Place, the adjacent street in the Ghetto.—Yesterday, a truck full of fish was driven into the Ghetto, at the cost of thousands of zlotys in bribes.—A man called Ehrlich* came to a foreman with a letter from the Germans ordering the foreman to give Ehrlich twenty-five of his men for his work.

The professor who is a *lover of Israel* came to say his farewells to *our brethren the children of Israel* the day after the Ghetto was closed. He says that barracks are being built in the city—no one knows for whom. The speech of the Jewish Council people is interlarded with threatening phrases like "Kawenczinska Street," "work camp," and the like.†—"You'll bring us the money between your teeth." Ruffians, nice boys all of them, wearing high shoes, have taken the reins at the Jewish Council. You have to bribe the mailman for your mail. Janitor service costs 300 zlotys; mail, 500 zlotys. Every service has a charge. For 600 zlotys you can be settled in a

* Ehrlich was a Gestapo agent (*see* p. 232).
† K Street was the assembly point for the work camps.

new apartment in one day. A gang of operators and swindlers, and there's no control over them. Some of the leaders of the Council are honest people, but without understanding of social problems. One of the guards said to his Jewish partner: "It was the devil who thought up this plan to strangle 400,000 people." Some of Them pretend not to see people crossing over to the Other Side to fetch produce.—The doctors and personnel of the Jewish Hospital (1,000 persons in all) at first received 75 passes (to leave the Ghetto); now the number is 200. The rest must come to 6 Twarda Street at 7 A.M. and from there walk in line to the hospital on Szista.—There's a lack of antityphus serum in the Ghetto because private people have bought it all up. Many Jews get letters from the Others recommending that they be granted various concessions in the Ghetto; the same is true for positions.—Today, at the corner of Leszno and Chlodna Streets, men and women were ordered to dance together and a passing band played. Besides, a lot of calisthenics.—The Jewish Council wanted to tax administrators [of houses] several hundred zlotys, but "the Thirteen" would not agree and forbade it. They were also against the requirement that 25 per cent of the administrators be Jewish lawyers. This was privileging one profession. "The Thirteen" will occupy itself with setting up merchandise depots. It has received administration of the Jewish houses on Leszno. It is also forming some sort of sanitation commission.—Heard about the heroism of the Jews during the fighting against the German invaders. There were a few antiaircraft artillery posts near Mlawa; everyone but the Jews fled during an air raid. The Jews shot down seventeen airplanes. Another incident: The Polish artillery was knocked out; everyone but one Jew fled. He ran a machine gun alone; afterward the others rejoined him. He was wounded, but continued to man the machine gun. The doctor who tended him in the hospital told me about it. Heard a great many such cases when I was in prison. The Jews set an example of endurance and courage. A Jewish doctor from Marszalkowska Street (the doctors' guild looked for him later) placed himself at the head of a division after its commander died, led the division to the attack, fell.

Dec. 10

Today, in the morning, at the corner of Chlodna and Zelazna Streets, sacks of bread, fats, etc., were taken away from Jews because a Polish guard insisted they had been smuggled in. Later, Jewish guards came and proved that the Jews had been walking through Jewish streets all the way, so the bread was distributed among the poor.—The Jewish Hospital will be evacuated by April.—There are 750 Jewish doctors in Warsaw.—The dollar is up again, to 108. This is explainable by two facts. First, the populace is buying merchandise, feeling that money is valueless now; and second, the Others are supposed to be buying dollars in large amounts.—It is said that four Germans were killed on the Other Side, which explains why a few streets have been cut off.—The Wall, to the people on the Other Side, is a symbol of the Jewish Council's graft. That is what the Christian and Jewish health officials say when they arrive with their steam baths for disinfection and want graft themselves.—Yesterday, a soldier sprang out of a passing automobile and hit a boy on the head with an iron bar. The boy died.—There was a massacre on Grzybowska Street yesterday. Some of the Others got drunk and beat and injured dozens of Jewish passers-by. The estimate is 100 wounded, one boy killed.—A great many dispatches are arriving from Oswiecim with news of the deaths of inmates. People are forced to exercise under showers every day for three hours there; this produces inflammation of the lung and death follows. Postcards have been received describing the difficult situation there, the writers wishing themselves dead.

Heard an interesting interpretation of the new mode in high shoes. The power and bearing of the Others is impressive. People are trying to rise above the general mass of mankind and make an impression wearing the same high shoes as the Others.—Juvenile delinquents ride around town beating innocent Jewish passers-by with their whips.—The dollar has gone up to more than 100 for soft (paper) currency; 115 for hard (gold); bread is 3.50 zlotys a kilo, potatoes 5–6 zlotys.—The Jewish Council is setting up a transfer office. For 150,000 zlotys they remodel a house so that the windows facing the Ghetto are screened off.

Dec. 15

My dear:

During the last few days, Jewish stores on the Other Side were opened up. It turns out they are empty. One can guess that the storekeepers were themselves the "thieves."— Jewish artisans will be able to transport their tools and family mementos from the Other Side into the Ghetto. But not their merchandise.—Today I was at a concert in the Judaic Library. Jewish artists appeared and sang in Yiddish for the first time. The program was entirely in Yiddish. Perhaps this is the beginning of a return to Yiddish.—It is said that the priest who came to the Ghetto Sunday to preach to the converts was not allowed to pass through the gate. Some were converted as long as forty to sixty years ago, and now they must suffer the Jewish exile in the Ghetto. Some of them have had to separate from their Aryan wives, who have remained behind on the Other Side.—A man came along with a pass. The watchmen on Grzybowska Street took him into the guardroom, tortured him there for two hours, forcing him to drink urine, have sex relations with a Gentile woman. They beat him over the head, then cleaned the wounds with a broom. The next day, they treated him humanely, gave him food and drink, took him to his destination, on the way saying that Jews are people, too.—The Jewish Council proposed thirty-odd names of possible commissars to the authorities for their approval. —They struck out twenty, and proposed replacements. The Others gave swindlers jobs at 3,000 zlotys per job.

There are some honest people among "the Thirteen" gang. —This reminds us that Adam Czerniakow was informed on some time ago. Our "fine fellows" tell the Germans: "We'll locate the rich Jews' money. Then we can split it." "The Thirteen" are on the same tack. They're supported by the S.S. and want to become a second Council and look after the Jews —and themselves, too, incidentally. They have some shady characters there.—The Council has taken over the administration of Jewish houses. It is said that people who refused to pay rent will have to live in barracks.—Heard this joke: Someone comes to a fortuneteller in a chauffeur's uniform and asks to have his fortune told. He is told: "You'll run out of gasoline, your axle will break, and your driver's license will be taken away."—Yesterday, there was a big to-do at the Council. They divided the administrative jobs amongst their own. Kaminar gave his daughters the biggest houses, such as 28, 32, and 34 Swientojerska Street, and the like.—A well-dressed man approached the corner of Leszno and Zelazna wearing a derby. He wouldn't take it off and was beaten. The hat was thrown on the ground, but he wouldn't stoop to pick it up.—An original way of smuggling into the Ghetto. Two trucks stand on either side of the boundary line near the market; a Jewish truck with empty milk cans and an Aryan truck with full cans. After a while, when both guards are busy, the cans are switched and the trucks drive off.

Today, the 17th of December, it is bitter cold: 14 degrees (Centigrade), and no coal to be had. Coal costs 1,000 zlotys per ton. The game of taking bread from Jews at the Leszno–Zelazna corner and throwing it over the Wall to Christians is continuing. Smuggling is persisting for the time being. The base of operations is said to be located in the night spot used by the courtyards in Leszno Street. The Poles have access from one side; the Jews from the other. German police chiefs execute the transactions. The last few days, a large amount of wheat grain has been imported, to be ground in the Ghetto mills.—Yesterday the rabbi of Praga was badly beaten, because, though he did take his hat off, he left the skull cap on underneath it.—The transport firm of Hartwig is doing wonderful business. They take finished merchandise out of the Ghetto and carry raw material in.—The difference in the price of coal—inside and outside the Ghetto—is very great: Here, it costs more than 1,000 zlotys per ton; there, 400 zlotys. Saw someone from Ger. He'll tell nothing about what happened to him, but he's lost 24 kilos (from 82 down to 58). "People live here, people live there; they die there, too. There are some ninety such places in the country. Jews are separated from the rest."—This is all he would say. It is said that it will be possible to leave [the Ger Ghetto]; only relatives will have to pay 700 dollars first.—For 300 zlotys, you can rent a truck and have as much merchandise as you want brought in [to the Warsaw Ghetto].

There is widespread fortunetelling among the Poles, all kinds, and concerned with their eventual victory. Saw one such prophecy, in rhyme, but amateurish. Some time back heard a story about a boy living on Panska Street who prophesied salvation. This reminds me of an account from the seventeenth century (in Zinnenberg's fourth volume of his *History of Jewish Literature*) about a boy from Gradek who shook the whole Jewish world with his prophecies. Similar conditions produce similar reactions.—The populace is trembling in fear of the 31st of December. They're worried that the Ghetto may be hermetically sealed. In the meantime it is still possible to receive anything through the mail, including money.—The reason why typhus is not widespread among the Jews while it is among the Christians is quite simple: They eat a great deal of (unwashed) fruit; the Jews eat very little of it. Yesterday, a Jewish woman was shot. A kindly watchman let her out of the Ghetto; when she came back the watch had changed. She ran away, They shot after her, and she was hit.

Saw today a whole division of Jewish workers returning from the Other Side, loaded down with bread and other good things to eat.—Large numbers of small Jewish children, nine or ten years old, are to be seen on the Other Side, walking about without arm bands. Christians who take the train to the Ghetto have everything taken away from them when they arrive here.—Christians are buying a great deal of merchandise in Warsaw, at any price. Hence, the price of merchandise has risen, and of diamonds too, bought by Christians.—"Africa is losing its [Italian] hair."*—In Czestochowa conditions are quite good. People are not impressed into work gangs. Himmler's son-in-law is the town commandant. Jews engage in business. If anything is needed, the Jewish Council supplies it.—Here's how a Jewess smuggles merchandise into the Ghetto from Otwock. When she returns from Otwock, she puts on her arm band and stands facing the Ghetto at the gate. Naturally, the guard tells her to go back into the Ghetto, which she does when a crowd has gathered around the guard and he is too busy to search her. When she goes out of the Ghetto, she takes the arm band off and faces the other way.

* "Italian" and "hair" are the same word in Polish.

Dec. 20

Today, Saturday the 20th of November,* a wagon full of Jewish workers drove down Gesia Street. The Jewish workers clambered down; a Christian watchman ordered them to sing. One of them, a cantor by profession, stood on the auto and sang *El Mole Rachamim*.† The street was filled with people listening.—Passage through the courtyard on Leszno used for smuggling costs 5 zlotys. Poles entering the Ghetto with smuggled goods put on Jewish arm bands as they come in. In the courtyard itself Jews and Poles meet to conduct their affairs of business. A scene: He an Aryan, she Jewish; they rendezvous at the border. The watch moves discreetly aside, and they have an intimate conversation.—The converts are fixing up Christmas trees. Caritas‡ is said to be giving them relief.—Parszawiak [the writer] is working for "the Thirteen." Gancwajch will run a symposium on the subject of the Chanukkah holiday.—The cryptic question about the value of the dollar, expressed thus in a letter: "At what number of Hard§ Street does So and So live; and where does his father-in-law, Mr. Soft§ live?" The answer came back: "At Nos. 48 and 90."

The Jewish Hospital must move during the next few months. They may not remove anything attached to a wall (and most of their best apparatus has just such attachments). —On the other hand, the Treasury men are taking anything that can be ripped out from the hospital at Leszno Street, even the faucets and wash basins.—Lately, twelve to fourteen Jews have been dying daily, compared to some twenty before the war. Suicides before the war were seven a week, now they're three or four.

* Should be December.
† "God, Full of Compassion," a prayer from the memorial service.
‡ The Catholic social-aid organization.
§ "Hard" and "soft" refer to gold and paper dollars, respectively.

Dec. 23

My dear:

On December 17, at about 3:30 in the afternoon, a taxicab stopped at the small shop of a merchant selling tailor supplies at 22 Smocza Street. A soldier emerged, with Jewish companions. They emptied the shop completely. Having finished this piece of work, they left. Suddenly, with a rare calm, the Gestapo man pulled out his revolver and shot point blank into a crowd of Jews that happened to be standing around. They were all merchants who worked on the other side of the street. The result was that an eleven-year-old child fell dead; a woman from Dzielna Street lay badly wounded.— Yesterday, an auto pulled up at the border, at Tlomackie Place, and a couple of soldiers got out. They began viciously beating every Jew they could find. One man was injured. There was an attempt to fetch a doctor, but it turned out that there's no quick emergency service in the Ghetto. No doctor could be found, and it was some time before first aid could be given. Today, there was another beating on Karmelicka Street. An auto appeared with S.S. men; the soldiers in the back of the truck had . . . in their hands . . . chased off the sidewalk . . . beating Jews. Today . . . a truck of men from the Death's Head Corps. Soldiers got out and beat up all the Jews in the street. The crowd in the street fled behind the gates into the courtyards, pushing and trampling one another down. People piled up in some of the yards. Later, the soldiers got back into their car and drove on.—At the border of Chlodna and Zelazna Streets, a [German] soldier on duty addressed a Jewish guard: "You know, our comrade is kaput." The Jew was afraid to say anything and shrugged. The soldier, seeing this, called out: "You understand, I'm talking about the Italians. They were never good soldiers." A few minutes later, he called out again: "If I were a Jew, I'd commit suicide. I could never stand the humiliation the Jews are going through." The Jewish guard could contain himself no longer and said: "The Jews are an old people and have endured a great deal." The soldier said: "You're right." But this didn't prevent him from stopping Jews afterward and making them do calisthenics holding a brick in either hand.

Dec. 24

Told of another incident on Leszno Street: A truckload of men from the Death's Head Corps appeared. Suddenly the truck stopped, the men jumped into the street, a terrible scramble ensued. Some of the Jews stood still and took their hats off. These Jews weren't beaten, but They chased those who ran away and beat them fearfully. They threw one Jew to the ground and trampled on him until they drew blood.— Today, a car appeared at Karmelicka again; the soldiers got out and beat up all the Jews. Men, women, and children. A woman was going down the street with her child; the child got so powerful a blow he fell unconscious in the middle of the street. Typical that people cried hysterically just looking at what was going on.—"The Thirteen" is again making efforts to attract respectable people of all kinds. Their men are out trying to recruit new blood. But they're not succeeding. The story is that anyone who accepts a post with them can never leave.

A woman tells this experience, that happened to her on the 19th of last December:

I was traveling by train from Lodz to Warsaw. The round-about route was through Kutno, and you transferred at Kalisz. That was the only route Jews could take at the time. We were wearing patches on our shoulders and backs those days, and were allowed to be out in the street [in the Lodz Ghetto] from eight in the morning till five at night. So one had to rush. . . .

Arrived . . . at Kutno around one o'clock at night . . . had to leave for Warsaw at ten at night. Everybody got off the train and went into the waiting room, which was very crowded, because this was before the Christmas holiday. There weren't many Jews, and after some time a few very young soldiers appeared and declared that the Jews stank up the air in the waiting room, and they would have to go outside. The Jews were forced to leave the waiting room by the exit to the trains going the other way, to the city [Kutno]. We sat down on our baggage. Then the very same soldiers came out and began to beat the men terribly. It got so bad the men deserted their baggage and fled. Then they began to beat the women. They beat us about the face. Not a single woman escaped untouched—we were all bleeding. Two of the soldiers became quite disturbed at this and began to protest. They were told that the Jews were responsible for the fact that the [ethnic] Germans in Poland were in a bad way. The two replied that it wasn't the Jews' fault, but the Polish government's policy. The soldiers who beat us up went away, our two defenders with them. But they both kept coming out to see us, particularly one of them. They brought us water to wash the blood off, and said they were sorry. One of them said he was going to see what he could do to have us allowed back in the waiting room. They went away and didn't return. [We thought] this meant they hadn't been successful. Around three o'clock at night, an auto drove up with some officers in it. The same soldiers who had beaten us got out and ordered us to carry the officers' things. I was given a trunk to drag. After a few steps, the officer, seeing me, injured, trying to drag a trunk, said it was too heavy for me and took it himself. One of the two soldiers who had defended us from the others called out to us: "Wait a while, the brutes will be leaving soon; you'll be able to go inside." A little later they told us they would see to it we didn't have to wait until ten o'clock for the train. Luckily, a special train came in at six o'clock; we were told in the station it had been ordered by the soldiers, and we left in peace. . . ."

Dec. 31

My dear:

Heard there have been demonstrations the last few days in Polish cities, the demonstrators' slogan: "No Jews in Warsaw." But heard that at the same time sermons have been preached in all the churches urging Christians to forget their misunderstandings with the Jews. On the contrary, the Jews are to be pitied because they are immured behind walls. Christians were not to allow themselves to be agitated by the enemy, who was trying to sow hatred among peoples.— Recently, there have been big parties in private houses. People drink wine and brandy and have themselves a good time. —Sawdust ovens have become popular of late. This oven costs 40 zlotys, and only 2 zlotys to heat, as compared with 6 or 7 zlotys if you use coal. Besides, the heat from an oven fueled by sawdust is hygienic.—The Ghetto has split up families. The wife goes off to the Other Side, to live with her brother, who is a convert. One of the daughters, who doesn't want to remain in the Ghetto, smuggles herself into a small town as a Christian. The father remains in the Ghetto with two other daughters.—In Radom in three days they collected 150,000 zlotys for the 2,000 Jews who were driven out into the neighboring towns.—Many people are said to be writing memoirs—Nergep,* and others.—"The Memorial Song" is very effective, though not very good from the artistic point of view. The poet calls for all the woes we are suffering to be avenged. He tells about the press gangs, the deathly fear stalking the streets, the work camps ("leeches that suck the blood of workers plunged in the swamp mud") from which no one returns. He tells of the scandalous behavior of the Council people, who are sometimes worse than the Others; of the sorrow of children growing up without schooling; of the death of martyrs; of the child killed because of his beauty.

* Code for Gepner.

The new telephone book, under the entry Jaraslaj on Jesuit Street [?] gives the telephone number of a brothel for the Others.—King Chaim Rumkowski's system: He distributes the administration of houses to his own people, and levies a tax of several thousand marks on each of them for socal relief. He has managed to obtain a couple of million marks from the Others. His chief income so far comes from the blocked Jewish accounts; he also gets some income from rents which he demands both from Christian and Jewish houses.—There is a convert living at 6 Leszno Street who yearns to rejoin the Jewish fold. He works day and night in the House Committee.

Today, the 31st of December, a Jewish woman was shot at the corner of Niska and Zamenhofa Streets while trying to smuggle herself across the border. But hundreds of people are successful in getting through to the Other Side to buy produce there.—Today Jews were forbidden to hold Christmas celebrations. The Sienna Street affair stinks. Swindlers from the Council are mixed up in it. They are said to have provoked the whole thing.—Heard from someone who was in a prisoner-of-war camp in Germany that he saw a farmer's statement testifying that a certain Jew was the best milker he'd ever had. He had had milkers of various nationalities, but the Jew was the best of them all.—The orgy of parties is unconfined. I have been told that people are seen coming back from all-night balls as late as six or seven in the morning, clutching balloons in their hands, half-drunk, singing in the street, just like in the good old prewar days. The Jewish Council has ordered that all windows facing the front of the house be covered, probably so as not to agitate the Others with views of brilliant windows.—Dozens of Jews are going on foot to Otwock and fetching meat back from there. Where exactly they go to and how they get there no one knows.— There is said to have been a pogrom in Lodz the last few days. No details or confirmation available.—Also the last few days, the Others have been visiting the modern restaurant at 16 Sienna Street and taking photographs of the Jews having a good time. The same pictures appeared in placard form, with the legend: "Carnival Time." Today it's so cold you can pass the Gibraltar of the guards without having to take your hat off.—In a Jewish dairy on Muranowska Street the cows are exchanged every day. Yesterday's cow is slaughtered. This is how it works: Every day peasants come to the dairy with a new cow. They tell the watch at the Wall gate that they left the permit to bring the cow into the Ghetto at home. They leave 700 zlotys as security until they fetch the papers. Then they conveniently forget.—Herring is sold in the street by the converts, who have received it from the Catholic welfare organization, Caritas.—Nazi means "Nehm-zu"—take away; Allemagne means "Alles Mein"—all mine.

11/JANUARY, 1941

Heard today, 5th of January, from someone who visited the Lodz Ghetto. The people there all look like beggars, hunchbacked, starving; many people are now receiving letters telling them of the death of relatives [in work camps]. —In the street met Mandeltort, a manufacturer I know from Lodz. He was hunchbacked, leaning on a stick like a beggar. —Rumkowski is said to have ordered everyone in the Lodz Ghetto to give him their furs, under threat of imprisonment. The people of Lodz [consequently] sold all their furs for a song. For example, they took 50 marks for a fur that could be sold for 1,000 zlotys in Warsaw.—You see mobs of children in rags begging in the street nowadays.—Walking down Leszno Street every few steps you come across people lying at the street corner, frozen, begging.—On the Other Side [I] saw few such sights on Marszalkowska Street.—Gancwajch is said to be forming a culture association, with the help of Samuel Stupnicki and Isaac Katzenelson.

Recently streetwalking has become notable. Yesterday, a very respectable-looking woman detained me. Necessity drives people to anything. Heard about a refugee who used to make a living out of being a proxy for forced labor for two or three zlotys per client. Days when he had no clients to proxy for he worked for the S.S. and was paid in food.—The news about Szymke* confirmed. The same for Simeon Stanislaw. The last few days (beginning of January) heard about a tragic incident in Lodz. A mob of hungry people rushed the Jewish Council food stores. Not knowing what to do, the Council called on the representative of the Occupying Power. Several hundred people fell dead; a large number (in the thousands) were wounded. Here, there was a street round-up. People were taken out of Gertner's restaurant, were seized on the street. All the coats were stolen from a confectionery shop on Nowolipki Street.—Heard marvelous stories of the smuggling that goes on via the Jewish graveyard. In one night they transported twenty-six cows by that route. The smugglers have code numbers which they shout across through the . . . .

Jan. 15–16

Today news arrived of the deporting of 150,000 Jews from Sosnowiec and Bedzin. *They desire that we carry out this thing, and on condition that we do it, will allow us the opportunity to save the money of those people* [who are deported]. This is a question of principle. Should we, with our own hands, do such a thing?—There are still Jews in the institutions in Drewnica. And They are eager to take the Zofjowka madhouse with its 400 patients away from. . . . The slackness of the Jewish Council. Doesn't give a groschen to the [Zofjowka?] institution.—A police chief beat up a Jew, and shattered his wrist watch in the process. Later he came around demanding a hundred zlotys from the Jew to repair the damage.—*Knepel told me that he tried with every ounce of his strength to give them no pretext to beat him when he*

* Lubelski, who was arrested and executed.

was in the Gestapo. The words "damn, shitty Jews" never absent from his [?] lips. The decree requiring Jews to do compulsory labor, especially the twelve-year-olds, and the talk about "work that will prove educational and fruitful" reminds everyone of the [old-time] cantonists.* Jews are to be used to clean up and rebuild the battle-scarred cities in the Government General of Poland, to do agricultural work, and, as one *Courier* article puts it, for "water control projects"—working in swamps.

The 7th of January the rumor spread that *the German moveth forward.* The cities of Bialystok and Grodno are said to have passed into the hands of the Others, too. Panic is said to reign in those cities, their Jewish residents fleeing deep into Russia.—They came over to a group of porters and took 50 groschen each from them.—Yesterday They took 15 dekos of butter from someone.—An unemployed man was at my place yesterday, inventor of an automobile that can go without gas. Has been working in three different cities, for reasons of secrecy. Suggested to him that he go to Pal.[estine], if there are any certificates for emigration.—Heard from someone that Jews may not address police chiefs by title. Heard about that and the story about the beard [?]. During the move into the Ghetto, a police chief came to the Jewish Council and asked: "What's this trouble in the Ghetto?" The reply came: "For Jews to move in voluntarily, they have to be beaten and driven. [sic!] We can't do that." "Then what are you doing?" the police chief asked. "Well, when Jews ask our advice, we tell them not to move." He [the police chief] thundered, but later said to another one of the Council elders: "Who was that brave Jew, the one with the courage?" The tactics employed toward the Others: To say one agrees to the most impossible demands, and later to demonstrate that only a few of them

---

* The Jewish children who were conscripted for thirty years of service in the Czarist Army.

can be carried out, for "technical" reasons. Like the case of the 2,000 chairs. Szymke agreed to supply them. But the next day he brought only 50 chairs; the rest had to be ordered in Radomsk. To do that special certificates had to be gotten from Mannes, etc.

Best regards,
Yours,
Faybush

12/FEBRUARY, 1941

My dear friend:

In Lublin some time ago (December, 1940) a decree was published forbidding Jews to salute the Others by removing their hats. A placard to this effect was posted in the streets. But now some of those people who fail to salute the Others are being beaten. Those who do take their hats off are dragged over to the nearest poster and shown that they were not supposed to. The Jewish Councilman Dr. Alter was arrested in this connection.

What was their motive in introducing the Ghetto? One opinion has it that They wish to concentrate all the Jews of Poland in four places: Warsaw, Cracow, Kielce, and Radom. This is in case of war with the East [Russia]. They want to be secure in the rear.—The situation in Cracow is very grave. Jews are being constantly deported, particularly toward western Galicia. Every day they catch Jews lacking identification cards, who are sent to 5 Mogilsko Street. (The name is ominous.*)—A great many houses are being torn down in Lodz, particularly office buildings, to relieve the congestion.

* "Mogila" means "grave" in Polish.

They are taking the walls apart looking for foreign currency, gold, diamonds. There are a few Jews working in factories in Lodz. They—the remainder of the Jewish population of Lodz—may not leave their places of residence. The ragpickers are no longer there.—

In the prayer house of the Pietists from Braclaw on Nowolipie Street there is a large sign: Jews, Never Despair! The Pietists dance there with the same religious fervor as they did before the war. After prayers one day, a Jew danced there whose daughter had died the day before.—There are pessimists who are afraid that the English will finally arrive, declaring, "We have conquered!"—to our graves.—You can buy Jewish books dirt cheap these days by the basket. One-acters are particularly popular. They sell for 10 zlotys a copy, because the House Committees are putting on plays. At Krochmalna Street they're performing the war melodrama *Tzipke Fayer.*—When Frank was in Warsaw several weeks ago (January), all the pastries were removed from bakery show windows. The operation was accomplished in forty-eight hours by the Jewish police. He was at a Jewish apartment in 7 Zamenhofa Street.—There was a carnival at Melody Palace, with a beauty contest for the prettiest legs. The Ghetto is dancing. The Law and Order Service tried to break up the good time, but it turned out that one of the owners of the Melody Palace was one of Them, and she couldn't be touched. The same goes for most Jewish entertainment places. One dare not play Aryan music, and only the music of those Jews who were Aryans by adoption, i.e., Mendelssohn, Calmann, Bizet, and Meyerbeer.—A large number of packages have been arriving from Russia and Yugoslavia lately (2,000 a day). They're very good: fats, coffee, and the like. They are important in feeding the populace.—The Jewish populace sides with the Jewish policemen: "You would have minded a Polish policeman, so why don't you mind a Jewish one!"

There are intelligent policemen who dislike to order people about, so they try to prove the necessity of some action by discussion. Bitter news from Lodz: Because there's a shortage of fuel, furniture and floors are being torn up and burned.—The Jewish Council is selling hot water.—A story about Rumkowski: "We have gold currency in the Ghetto!" he declares. "How's that?" someone cries out in amazement. He raises his fists and says: "The labor of our hands is our gold!" "That's a German theory!" "We're willing to learn from everyone," replies R. . . . Polish policemen made their living this way during January: They'd throw Jews into prison even if they had passes and take 10 zlotys for letting them out.—In January a decree was published making leaving the Ghetto without a pass punishable with a fine of 1,000 zlotys.—In Lublin the Polish merchants intervened to have Jewish businesses removed.—A district officer made the notation "Not so fast" to the request of a Jewish family that their son be freed from a work camp. "And where were you when the Bydgoszcz affair happened?"* The infamous Professor Joachim Seraphim, together with Mr. Mayer Balaban, took away the best Judaica from Samuel Adalberg's collection of Polish proverbs. Seraphim was far too zealous. There are 700 prisoners of war from the other side (Russia) working in Lublin. Recently, there was an attempt to get them to put on arm bands, but they opposed it even at the risk of being shot.—Diamonds are said to have gone up recently (February), the reason being that the Others are buying them on a large scale.—Barracks are being put up on Stawki Street. That is where the Jewish population is to be transferred to wagons to take them directly from the train.† There was a poster hanging at 17 Krochmalna Street: "The first man who pays the Jewish Council a single zloty for

* When, according to Nazi propaganda, the Jews and Poles murdered 60,000 Germans.
† The infamous Umschlagplatz.

an antityphus inoculation gets a dagger in the belly." Most of the street beggars are from the refugee centers.

Feb. 27

On the other side of the Jewish graveyard, young Poles have formed bands that attack Christians as well as Jews. There have been cases of their stripping Jews naked.—Heard this story about Plonsk: In the ancient synagogue of that city there is a historic Ark of the Torah. A group of Jews were locked up in the synagogue until they hacked the holy ark to bits. Heard this explanation: The only purpose is to see to it that no vestige of the Jewish past survives in Poland. And this is necessary to prove that the Jews are a newly arrived element in Poland, with no real roots there.—The Cracow rabbis who were sent to Oswiecim are no longer alive. Their only sin was that they appealed to the Metropolitan Sapieha and Count Ronikier to intervene in the matter of deportation. The last few days the question of the deportation from Cracow has become more acute. Only 7,000 Jews have identity cards; the remaining 20,000 must leave Cracow.—One thousand Jews from Vienna arrived at Opole.—Almost all the important Polish museums have been emptied, their contents removed. At Kozla Street smuggling is through a door in a wall bordering on the Aryan side. It costs 5 zlotys to pass through. The Jewish owner of the apartment is making a fortune.—A few days back (23d–27th of February) there was a reception for the more than twenty families of converts that were on Ronikier's list.* Passports were prepared for them in the Jewish Council offices.—The last few days a ban was published on selling merchandise to Jews. Both parties are subject to a fine of 1,000 zlotys. This is a powerful blow at commerce, particularly smuggling.—The Pietists from Lubowicz have secured visas

---

* They had tried to secure permission to stay outside the Ghetto.

enabling them to emigrate to America.—There is an intense cultural activity. More than ninety-nine courtyards have conducted Mendele academies—Yiddish schools. Libraries of Jewish and Polish books are to be found in dozens of courtyards. Besides studying, 1,002 young Pietists are carrying on mutual-aid work.—A Jewish writer (Gilbert) walks into an office. His only request is twenty minutes to warm up.—A scene on Leszno Street: The head of a Jewish smuggler is thrust through a hole in the basement of the gutted post-office building. Six guards see him, call over two Jews, and order them to pull the man out. They do it, receiving a blow from the guards in the act. They order the smuggler to crawl back into his hole again, and, as he crawls, pierce his head with their bayonets. His screams ring through the quiet street. Another scene: An operation is being performed in the Jewish hospital at the former Treasury Department building on Leszno Street. Officials from the electric company come in. The hospital is 60,000 guilden behind in its payments. Dr. Borkowski asks five minutes to complete the operation. "It doesn't matter," the electric company officials say. "So there'll be one Jew less." The operation had to be completed by candlelight.

Today, the 27th of February, a young Jew was killed by the Jewish Law and Order Service. He struck a Jewish policeman and was executed in the Jewish Council building.—This is how taxes are collected from Jews in the provinces: They take away one of your garments, and give you a deadline of two weeks to buy it back. If you don't, the garment is sold.— The other week there was an incident in which three Jews *were killed by guards*. They were trying to disperse a crowd standing at the corner of Leszno and Zelazna Streets when a rifle fell to the ground and was broken. There were shots from a passing auto, and three innocent Jewish bystanders fell dead.

Feb. 28

Today, Saturday, learned about placards posted on the Other Side supposedly announcing that Aryans who are not Germans are to report for camp service to guard the Jews from the Warsaw district. The populace understood this to mean that Warsaw Jews are to be removed and sent to extermination barracks; hence there was great uneasiness. But the fact is the announcement refers to work camps.—Among the converts who have moved into the Ghetto are Professor Hirszfeld, who has a European reputation in the field of bacteriology, and Nathanson. Czerniakow showed him [Nathanson?] the picture of his grandfather, formerly the head of the Warsaw Jewish Council. The grandson acknowledged that his grandfather had acted more wisely than he.—News of a killing, that of a baptized Jew in Oswiecim. His crime, and that of two of his comrades, was that he told a Polish policeman that he was worse than a German.

Eight thousand Viennese Jews have arrived. In Opole, 2,000 [Viennese Jews arrived], in Kielce, and other cities. The price of butter has gone up to 35 zlotys. . . .—More than fifty Jewish craftsmen have returned to Grodzinsk. They have to repair houses for Germans soon to be billeted there.—To a Jew who had lost his arm band, a German police chief cried: *"Sie, Jude, Sie haben das zwanzigste Jahrhundert verloren!"* ["You, Jew, you have lost the twentieth century!"].—From one to three o'clock the Jewish police detail on Karmelicka Street is strengthened, so as to give the Others no grounds to beat Jews on their way to the Pawia Street prison. It is said that They visit the prison every day to beat the prisoners.— When negotiations were under way at the Council for deciding on a day of rest acceptable to all residents of the Ghetto, a curious situation developed. The Orthodox Aguda people were for keeping Sunday as the day of rest, because it had been established as such by the former Polish government; but the baptized Jews were for Saturday—and that's the way it was decided!—There's a new source of livelihood associated with confectionery and caviar stores. A woman stands at the door lending a Jewish pass to those who go in. She gets 10 to 20 groschen for this.—Almost daily people are falling dead or unconscious in the middle of the street. It no longer makes so direct an impression.—The streets are forever full of newly arrived refugees. The wagons or cars loaded high with the mattresses of poor Jews make a remarkable sight.— The large conference on Jewish cultural activity. More than ninety celebrations of Mendele's* anniversary in the court- yards. Greetings from the world outside.—A refugee woman lived a whole year in the free refugee center at 7 Dzielna Street, though she had jewelry, coins, and the like valued at 120,000 zlotys.—A tale of altruism: Epstein, a refugee from Silesia, spent a whole night in the bathhouse on the quiet, to protect Jewish refugees from being exploited by Polish police- men during the disinfection. He had learned that the Polish policemen intended to demand 5 zlotys for each bundle they allowed to escape disinfection, anticipated loot of 1,500 zlotys. Epstein woke up the Polish director of the bathhouse and appealed to his conscience, asserting that so long as he was alive, they wouldn't get the money. He succeeded in moving the anti-Semitic director to fire the people who were taking graft from the refugees. In general, community workers often were forced surreptitiously to carry the refugees' bundles at 109 Leszno Street—the disinfection bathhouse—suffering the blows of the guards, who insisted it was taking too long to carry the sick and old people out of the wagons.—There are 107 patients left in the Warsaw Hospital on the other side, who have been there since 1939. They all have papers from

* Mendele Mocher Seforim was the father of modern Hebrew and Yiddish literature.

the Polish Red Cross permitting them to remain. The Red Cross is liquidating its activity in the Ghetto quarter.

My dear friend:

A wooden bridge has been put up on Mlawska Street, linking the Ghetto streets. Two Jewish streetcar lines, 15 and 28, have been canceled. Now only one streetcar line is still operating—there's a big Jewish star on it. The Christian apothecaries are doing a tremendous business. All their drugs are bought up immediately. An epidemic of tuberculosis threatens; because of the closeness in the Ghetto, it would spread like wildfire. Frequent cases of scavenging in garbage cans. On the other hand, houses where they eat oranges daily, 25 zlotys per kilo, and grapes, etc. More entertainment spots opened. Many of the partners ethnic Germans. There are Jews who collaborate with the S.A., S.S., and the like. They make the rounds of Jewish organizations demanding clothing and the like, on the basis of their connections. At the least sign of opposition they threaten to denounce you to Them. A whole body of legends surrounds Dr. Schubert, a high official of the Warsaw Municiple District, the protector of Gancwajch. Is said to put on an arm band, and walk through the Ghetto. Is said sometimes to save Jewish goods from confiscation. He is a Baptist.

Misericordia et justicia, the slogan of the Inquisition. Scabies widespread, because of dearth of soap. Terrible case of three-year-old refugee child. En route, the guard threw the child into the snow. Its mother jumped off the wagon and tried to save the child. The guard threatened her with a revolver. The mother insisted life was worthless for her without her child. Then the guard threatened to shoot all the Jews in the wagon. The mother arrived in Warsaw, and here went out of her mind. In provinces, huge sums extorted; in Radom

50,000 zlotys had to be raised in three hours for 500 deportees.
... Another explanation, the reason for "location" deportation
of Jews from the Warsaw District [to Warsaw Ghetto] is the
arrival of Poles from Pomerania. In fact, Pomeranian Poles
did arrive in Piaseczna shortly after the deportation of the
[local] Jews. A short time ago group of twenty Jews was sent
out to work for a German farmer in a village from which Jews
had been deported. So work can open the Ghetto doors.

Big to-do recently in the Transfer Station,* involving a
German army officer and Jewish workers whom he refused to
give work certificates. Wouldn't give work to any Poles, out
of fear of sabotage. There are illegal traveling libraries that
circulate from house to house. There is a Talmud Torah attended by 700 students; rabbis are the teachers. "Grind the
Organ" is the most popular name for Jewish Council. Throw
a coin to the organ grinder, and the organ plays. In February
some of the streets had their names changed: Zamenhofa
back to Dzika, etc. Sienna got its old name back. For this
privilege Jews had to pay 160,000 gold zlotys. Jews were
given certificates to be able to buy gold on the Other Side,
rings, junk, and the like. The money goes to the Winter Relief for the Nazi Party. One S.S. man came looking for a Jew,
but took nothing when he found him. Instead, asked for a
Jewish holy volume—as a charm. Hawkers cry their wares in
the street: "If you must buy a rag, buy a clean one!"

Beggars ply their trade in various fashions in the street. The
Pultusk cantor, his assistant at his side, trills *El Mole Rachamim.* A preacher delivers complete sermons rushing back and
forth, as though someone were at his heels, and gesticulating

* German office, through which all business dealings involving the Ghetto
passed.

wildly with his arms, as though he were in the pulpit. Child in arms, a mother begs—the child appears dead. The begging of three- and four-year-old children, and that is the most painful. Some beggars strike studied theatrical poses, for the sake of effect. The drive to write down one's memoirs is powerful: Even young people in labor camps do it. The manuscripts are discovered, torn up, and their authors beaten. Rumor that the staff of the Lubawicz rabbi are receiving exit permits for America and are leaving any day now. Arrival of Germans from Lodz to buy furs, diamonds, gold, foreign currency. They want to insure themselves for the future—so they buy their insurance in the Warsaw Ghetto. As a result, the price of diamonds has gone up. It's characteristic that there's trade in real estate in the Ghetto. . . . They say Count Ronikier is trying to obtain permission for some converts to remain on the Other Side. He presented a list of the converts to the Authorities. The men on the list were arrested, the women transferred to the Ghetto. Many of the converts are said to be living in Sienna Street. In one town Jews wrote to a relief organization, ending their letters with S.O.S. . . . They were ordered arrested by the district governor. Of late some courtyards, complete streets in fact, have been closed down for nonpayment of rent. They turn off the electricity. Karmelicka Street makes a dreadful impression. It's so dark people stumble over each other. They've been making up ditties about the Jewish Council, about the brothers Lichtenbojm who have the contract to build the Ghetto walls and make fortunes with the help of their father.* He gives his sons all the work. To repair the Merchants' Association building, using simple fir wood, they demand 60,000 zlotys—other contractors a fourth that much. On the Other Side they say that the Jews are having a

* Engineer Mark Lichtenbojm, a member of the Warsaw Council from the first, became its president at the death of Czerniakow. Lichtenbojm was universally hated.

good time in the Ghetto—with dancing, new night clubs being opened all the time: Palermo on Zelazna Street, Casanova at Nowolipie Street (by "the Thirteen"). In Bedzin, Sosnowiec, *shleppers* are sent into homes to occupy them until their residents meet the extortioners' demands.

13 / MARCH, 1941

March 10

My dear friend:

A scene: An auto with Others riding in it comes along. A Jewish hand wagon blocks the way at Karmelicka Street. The car can't move. One of the Others gets out and begins beating the Jew. A shudder runs down the Jew's back. A man in the car calls out: "Let him alone. He's contagious." The attacker reconsiders and lets the Jew be.—Several days ago there was a tragic incident at the corner of Zelazna and Grzybowska Streets. A large group of poor Jews were standing at the corner, looking for an opportunity to smuggle themselves across to the Other Side. A guard ordered a Jewish policeman to clear them away within five minutes. He was unsuccessful. The guard shot and two or three people fell.—A few days ago, a secret hospital for typhus was discovered in a house that had no water pipes. There were eight sick people lying there, including two from another house. Implicated were two doctors and one male practical nurse. A huge poster showing a *Stuermer*-type Jew with a big louse crawling into his beard, with the words: "Jews Are Crawling with the Typhus."

The posters are put up in Aryan streetcars, too. They've been torn down wherever they were posted in the Ghetto. The fact is, typhus isn't spreading much among the Jews. It has been decreed that Jews working in German work brigades outside the Ghetto must bathe every day before going to work. It is also said that every Jew applying for a pass will have to show a delousing certificate. They're exploiting the danger of typhus to seal the Ghetto so tight a bug couldn't get through.

This incident takes place in a German institution: A Jew who's there every day of the year is greeted by the official with a brief hello, instead of the usual handshake. The official later calls the Jew into a separate room and apologizes. It is not that he, personally, has anything against the Jews. Only, it's war. Jewry is against the Others, so he can't shake hands with Jews. But personally, he has nothing against *this* Jew. There's a regular factory for exempting Jews from forced labor in the work camps. Mixed commissions composed of both Others and Jews will give you an exemption if you pay. More than 50,000 Jews are said to be needed for the work camps.—A few days ago it was announced that the resettlement operation would be interrupted until the end of March.

But today, the 10th of March, a train arrived with 2,000 Jews from Danzig, Bydgoszcz, and Pomerania generally. At two o'clock Friday night, they were awakened and ordered to pack their things within two hours. They were allowed to take 20 marks with them, which were exchanged at Tczew on the border for a worthless 40 zlotys (20 zlotys were deducted from the sum).

A number of caviar shops have been set up in partnership by many families—e.g., Stuka's (at 2 Leszno Street), where twenty-odd families are involved.—Much of the smuggling is via the streetcars. Passing through the Jewish quarter, Christians spring off the streetcar carrying bundles, particularly at

Muranow Place. There, the conductor and policeman on guard are paid 100 zlotys per trip. The conductor slows down, and they jump off with whole bags of groats or flour. A vast amount of smuggling goes through the Jewish graveyard, Christians entering the Ghetto and Jews leaving it. The "rubes" can be seen moving about the city again.—Regards from Lodz. The food supply is fair there. Jews get 400 grams of bread per person. Everything is orderly and clean. Warsaw is pandemonium to anyone coming here from Lodz. Fifteen or sixteen thousand people are working in factories outside the Lodz Ghetto. Several thousand have left voluntarily to build roads in Germany. Heard from a Jew from Glowno that the peasants hid the local Jews for the whole winter; there wasn't a single case of a Jew coming into a village and leaving without a sack of potatoes.—Though it is against the law there have been frequent instances of places and houses in Warsaw being sold by Jews to Christians. Lawyers write up the contracts. This practice has become less frequent recently. On the other hand, tracts in Pal.[estine] are being sold. Heard of a few such cases.—During the last three days, since the 7th of March and the killing of the artist Igo Sym by the Polish underground for collaborating with the Nazis, Warsaw has been going through hard times. Two hundred twenty Poles have been put in prison: the greatest Polish artists—Stempowski, Jaracz, Malicka, Prszibilko-Potocka, Prof. Michalowicz, Prof. Radlinski, Gebetner, Spiss, Pakolski—judges, lawyers, etc. They are all threatened with death, if Sym's assassin doesn't give himself up. Yesterday forty-four Polish women were said to have given themselves up—among them, the artist Bzszeszinska, who was said to have surrendered in a letter and then to have taken poison. There's a story about a similar incident in Lowicz, where the whole Polish intelligentsia was put in prison.

March 18

My dear:

The number of the dead in Warsaw is growing from day to day. Two weeks ago some two hundred Jews died. Last week (the beginning of March) there were more than four hundred deaths. The corpses are laid in mass graves, separated by boards. Most of the bodies, brought to the graveyard from the hospital, are buried naked. In the house I lived in, a father, mother, and son all died from hunger in the course of one day. Pinkiert, the King of the Dead, keeps opening new branches of his funeral parlors. He recently opened a branch on Smocza Street, where he offers burial in "luxury" (i.e., for 12 zlotys, you can have pallbearers in uniform).—A scene: There's an apartment in a Jewish courtyard where traditional studies are secretly going on. The door of the apartment is opened only to the password (one knock). When you come in, you see a large group of Talmudic students sitting over their studies.—Every day another attack on the Jews in the Polish newspaper for supposedly spreading typhus. Every day they repeat the warning to keep clean and avoid Jews.—There's a new fashion for women—wearing kerchiefs instead of hats. The mode, in imitation of Christian styles, is flourishing.—Rubinstein,* the mad jester, walks through the streets, shouting: "All are equal —in the Ghetto all are equal!" and "The rich are dissolving— we're going to have some fat!" The rumor about mobilization in Russia (spread on the 13th of March) sent the dollar up four points.—One of the baptized Jews in the Ghetto is the infamous anti-Semitic National Democratic Party agitator and writer Susanna Rabska.—There are a hundred baptized Jews serving in the police force in prominent positions. They are also thrusting their way into chairs of responsibility in the House Committees, particularly in the Fifth District. Their

---

* An eccentric from Lodz, composer of many popular songs, who was a famous Ghetto character.

neighbors are debating whether or not to permit them to hold important positions.—In the church on Grzybowska Street one of the baptized Jewish policemen shouted: "Down with the Jews!" It was impossible to establish who he was. But that's characteristic of their arrogance.—The past few days there has been a deportation from Plock . . . under very difficult circumstances. The Jews were awakened in the middle of the night and driven out, literally naked. Those who put up opposition were shot on the spot, others en route. The deportees are now in Radomsk.—There were assemblies in celebration of Purim this year. People hope for a new Purim—to celebrate the downfall of the modern Haman, Hitler—one that will be commemorated as long as the Jewish people exist. The new Purim would surpass all previous Purims in Jewish history.—The last few days the Jewish droshky drivers all have had their horses taken away from them, so now the only means of transportation are the hand wagons. The same thing is supposed to have happened in the Aryan part of Warsaw.—Today the rumor spread about great changes coming for the Ghetto. Some of the streets are to be excluded: Sienna, Wielka, Pruzhany, etc. Others are to be included—part of Dluga, Pzriazd, Zakroczymska, etc.—The deportees from Danzig* were received very warmly in the Ghetto. A good assembly point was assigned to them (14 Prosta Street). One of them, an old post-office worker (forty years' service) could not understand how Jews could be forbidden to enter a post office of the Reich. A wagon of vital supplies that they had bought got lost en route.—The last few days the price of produce has risen steeply. Because of the Igo Sym affair,† Aryans have been denied access to the Ghetto and the price of bread and other items has gone up.—Smuggling now takes this shape: Christian boys spring off streetcars as they enter the Ghetto

* See above, p. 136.
† See above, p. 137.

carrying sacks of flour and potatoes, dash into the nearest gateway, put on an arm band, and run out into the street.— Maximilian, the medieval German emperor, took the position that Jews were the hens that laid the golden eggs; they had to be well guarded. He put them in prison, so they couldn't run away.—The arrogance of some of the Council grafters. It reaches the point where a post-office worker, knowing that a certain Jewish family is receiving a great many packages, comes to them and demands that they sell him cheap the produce they are receiving on threat of informing against them.—The abandonment of children in offices of institutions and Jewish police headquarters has become a mass phenomenon. The establishment of a home for 100 beggar children has not helped. Children are continuing to beg, no less than before. The beggars have a new line. "I'm short 10 groschen for a place to sleep; I can't sleep in the street."—After the news of the deportation from Lublin (15,000 Jews expelled), the Jewish populace of Warsaw was in a state of vast confusion. Cracow, Lublin, Radom—Warsaw is next, get on your mark. The Lublin Jews were deported in their turn: Rejowiec, Belzec, Parczew—and then Lublin. Most of those deported were women, because the men hid, so women were seized on the street and sent away.—Children's badges reading "Law and Order Service," are being sold on the street—in a word, the police are now in fashion. "Hold out, boy, help is on the way"—a very successful popular song. Some of the converts live in the courts outside All Saints Church on Leszno Street. The baptized Jews who live near the Grzybowska Street church want to have nothing to do with Jews. They are getting help from the Catholic Caritas society. The literary output against the Jewish Council is growing—the song about the Lichtenbojm brothers, who are dominant in the Council, is popular. The refugees from Danzig in Warsaw believe they'll be able to return to their homes soon, since the Fuehrer has announced that the war will be finished this year. The hunger is so great that the poor people are snatching bread from the equally poor bread vendors. They tear the bread in two and bite into it immediately afterward—in that condition, bread can't be sold.—The court of 56 Leszno Street is the meeting place for Jews and Christians. When a Jew has business in court, he telephones his lawyer to come out and meet him there, and discusses the matter with him. The professor meets his assistants here.—The beginning of March, news that Grzybowska and Pruzhany Streets have been excluded from the Ghetto. The reason: Swieca, a large scrap-iron firm, has a warehouse on G. Street; it would take a long time for the supply to be transported to the Other Side, so, at Swieca's request, the commissar saw to it that Grzybowska and Pruzhany were excluded. The porters are downcast because of Swieca's intervention. They would have earned *some* money if the residents had to move.—The Danzig refugees purportedly had half a million marks taken away from them. Rumors about the arrival of Jews from abroad: from Vienna, Belgium, and Holland. Stew has become very popular in the Ghetto, even a proletarian *chalent*. Tens of thousands of them prepared.— The number of thieves is increasing. There have been thefts after which it wasn't possible to buy the stolen items back from the thieves' guild—as used to be the case. The reason: The new thieves aren't organized yet. There's also been an increase in the number of operators who specialize in taking over apartments. They're real artists at it.—The police have a new practice: All the money taken in during the week is split among the platoon at the end of the week. But it's turned out that the money grabbed in haste is false. In one platoon it came to 80 zlotys for each man.—Nine Christian pharmacies are about to be bought up by the Jewish Council. Jews are to collect a capital of 300,000 zlotys for the purpose. Recently, four transports of Viennese Jews arrived in Kielce

—6,500 persons in all. They came with fashionable valises, in special wagons. On Jagelonsko Street there's a large storehouse for merchandise where 300 Jews are working. Their daily earnings are 4.80 zlotys. Lately, they've been getting 15 per cent less, because 10 per cent is deducted by the Transfer Station, another 5 per cent is a general deduction for all workers. There was a theft recently, so every worker has had 1 zloty a day deducted from his wages. They've been digging up potato heads; it turned out they were all spoiled. They had made the potato cairns too warm. They had buried the potatoes deep in the earth, laid a couple of layers of earth and straw over them, which was according to the German scientific method, but unsuited to the Polish winter, which was mild this year. They were paid by the Transfer Station in the Jewish Council building.

Yesterday, the 17th of March, I saw this scene: For some offense (presumably smuggling), a few seven- or eight-year-old children and a Christian woman were forced to do calisthenics for more than an hour, touching their toes. Afterward, the Polish and Jewish guards took the children and the woman into a café and stuffed them with food. One child couldn't move. The sight of children bending up and down, up and down, and the sound of the guards screaming at them, are unforgettable.—The converts are behaving miserably. One of them, a Dr. Szeniszer, is angry at the "filthy Jews" in the hospital. Dr. Werthajm, another convert, is said to have appealed to the authorities, stating that he had been converted thirty rather than twenty years before, and his attitude toward the Jews was hostile; consequently, he was made the administrator of the Jewish Hospital.—From tomorrow on, the streetcars running from the Other Side to the Ghetto are to go via Chlodna, rather than via Leszno, to make smuggling more difficult. Meanwhile, the tailor and hatter shops are inactive. The craftsmen spent a great deal of money setting up these shops, but for the time being they've realized nothing from them.

Most of the machines from the Jewish factories and shops have been dismantled and hidden. Almost every day, I see two or three people fall dead in the street from hunger.— The inhabitants of houses on Pruzhany Street have received an order to leave their apartments by the end of March.— Jewish apartments are again being emptied of their furnishings. The Jewish populace's outward appearance [is] very distressing. At every step one comes across people who are badly dressed, wearing torn coats, or tattered ones, or coats held together with a safety pin to conceal the fact that their wearers have no shirts on underneath. . . .—Beggars have been going into partnership: One beggar sprawls on the ground in a faint; his partner calls on passers-by to take pity on the poor man lying on the street.

End of March

Rajtnemer, the owner of one of the largest libraries of Hebraica, died a few days ago. The cause of death was heartbreak; he missed his library, which remained behind in two large rooms on the Other Side. Puttering around his books was his whole life. When this ceased because of the Ghetto, he moved aimlessly about his apartment.

All the Jewish Council's correspondence with the special offices assigned to the Ghetto goes through the Transfer Station, which is the Jews' only connection with the outside world.—Sunday, forty men from the Transfer Station visited the Jewish Council building. When shown the handicrafts school, they asked whether the Jews had always worked, or were just working now. At the end they declared that the Jews benefited by their work.—Grochow, the Warsaw suburb, where nineteen *chalutzim* [prospective farmers in Palestine] support themselves by agricultural work, is like an island. Originally, there was a project to put up a wall around Grochow, but it was abandoned because of the excessive cost. Some fifty *chalutzim* are to be engaged in the village of Czerniakow, too. Last year they worked there.—The illegal Polish publication *Your Freedom and Ours* has come out sharply opposed to the employment of 5,000 young Jewish volunteers in agricultural work. They maintain that it is collaborating with the enemy.—During the last ten months, the Jewish populace of Lodz has been diminished by the death of 23,000 individuals.—Serious literature in Yiddish has begun to be sold in baskets; this seems to be a good business, and the prices of books have gone up.—A number of Them who are decent human beings and have important positions have left Warsaw; They can't bear what's happening to the Jews.— Hochmann's [?] seventeen-year-old son was killed when struck on the head with an iron bar. His mother visits his grave daily; his father has devoted his whole life to helping poor people. He has become their advocate, pressing their claims against the rich. He has organized an honorary fighting squad that sets up a blockade around the apartments of rich people, until the rich meet their demands. He settles refugees in the confiscated apartments. The finest embodiment of the just popular anger at the rich for failing to do their duty to the poor.—One of the greatest cultural losses of Polish Jewry has been the destruction of the synagogue in Pinczow—built in the Renaissance style, it is perhaps the only one of its kind in Poland. In 1938 German Jewry lost its oldest synagogue, that of Worms, built on a Roman base with Gothic superstructure. Kupcziker, one of the biggest grafters in the Jewish Council, is known in popular parlance as chap-zucker —because he takes a large part of every sugar ration for his own confectionery factory.*—Sachsenhaus has been ar-

* *Chap* in Yiddish means "grab"; *zucker* is "sugar," as in German.

rested and is said to be in Oswiecim. The same for one of the worst police scoundrels—Ehrlich, the police administrator for the graveyard region. At the end of every day he used to keep for himself whatever was taken from captured smugglers. They seem to be systematically getting rid of those agents who have outlived their usefulness.—Blackmail and "fixed" arrests are becoming a large-scale system. This is how it works: Around eight o'clock a Jew is arrested and put in prison at Danilowiczowska Street. Some two or three hours later, another Jew comes along, says he is here about the poor man who's been arrested—it just so happens. The visitor wants to help, and in fact, by paying a specified sum, the arrested man is released after two days. The Jewish middleman has an affidavit certifying that he is in the service of the Gestapo. On the day of the Yugoslav revolution (29th of March),* a Jewish Councilman came to see a high official in the Transfer Station and was greeted with a slap in the face. "I'll come back tomorrow—you are out of sorts today," said the Jewish official.—A number of work bureaus in the towns that Jews were driven out from are said to have appealed for Jewish labor. It is said that this is the reason why further resettlements have been temporarily suspended.— The avarice of the Jewish police is such that they take 20 groschen from smuggler boys for every loaf of smuggled bread.—Every day a captain of the watch visits the graveyard to check the number of those who have died that day. They can't understand why so few Jews are dying here, while the mortality on the Other Side is so high. He wonders aloud whether the d.n. [daily number] of deaths is not being concealed, or whether the bodies aren't being disposed of in some other manner.

* On March 27, 1941, King Peter of Yugoslavia took over the government of Yugoslavia, leading a revolt against the pro-German government. But on April 6, the German army invaded Yugoslavia, as did the Bulgarian.

April 6

My dear:

The system of collective responsibility. A Jew stole electricity by tampering with the electricity meter. He couldn't pay the 100 zlotys fine. So his neighbors had to pay it.—*Wolnosc,* the illegal paper, berates the Polish populace for having completely stripped their apartments on Dzika Street when they had to move out of them: They tore out window frames, doors, broke windows, stoves, roofs.—The poison is bearing fruit. There are sixty-one night spots in the Warsaw Ghetto. Extraordinary slackening of kinship ties. There are frequent cases where They come and search behind one particular picture [concealing a wall safe] because they know there is foreign currency or gold hidden there. Who but members of the household could have told them that?—The rabbinate is about to declare various types of beans and gourds kosher for Passover use, out of fear lest there be a shortage of matzoth—and the Orthodox go hungry rather than eat fermented food during the Passover holiday.— When complaint was made to Czerniakow that, as head of the

Jewish Council, he not only tolerated baptized Jews, but actually placed them in important positions, he replied that he could not approach the problem from the Jewish standpoint, but as one affecting the general government of the Ghetto. The Ghetto, he said, is not a Jewish state, but an area where baptized Jews are residents, as are Jews—consequently, they must be given equal treatment. Some people have pointed out that, rather than the baptized Jews assimilating to the Jews, a contrary process is taking place, particularly on Sienna Street, where converts comprise a significant part of all the residents. They are influencing the Jews to become more assimilationist. On the other hand young converts made a ceremony of putting on the Jewish star arm bands. There was speechmaking for the occasion. The last few days (beginning of April) the man in the street has been nervous. From the Other Side have come reports of preparations that seem to point to war. Antiaircraft artillery has been set up, some houses have been scrubbed down to serve as hospitals. The Mirkow paper factory is producing nothing but blackout paper. German wives (of ethnic Germans) have been given till the 15th, some say till the 10th, to leave Warsaw; the hospitals have all been scrubbed down. All these preparations arouse fear of imminent war with Russia.* The cost of living keeps rising. Nowadays (the 6th of April) a kilo of potatoes costs 1.50 zlotys, black bread 6 zlotys, white bread 7.50—it's simply intolerable. The popular mood has been badly affected by Czerniakow's arrest. Arrested with him were Engineer Lichtenbojm, and a man called Ehrmann, who had the concession for garbage removal in the Ghetto. There's an ethnic German in "the Thirteen" who makes it his business to remove garbage. Three garbage removal bids were submitted to the Jewish Council: one from the City Cleaning Company, another for 27 groschen, a third for 25 groschen. The CCC was

---

* On June 22, 1941, Germany invaded Russia.

rejected because it is an Aryan company. But the Jewish Council accepted the bid to remove garbage at 30 groschen, hoping to beat the price down to 25. The Transfer Station accomplished this. The Jewish Council is said to have been found guilty of taking graft, in that it accepted security of only 50,000 zlotys from the garbage removal company. Another opinion ascribes Czerniakow's arrest to malfeasance in potato distribution; the Council sold a shipment of potatoes at market prices, instead of giving it away free to the populace. Rubinstein, the mad jester, is the voice of the people in his insistence that C. was arrested because of the potatoes. Still a third opinion has it that C.'s arrest is connected with the arrest in Radom of the head of the Jewish Council in Siedlce and Lublin (Dr. Alter).—Roosevelt sent a dispatch to Pétain: "Hold out, young fellow!"* There's a shortage of disinfectant supplies in the Ghetto, and of medications in general. Representations have been made at the Transfer Station for some time now, but there has been no answer. The Transfer Station has justified its taking of 50 per cent of all merchandise passing from and to the Ghetto on the grounds that the Ghetto is an "extraterritorial payment area."—There's a Central Agency for Lies in the Ghetto. It disseminates what is purportedly news picked up from radio broadcasts, but is actually only newspaper items, highly seasoned. Thus, for example, a couple of days ago I heard that the [Ethiopian] insurgents had taken Addis Ababa, thrown out the Italians, and burned their women and children on the Plaza Balbo.†— Heard that the city magistrate's office is favorably disposed to the Jews of Warsaw, helping them as far as they are able— such as letting Jews know about the arrival of produce and

* On April 7, 1941, Marshal Pétain stated the French Vichy government's policy; it would not engage in "action against our former allies."

† The basis of truth in the report was that on April 7, 1941, in the Gojjam area of Ethiopia, patriots captured Debra Marcos.

the like.—Heard about the remarkably warm reception given the Jews deported from Plock to Konskie. When they arrived in Konskie, several dozen of them were found lying in the wagons in pools of blood, with broken arms and legs; there was one sick woman who was completely naked. One of the Konskie community workers wept at the sight. Even the local district chief, not a particular lover of Jews, moved aside and wiped away the tears from his face. He permitted the injured and sick to be removed from the wagons in his trucks. The Jewish population of Konskie received their brethren from Plock very cordially. They had bread and coffee waiting for the deportees. The Jews of Konskie did not sleep that night, having given their own beds to those newly arrived from Plock. All the next day the newcomers were flooded with gifts. Three days later the order came for the Jews from Plock to disperse into the neighboring towns. The Jewish Council of Konskie sent messengers out with money, set up a Jewish Council in Paradyz—in a word, took particular care of "their" Jews from Plock.—An interesting phenomenon: The Others never show any humanity when they get together; on the contrary, They vie with each other in cruelty. For example: Dr. Hagen,* when appealed to officially to provide milk for sucklings, replied: "How dare the Jews make such a proposal when they can satisfy all their needs with contraband?" And yet, his attitude has been a generally humane one up to now.—A notebook was supposed to have been found on Czerniakow with a notation for 60,000 zlotys which does not figure in the general Council books. He cannot explain the source of this figure. Another reason given for Czerniakow's arrest is competition with "the Thirteen." Still another theory is that Czerniakow complained that he had no power in the Ghetto, for some of the Others were supporting individual Jews, thus weakening his authority.

* Medical officer for the Government General of Poland.

April 13

The city magistracy does not see to it that the city is kept clean, particularly in the Jewish neighborhood.—In the Sejm building* Rabbi Mendele was told: "Aren't you responsible for the war?" They beat him so hard on the hand with a rubber truncheon that the hand swelled.—Hasensprung, one of the Jewish war veterans, and an idiot, came to the Jewish Council. He said to Penger†: "You can't do anything with Jews unless you use force."—The Nazi line: Cast fear into the whole population, and then you'll be able to run them with a handful of people.—"Mr. President" is what Isaac Giterman was [derisively] called in the work camp.—Hitler is wearing a vest nowadays, because he has lost his "flotilla jacket."‡— S. told us of the ignoble behavior of the Poles. How they behaved after the Germans entered Warsaw.—Old Herr Professor Majer [Balaban] was made to work in a garden. Gepner was set free: *"Sie sind so sauber"*—"You're so clean." —"You'll see," says a German soldier to a Jew during the Norway affair. "The big fellow will make peace with the Jews yet, and win the war."—"If we kept the law, we'd all have to jump into the Vistula," said a merchant. "We can't mind all these regulations. If we did, we wouldn't be able to operate at all."—The Passover holiday eve (April 11) Jews were pulled out of the lines for holiday supplies and taken to work camp.—The Jewish Councilmen who went to Cracow came back with a work pass allowing the prophet Elijah to be out in the streets after nine o'clock on the nights of the Passover Seders. The Warsaw streets, particularly Leszno, have become very lively. All the young people are out on the street.

* *See above*, p. 26.
† Code for Gepner.
‡ "Flotilla" and "jacket" are the same word in Polish. On April 7 and 8, 1941, the British Air Force raided the German fleet at Kiel; and again on the night of April 8–9.

From lack of schooling, they're becoming wild, undisciplined. Saw the typewritten number of *Liberty*, a Zionist Young Guard paper (probably the March number). A lead article by Simon. Another paper of the Young Guard's, *Against the Stream*, No. 3, had a fine lead article: "It's the thing to say that the war is turning people into beasts. But we did not wish the war, and we do not wish it now, and we will not be turned into beasts. We were, and we will remain, human beings."—The last few days (since the 20th [12th?] of April), young flyers [?] have been going around accompanied by petty police officers from the Jewish Council, dragging Jews out of their homes for forced work. The head of the group is said to be an honest man; he doesn't want to do the dirty work alone.—An acquaintance of mine saw Jewish petty police officers walking around during the holiday (Passover) without their badges on, and with pockets full of eggs. That was their graft. They are also said to have begun collecting "polls" —people for work camp. In a word, we've a new style—Jewish body-snatchers.—Yesterday, the second day of Passover (April 12), Jews were taken off streetcars for work camp. One man jumped off the streetcar; they shot into the air after him. A guard tried to hit the running man with his rifle, missed, and broke it. It is said that the press ganging will stop soon. The "question of Jewish labor" will be "regulated."— Accident and free will: Mrs. Bach [?] went to the Gestapo to see about a permit. The first time she went, for no good reason she was ordered to go home. The second time she was told to come in a month, although it only takes a few days. The third time the man said, "What do you mean you were told to come back in a month? That's the way Jews do things; the German way is to do things fast (!). Get out!" The fourth time she came, there was someone else there, and she got the permit.

The Polish book stores have closed not only their English and French departments, but their Yiddish ones as well. After lengthy appeals, they were reopened.—In the *Voelkisher Beobachter* there was an article about the showing of *Jud Suess*, how they went to Berlin to produce the scene. The Jews sang [for the film]: "We shall survive them." That is how the song has been filmed for all eternity.—Gossip that the Gestapo has hired 4,000 Jews to fill listening posts in every courtyard.—Saw an edition of *Liberty:* "The war's end will see the end of all imperialism."—Saw a fine Polish-language Purim number of the paper, called *Laughter through Tears*. —It is said that, for a small fee, priests are glad to give Jews papers certifying they were converted, to make it easier for those Jews who wish to pass as Aryans.—At the beginning of the Ghetto period, *men of valor* tore down the mezuzoth from the door posts of Jewish apartments and shops. Most of the Jewish places have none now. There's a copy of his exemption document hanging on the door of the home of the elder of the Jewish Council of Warsaw, Adam Czerniakow. If she [his wife?] could not show the original, she would be shot.— Spent the two Passover Seder nights at Shachna [Zagan's]. There was an interesting discussion about vengeance. Mr. Isaac,‡ who had been interned in a German prison camp in Pomerania, demonstrated that vengeance would never solve anything. The vanquished would in turn plan their own vengeance, and so it would go on forever. There was talk that raising the moral level of all humanity was the only solution. Mr. Isaac told us a story about a young Jew who committed theft in his camp. The leftists ganged up to beat him, but the Talmudic academy comrades rallied and protected him—the morality of the "Fourth Classroom." Where group and

* *See above*, p. 151.
† Giterman.

national hatred comes from—the camp inmates fought over a couple of centimeters of sausage. They liked only their room-mates.—Everyone else was "the enemy." Seven Jewish fam-ilies have remained in Starogard. They all live in one court-yard. The German workers bring them food and delicacies. They have only one hour a week to leave [Starogard] to buy things. The Jews are employed as day laborers. The magis-tracy pays them. The worst anti-Semites became Mr. Isaac's friends in camp. The Jewish revenge: The Jews are very for-giving. The Germans are only people after all—except for the Gestapo!—RSJF [stands for] Radio Station Jewish Fan-tasy, the rumor mongers. "Anything new?" "What's the mat-ter—are you too lazy to think up your own news?"—A Polish society has been formed in Warsaw, called Hammer and Cross, whose aim is to "liberate Polish life from Jewish influ-ence."—The first few days after the appearance of the new money, some false 50 groschen pieces turned up. They sold like hot cakes.—The odd letter—in code: "Bronek [England] has married [been defeated by] Helena [Germany]. We drank 40 flasks of wine bottled by the firm *Broken Ships*."*—The *big fellow* ordered three different tailors each to make him a suit and furnished the material. One tailor said, "There's only enough material for a vest." The second tailor said, "There's enough material for a whole suit." The Jewish tailor said he could make three suits out of the stuff: "He may be very big to Them, but to us he's a pigmy!"—Code message: "How many volumes are there to Brodecki's encyclopedia in the Polish translation?" ("What is the English pound worth?"). [Trustees]: They published a decree that every Jewish woman must bear one child, or They would assign a trustee to see to the matter.

* On March 30, 1941, the British announced that British, Allied, and neutral shipping losses caused by German submarines had been 77,575 tons the previous week.

April 17

My dear:

There were fearful scenes in the office of the refugee organization on the eve of the Passover holiday. A crowd of 7,000–8,000 refugees gathered, waiting for matzoth and other packages generally. The whole horror of the present situation was revealed. People applied for free packages whose neighbors considered them to be persons of means, and who a short time before had been able to help others. The disappointment of those who could not receive packages is indescribable.—The high cost of living (bread is 11 zlotys a kilo, potatoes around 3 zlotys, matzoth 16–18 zlotys), the political developments (the fall of Yugoslavia),* and the work camps —this is the awful trio that determines our situation in the Ghetto. Hunger is rampant, because neither bread nor potatoes can be secured, even with ration cards. A friend whom I wished a "calm Passover" (that was last year's motto) replied: "Rather wish me an easy fast."—People are being seized for the work camps because the Jewish Council has not met its quota. The Jewish police, joining with the Polish police, have had to form press gangs. What had happened was that Jews who had been accepted as fit for work duty and had been called up had not presented themselves. Of course, they spent the night away from home. So the police seized whomever they could find, even people over fifty. The Jewish and Polish police took advantage of this opportunity to do business. They took hundreds of zlotys from innocent people and from complete courtyards. It was a real orgy. The young people hid out on roofs, in cellars, in the public kitchens, and in other public places.—The news from the camps is not bad. This will doubtless influence Jews to go there. The refugee centers have been depleted significantly. Gen-

* On April 13, 1941, the Germans occupied Belgrade.

erally speaking, the Jewish police are fearfully corrupt. There have been 700 disciplinary trials for a force of 1,700. This is because of the fact that Kupcziker was the man chiefly responsible for recruiting policemen, and recruits had to pay him to be taken on. The result was that a very bad element was accepted in the police force.—One of the guards calls a Jewish policeman over. The Jew has to stand 10 meters away to speak to the guard, 50 meters away otherwise. For Jews, They say, are like gangrene—the place where they set foot must be cauterized.—A week ago (around the 10th of April), a terrible incident involving a Jewish policeman took place with the arrival of a new company of guards in Warsaw. Reportedly, it was the same platoon that was present when the Ghetto was first introduced, the one infamous for forcing Jews to do calisthenics. On Solna Street one of these guards took a sack of potatoes away from a Jewish woman. Ginsberg, a Jewish policeman from Lodz, asked the guard to give the potatoes back to the poor woman. As punishment for Ginsberg's audacity, the guard knocked him to the ground, stabbed him with his bayonet, and shot him as he lay there. Weak from hunger, Ginsberg died in the hospital. Another Jewish policeman was wounded by a guard's bullet at the same place. The same evening a group of people who had been out late were shot at after nine o'clock and two of them were injured. Passover Seders, complete with meat, dough balls, and wine, were held at many of the refugee centers. For a brief moment, the refugees were able to forget the sadness of their situation and their misery. The Seders were a source of spiritual strength to the exhausted and homeless refugees.

The 13th of April people were seized in the streets for forced work. Many of them did not run away, preferring to work for 3.20 zlotys a day. Merin was here a few days ago. He received a royal reception. In the theater actors saluted him. Menachem Mendel [Kirshbojm] presented him to the audience as the redeemer of the Jewish people! Thanks to *his* efforts, ghettos had been averted in Bedzin, Sosnowiec. The mortality in those towns was actually lower than it had been before the war. There were no beggars in the streets. Merin had quickly organized the resettlement of 6,000 Jews from Oswiecim and vicinity [in Bedzin and Sosnowiec]. The refugees had been able to take everything with them, even their furniture. The housing problem had been solved by boarding refugees in every Jewish house in town. Any family that would not voluntarily accept a refugee was threatened with eviction.—During the night visits by the Jewish and Polish policemen, the most acceptable papers are said to be those bearing Mlinarski's photograph.*—A group of seven *chalutzim* managed to smuggle themselves into Bratislava via Najsanc recently, to migrate from there to Pal.[estine]. The trip costs 1,200 zlotys a person.—The scene at the laying-out shed at the graveyard is horrible. Every day corpses are found sprawling in the streets, half naked. The heaps of raggedy corpses are a macabre sight.—The rent receipts, which formerly came to an estimated 60 per cent of rent due, have recently fallen another 10 per cent. When appeals were made to the Warsaw rich to levy a tax on themselves for the benefit of the refugees, they replied: "That won't help. The paupers will die out, anyway." That's how they think; they won't give a groschen for the refugees.—The freeing of Czerniakow is said to have cost the Jewish Council 20,000 zlotys. That much money is thrown away on drink every night at the Casanova night club. Szternfeld, the chief of police, swears he's not touching the money that comes in to the police as graft. He must be spending it on drink say the cynics; how much truth there is in that nobody knows.

* Notes issued by the bank whose director was Mlinarski.

April 26

My dear:

Heard the following interesting theory, which is intended to justify the martyrdom They are inflicting on the Jewish population. Jews, They say, are on the side of the enemy—so they must be the victims (Mr. Ignacy's* theory). During the campaign in the east in 1939, some Polish soldiers held a meeting to consider whether to go back to Warsaw or on to the East [Russia]. Characteristic of the decline of the Polish army.—In one of the prisoner-of-war camps (according to Mr. Isaac Giterman), the Jewish prisoners were ordered to repeat: "There will be no peace until the last Jew and the last Papuan will have disappeared from the face of the earth" (probably a quote from one of Their favorite works).—The Jews are reviving their spirits with political smelling salts: Yugoslavia fell, they say, because the English are trying to contract the front, they are looking for breathing space. The military defeats of the Allies have had a depressing effect on the Jews. Despair and a sense of hopelessness are growing. There is the universal feeling that They are trying to starve us out, and we cannot escape, save through a miracle.—A few days back this happened: Some rich men were found in a cellar on 31 Muranowska Street, with two radio sets. The extortioners demanded 20,000 zlotys. The whole courtyard appealed to "the Thirteen" for help; the latter reported to the authorities that they were conducting an investigation themselves.—Heard the opinion expressed that war reveals the best and the worst in people. It's like a high fever, in which everything is clarified. On the one hand, some Christians offer to help the Jews; on the other hand, bestial anti-Semitism; on the one hand stony hearts [among the Jews]; on the other, devoted self-sacrifice to aid those suffering from hunger.—Saw a beggar with a cradle in the

* Giterman.

street—another good technique for getting money.—Three-year-old children are out begging in the streets. You can't rest nowadays in a Jewish apartment. You hear beggars rapping on doors on either side of your own apartment. These early spring days they're playing music in the streets. Unemployed Jewish musicians are playing outdoors for their livelihood. At the beginning people used to snatch loaves of bread because they were hungry; now it's become a livelihood.—There are cases where part of an apartment is sold, though apartments are under the control of the commissariat.—During the Passover operation, Rawicki, the millionaire from Lowicz, fainted twice on the road from hunger. Kohn and Heller have left "the Thirteen" and are going into business on their own. For 500 zlotys you can become one of their middlemen.—Recently, this happened: The Others came to a man and ordered him to appear at the Gestapo the next day. He called up Kohn, who, it just so happened, had heard about this matter, and, for 1,000 zlotys, the man didn't have to go to the Gestapo after all.—In Lodz the poor people receive 9 marks from the Jewish Council. There are no beggars in the streets.—The director of the Transfer Station makes it a practice not to talk to Jews. There are dignitaries like that, who won't see a Jew to talk with as a matter of principle. They order the windows of the Transfer Station kept open because of the stench the Jews make.—The Jewish madmen from all over the country are concentrated in Zofjowka, where more than one hundred madmen from Tworki and thirty from Kobieszin were transported. In all there are some four hundred patients there, dying of hunger.—"The Thirteen" recently got permission to import a big load of potatoes and made good money at it (over 100,000 zlotys). "The Thirteen" is to have its own jail and criminal court.—The 19th, 20th, and 21st of April will remain indelibly fixed in the memory of the Jews of Warsaw. On those days the Jewish Council, with the help of the Jewish police, revived the melancholy practice of kidnaping. It was like a literal photograph from the past. The reason for the press gangs was that the Jewish Council had to send 1,500 people to work camp. Only 50 persons turned up. When the police (both Jewish and Polish) went searching for the missing persons, they could find only 130 at home. The rest were spending the night away from home —remembering what had happened in the work camp last year, when almost 100 per cent of the workers returned injured, physically and psychically broken. Another reason why people evaded work service was the criminal attitude of the Council, which, neither last year nor this, did anything to help the campers' families. Nor, for that matter, have they helped the campers themselves. The Council representatives who went to see the camps last year didn't even visit them; still they came back with the good word that everything was all right. A third reason for the large-scale evasion of work camps is an evil that cries to the very heaven—only the poor go to camp. The rich boys are working on the police force, in community organizations, or are registered with the sick fund as supposedly employed by various firms—but, most important, they can always buy their way out of work-camp duty. It costs very little. I know one rich man who pays 100 zlotys a month to keep his son out of work camp. Many rich men's sons bribe the Jewish doctors during the medical examinations. The Jewish doctors are in partnership with the Other doctors, who have to countersign the medical certificates. There are middlemen in this business, too. With such corruption rife, it is no wonder that the poor have banded together and refused to go to work camps. It is notable that of the 45,000 men who were supposed to register for the work camps, 11,000 did not appear. However, it would be a mistake to suppose that so large a number of men deliberately absented themselves. The Jewish Council's work department is not only corrupt, it is completely indolent as well. Every little thing (a special registration, for instance) seems to require superhuman effort on the part of everyone concerned. To get a medical examination you have to spend some two or three days waiting from five in the morning—of course, you can go into the examination room by a side entrance for 5–10 zlotys. Nothing was anticipated. Complete anarchy and dry rot. Because of all this, the heads of the Council's work department lost their heads, and, unable to control the situation, took to kidnaping people. The first day—the 19th of April—was horrible. It earned the Jewish police the honorary title of "gangsters," the name that was flung at them hundreds of times during meetings that the House Committees held to discuss the subject. Instead of searching for those who were hiding out the nights of the 19th and 20th of April, the Jewish and Polish police took over complete houses and demanded to be paid off. One policeman is said to have made 5,000 zlotys that first night. They forced their way into the apartments of people over forty, of people who were sick, and insisted on being paid off. Of course, the only people taken for work were those who couldn't buy their way out, or those who had been exempted previously as being sick, or as the only breadwinner in the family. Those pressed for work included a father of seven children, the youngest two weeks old. There were special raids on the refugee centers, where men were taken away who were starving and had been tortured during the deportation from their home towns. A police officer told me that in one of the centers a refugee had kissed his boots and begged him on bended knees to let him stay with his family, whose only support he was. The officer said to me: "I am willing to give away five years of my life not to have to live through such a terrible experience again."—There were more raids the second and third days (the 20th and 21st of April) and these completely paralyzed normal life in the Ghetto. The markets were practically inactive, because the police refused to honor the exemptions issued by any of the charitable institutions. The police barricaded complete blocks looking for young people, and graft flourished. The searches were pretty fruitless, because the populace hid out in cellars, attics, warehouses, concealed rooms, and with friends on the Other Side. The young people stayed awake all night waiting for the janitor's signal that the police were coming. Those were hideous days, and they will forever be remembered unto the Jewish Council as a mark of shame. The Jewish populace's wrath at the Council was indescribable. It was most sharply expressed at the meeting of the H.C.'s [House Committees] called by the Council to persuade the populace to report for work service. The official speakers were continually interrupted during the meeting. A number of cries of protest expressed the popular sentiment. It was on this occasion that Councilman Rosen, director of the work department, made the brilliant statement that the chairmen of the House Committees would be held personally responsible for the failure of registered campers to report for work service. As is the wont at Council meetings, no discussion was permitted. The meeting was quickly concluded to the sound of protests from those assembled. This was the meeting where Shapiro, the chairman of the 2 Leszno Street House Committee, cried out: "Where is the leader of the gangsters whom we have had to buy off the last few nights?" Shapiro, along with two other people, was subsequently arrested by the Jewish police; but a few minutes later they had to be released because of the stormy protest of the audience.

Last year there were cripples in the work camps; there was a man with one foot. In Lublin and Zamoszcz people were picked up on the street to meet the quota. Mannes, the head of the department of internal administration for the Warsaw district, sent a letter to the Jewish Council threatening that in the event the Jews did not meet their quota the food supply for the Ghetto would be suspended, and the work camps would be turned into penal camps. This is what influenced the Citizens' Committee to call a meeting of H.C.'s to persuade the people to do their duty. The late advocate Ludwig Berenson suggested that it was the duty of fifty community leaders to report voluntarily to the camps themselves, if they wished to set a good example of doing one's duty. There were speakers, such as Dr. Wielikowski, who maintained that work service was a national duty. Other speakers, more sober than he, pointed out that tens of thousands of men could not hide out, and we were obliged to think of the terrible consequences this could have for the people as a whole. A representative of the Jewish Council labor bureau declared: "We have found a way of getting along with the Others; why can't we find a way of getting along in the Ghetto?" There was the threat of a retaliatory raid by the S.S., who would seize people for work. Last year the several thousand campers from Warsaw worked in fifty-six different camps. This year it's been decided to keep all the workers from the same landsman's society together. Luxury barracks have been put up in some of the camps, such as Kampinos Puszcza, for example. The first few days as many as 2,000 men volunteered for the work. The first reports from the camps were bad, particularly from Lowicz. Two hundred grams of bread daily rations per man, besides working in water, in a project to control the Bzura river. Handicraftsmen and "economically active persons" have been let out of the camps. The Jews showed such repulsion toward the press-gang men that a police delegation reported to the Jewish Council that they did not want to be used for the dirty work. Some of them declared they were prepared to go to the camp themselves, rather than have to press others to do it.—A few of the policemen (a small part of the culprits) who had been particularly skillful at extortion, were actually sent to camp themselves. One of them, the one who had made 5,000 zlotys in one night, came riding back in the company of a guard a few days after he'd been sent off to camp—to buy up produce for the camp. He announced that he could get people freed from camp service for 200 zlotys.—The camp guard, mostly Ukrainian recruits, are scoundrels, and they made sure to let the Jewish populace feel their presence. Yesterday, the 25th of April, they tried to hold up some Jewish businesses. The Others caught them, placed them in chains, and took them away. The same thing happened today, the 26th.—In Lowicz one of the C.G. [Camp Guards] poured benzine over a young Jew and then set fire to him. The C.G. carry rifles and are dressed in green uniforms. At the 84 Zelazna Street commission, the Polish police let 400 of the 700 people seized for work camps go free, for a price, so that in the end only the poor people remained. The extent to which the Jewish Council is disliked and what they are thought capable of may be gauged from the report circulated that, in fact, many volunteers had reported for the work camps, but they had been ordered to pay 50 zlotys. Apparently, this was only a rumor. The Councilmen are accused of really not wanting volunteers, so as to make money from those forced to go to camp. The H.C.'s are helping the campers tremendously, supplying them with linen, clothing, shoes, money, supporting their families, etc. . . . It costs some 500 zlotys to be assigned to the police force.— The police have an important problem with getting rubber tips for their shoes. It seems that the wooden tips are dangerous, because when the police kick offending persons, they break their bones. But for the time being rubber is not available in the Ghetto.—What the streets looked like on the 19th, 20th, and 21st of April, during the work seizures: There were only women in the streets. Crying women surrounded the men who had been seized; they were sent off to camp the first day empty-handed. A three-year-old child tearfully asked a policeman not to take his father away: "Who will give us bread?" The policeman swore to me that those words would torment him the rest of his life. The Jewish Council's inefficiency: People who had been released from work camp a long time before had not been issued release papers because the doctors had given all [the release papers] away to those who had paid for them—and had not done service—so the Council had not had the time to issue them to the people who had really been in work camps. So, naturally [!] people who had already been released were seized again by the press gangs, because they had no proof they'd already served. It reached the point where people were seized for the work camps while standing in line to register for them. Anarchy and complete lack of common sense.—One thousand three hundred "rabbis" were exempted. There never were that many in all Poland. [People had bought exemption as rabbis.] —Heard from a Lodz refugee that the editor of the Lodz newspaper, a former anti-Semitic National Democrat called Kargel, ordered the Jewish artist Hanemann to paint him standing on the ruins of Warsaw in the pose of a conqueror. Naturally, the portrait was to be signed by an Aryan artist. —The children call Karmelicka Street "The Forge of Death." —One of the camp guards wounded (or killed) a woman and child on the 20th [of April] while the woman was looking into the commission to see her husband.—The Jewish Council has adopted the old Czarist slogan: "Keep quiet. Don't argue." No discussion is permitted at any of their meetings, and certainly no questioning. They held a meeting of doctors dealing with antityphus inoculations; no discussion was permitted. Czerniakow is regarded as an idol. His edicts are not to be questioned; his word is command. In general, they have taken over the Fuehrer principle.—The following is typical of the general attitude toward the Jewish Council. When the Toporol organization held a public meeting for the purposes of agitation, the first question posed by the audience was: "Do you people have any connection with the Council administration?"—Private individuals get tons of coal free, while public kitchens [and] children's homes have to pay 1,500 zlotys a ton. Nor can the buyer watch the coal being weighed. He's forced to take a ready wagonful. But if you give the coalman some 20 zlotys, you can get whole coals, not pieces. There's an organized gang that steals the coal from the wagon en route to your house, unless you pay them off. The mortality among the Jewish populace is colossal. Has grown from 150 to 500–600 a week. People are dying in the street. When a woman was asked why she went out in the street with her children, she replied that she would rather die in the street than at home. There are hundreds of people lying unconscious in the street. Besides those who are really unconscious, there are the simulators, who fall down in a faint every couple of minutes. You may be able to bear their screaming for bread, but when they fall unconscious at your feet, you have to stop. Usually you give them bread or tea.—The cost of living and the value of the dollar are rising, because of the rumors about war with Russia being imminent.*—The 21st of April there was talk of a black-out. So bread rose from 7 to 11 zlotys a kilo, the hard gold dollar to 240, the soft paper dollar to 60 zlotys. This has been a recurrent thing. Whenever there is rumor of war, produce disappears, and bread as well as the dollar rises. The same is true of potatoes, which have gone up as high as 4 zlotys.—Today, the 26th of April, potatoes are 2.40 zlotys.— . . . There's been a flight from Warsaw recently, because it's cheaper to live in the provinces. People go by auto. Recently all (!) of the newly fashioned exits have been walled up. This lessens the chances of smuggling, and the

* Germany invaded Russia on June 22, 1941.

Ghetto faces the danger of death through starvation, because the food rations are so meager.—A scene: A Christian smuggler climbs the Wall at Sienna or Sliska Street. The guards hiding in the gateway shoot him. He falls dead into the Ghetto. One of Their train or postal officials appears at the Wall, rummages through the dead man's pockets, cleans them out, and climbs back over the Wall. All this happens at twelve o'clock noon before the eyes of the guards on both sides of the Wall.—When there's a storm, refuse flies through the air.—About corruption in the Ghetto: Led by the Jewish Council's commission that finances the work camps, abetted by its director, the Council chairman holds to the theory of "democratic taxation," because, they say, there are no rich people in the Ghetto. The Council takes 40 per cent of the cost of medication—another "democratic tax."—Of the 500 sent to the work camp at Lowicz, 150 returned sick, 3 died. The reason, a simple one: Refugees lay exhausted in the commission for two days without food. In Lowicz they got 200 grams of bread a day while doing hard work.—Even the dead have no rest in the Ghetto. There's the continual sound of gunshot in the graveyard in connection with the smugglers.—Fourteen Leszno Street is the name of the organization Kohn and Heller have formed, after leaving "the Thirteen."—Prices have been jittery. When the loud-speaker broadcasts unfavorable news at one o'clock, prices jump. When it denies the rumor, prices go down again.—"How far is it from Bardia to Sochaszew," asks a Jew when told that the English have occupied Bardia.*—The professionals are in desperate straits. By now everything they had has been lost or sold; their bodies are swelling from hunger. Packages are arriving from abroad, several thousand a day, but not enough to solve our situation.—Reports from Lodz that the

* On April 13, the Germans announced the capture of Bardia in the North African campaign.

Passover operation was successful. Every Jew received 2.5 kilo of matzoth and nine eggs for the eight-day holiday period. The Jewish Council of Lodz received permission to open schools for 5,000 children and four places of worship. The schools' languages of instruction are to be Yiddish and Hebrew.—The tablets bearing inscriptions in honor of the founders of the special pavilions have been walled up at the Czista Street [Hospital?]. One of the Jewish scholars compared the Ghetto with the spoliarium where the Roman gladiators lived. The Romans used to tear the slain gladiators' clothing off their backs and leave them naked.

April 26

The walls enclosing the epidemic area in Warsaw are known popularly as the "Siegfried Line Extension."*—Jewish body-snatchers (petty officers) from the Jewish Council have been moving about lately. They'll be lounging around outside a gateway, then suddenly dash into the courtyard, where Jews are hiding. The guards wait for them there.—A week back, i.e., around the 20th of April, the press gangs were active. They dragged people out of streetcars [and] out of their homes.—Heard how the rabbi from Wengrow was killed on Yom Kippur. He was ordered to sweep the street. Then he was ordered to collect the refuse into his fur hat; while he was bending over, They bayoneted him three times. He continued working and died at work.—Jews may not be sold wood from the state forest.—There are Jews who wear ribbons on their arms that read: "Jews Useful for the Economy."— Fifty Jews were seized on Okencia Street. Twenty of them were ordered to bury a dead cat; thirty of them were ordered to turn their backs while the cat was being buried, then, to

* The Siegfried Line was the network of underground defenses Germany had constructed to face the French Maginot Line.

turn around and look for the grave. They pretended to look for a few hours and then found it easily. The soldiers laughed. Another time, They came along, had nothing to do, played a soccer game against the Jews. The Jews won, 2 to 1. It's characteristic that when alone individual Germans behave humanely. That humane captain of the watch in Mr. Isaac's camp, when he was in a room with the Others, said "The Jews are responsible for the war," and so on.—Disinfection methods in the camp: lysol on the head and on the bare body.— The letter in code to Talyn: "Uncle Amcha [God's People] Israel is living under bad conditions. He is suffering from the trouble his son Yeke [Germany] is causing him. Yeke is behaving very badly. He does scandalous things in the street. He drags Uncle about all day. You know how he used to behave at home. Now it turns out he's a hundred times worse [abroad]. Uncle would like to live in the south [Palestine] but he has to live in the north [Poland]. . . ."—A Jew has to pay more for the same pair of gloves than the Christian, who can buy it cheaper, because the Jewish artisan has no more raw material and knows he won't be receiving any more, so he has to ask a much higher price than the Christian artisan. —In Lodz there's a path running through Zgierza Street and through the Ghetto. The path is bounded on either side by barbed-wire fence, so that Christians taking this path through the Ghetto need not meet Jews. Christians may not enter the Ghetto.—A mark is worth 4 zlotys there.—This is the kind of trickery They resort to in making the film about the Ghettos of Poland: A German guard stands in the middle of Zgierza Street in the Lodz Ghetto; he is flanked on either side by Jewish guards. The German guard detains a German police officer for jaywalking; he orders the Jewish guards to hold the German police officer. And they film that.

15/MAY, 1941

During the last few days of April and the 1st of May, the situation was tense. People rarely showed themselves outside their homes—in any event, there was less movement in the streets. The reason: the arrest of Poles, taken out of Gajewski's confectionery shop in the Polish neighborhood.—One hundred sixty Jews are in the Pawia Street prison, including one couple and twenty women.—Several autos loaded with soldiers drove down Karmelicka Street, in the Jewish neighborhood. They shot into the air as they passed.—Heard that the Jewish patients were taken out of Poznanski's hospital in Lodz. It is said *they were killed.*—The plague of disinfection steam baths in Warsaw. Everybody living in a courtyard where there's a pile of refuse is forced to go to the bath. People have been able to escape the baths by paying Polish doctors as they did the health service. The courtyard at 32 Leszno Street paid 1,200 zlotys to escape the steam baths. There are families that make a living by going to the steam baths for others who have been ordered to go. The same courtyard paid 3,000 zlotys to escape being quarantined because of one case of typhus. Straw sacks, pillows, and the like are burned in the filthy courtyard.

. . . Scenes from Jewish life in Poland. Particularly interesting a prayer quorum in the field: Small-town Jews are working outdoors clearing away the snow. An elderly Jew has to recite the mourner's Kaddish prayer. When he observes that the guard has moved on, he turns his back to the work, recites the Kaddish, and a quorum of ten Jews say, "Amen."

Heard that once sometime during October–November some Jews fetched water from a distance; *men of valor* poured it out.—The Catholic populace permits Jews to fetch water from the Powonzk graveyard. The Catholics displayed a far-reaching tolerance.—The Passover program had a great moral significance: It evoked great respect among the Polish populace, who marveled at Jewish solidarity.—Heard of four artists' clubs.—Mr. Isaac estimates the percentage of *saintly Gentiles* in Starogrod at 95 per cent.

May 11

My dear:

Now, at the beginning of May, the Jewish populace is shaken up by the fearful news from the work camps, as well as from those who have fled the camps or have been released from them for reasons of sickness. The basic cause of the large number of deaths (as of the 6th of May, there were ninety-one) has been the terrible treatment of the campers by most of the Ukrainian camp guards; the very bad, actually starvation, rations have also contributed to the high mortality among the campers. The Ukrainians made their presence felt among all Jews, not only those in work camps.—The last few days have seen a series of thefts from Jewish small businesses —for example, a watchmaker whose shop was at 18 Leszno Street was forced to sell a watch ordinarily costing 50 zlotys for 10 zlotys. In every instance the Law and Order Service or "the Thirteen" intervened successfully. The police arrested and disarmed "the Ukrainian boys." Their comrades serving as camp guards used this as a pretext to wreak vengeance on the campers. It was worst in Puszcza-Kampinas, where there were thirty-seven Jewish victims, i.e., 10 per cent of the campers. The guards simply stole the campers' rations (18 dekos of bread, a thin soup, and a glass of black coffee).— When they came back, the campers died in the Jewish Council house. Some of the inmates were shot while trying to escape from camp. The camp regime was dreadful. The returnees were dreadfully exhausted. Some of them suffered the effects of a camp psychosis and trembled at the sight of a uniform. The Jewish Council is now concentrating on having the camp guards removed—Mannes, the commissar for the Jewish part of Warsaw, is to appeal to the Governor General for this purpose. You can guess the mood of those who have to go to camp. Yesterday's transport actually rebelled and refused to go. Now you can see how much reliance can be put on the promises of the Council that things would be better in the camps this year than they were last year. No words are used in camp—just blows.—A Jewish glazier worked for a Gestapo collaborator, whose servant had the unhappy thought of treating the Jew to a plate of soup. When the master of the house came home and found out about this, he ordered the servant girl to break the plate in his presence.—On Sienna and Sliska Streets the guards make money by advancing the hour. When it is fifteen or twenty minutes before nine, they detain passers-by with the complaint that it is really nine o'clock and after the curfew. By paying 10–20 zlotys, or offering a watch, ring, etc., one can buy them off.—It is said that it will be possible to telephone only through the Transfer Station, which will censor all communications. Nowadays the telephone is the most important means of communication in smuggling. You use it to tell your contacts on the Other Side when it will be possible to smuggle out a wagon of merchandise, or the like. This is the way stuff is smuggled through Sienna Street: The street cleaner stands on the Other Side of the Wall diligently sweeping. He pushes various objects through the rain-water culvert with his broom; he receives money through the same channel. Emaciated three or four-year-old children crawl through the culverts to fetch merchandise from the Other Side. Imagine what a mother must go through when her child is in momentary danger of death. —Recenty, the mortality has become catastrophic. According to the statistics, there were seven times as many deaths in April, 1941, as there had been in November, 1940. At this point it is worth noting that even before the war the mortality in Warsaw was high, because critically sick Jews from the provinces came to Warsaw to be cared for in the Jewish Hospital here. And yet, the mortality nowadays is high even compared with prewar days.—The Jewish newspaper (*Gazetta Zhitowska*) has received a notice from the Occupying Power that no German or Polish newspapers will be allowed into the Ghetto, as of the 1st of May. Obviously, this order was requested by the Jewish newspaper, which doesn't have much of a circulation. But the only result is that the other newspapers are smuggled in and are more expensive. *Nowy Kurier Warszawski* costs 35 groschen instead of 20 groschen, and the Cracow paper (*Gazetta Zhitowska*) is 50 groschen. Rickshas have become very common. Hundreds of young people make a living from them. Somebody took a funny picture of a thin young man pedaling a fat woman and child in a ricksha.—Last week (beginning of May) there was a tragic incident. On Walicow Street, where it's impossible to get through, a military car was held up by a ricksha. The soldier driving the car got out, shot one Jew dead, and wounded several others.—One of the most fearful streets is Grzybowska. Coffee with saccharine in it is sold there for 10 groschen a glass. Women stand outdoors at their old-fashioned samovars, as in a small town.—People are deserting Warsaw in hordes. They drive out in German autos (a seat costs 100 zlotys); most everyone else takes streetcar No. 3, or passes the watch at the gates on foot, paying the guards 5–10 zlotys a head. Once out of town, they all walk. Within a period of two weeks (the second half of April), 1,500 Jews, many of them women and children, arrived in Rembertow in a terrible condition, exhausted from walking, barely able to breathe.

Last Thursday, the 8th of May, was one of the worst days; 210 Jews died, a record number.—Passover, when many provincial Jews fasted—because they had no food that was kosher for Passover—was a factor in the significant rise in mortality. —Rubinstein, the mad jester, says: "Number One is all right; Number Two is not; Number Three and Number Four—may they burn!* Sixty-three people died in one day. Twenty of them were from Warsaw, forty-three from the provinces.— Recently, Saturday was declared the official day of rest. The shops are busy on Sunday.—The rich squirm out of service in the work camps in various ways. One way is through the shops, which meanwhile are not busy. The rich pay to be listed on the shop rolls and are thus exempted from forced work service.—At the same time, they don't have to pay the Jewish Council. Other rich people get themselves exempted by commissar firms, by bribing them, of course.—The Jewish populace is in a depression these days because of the Allied defeat in the Balkans, the German victories in North Africa, and their nearness to Palestine.† The high cost of living, the

* Number Four (*Der Firter,* in Yiddish) presumably refers to Hitler, *Der Fuehrer* in German.

† On April 27, 1941, the Germans entered Athens, after having virtually destroyed the British Royal Air Force in Greece. On May 1, they invaded Tobruk in North Africa, piercing the outer defense perimeter. On May 2, the British evacuated Greece. On May 10, British forces were announced as having come to the defense of Palestine and Transjordan.

work camps, the rising mortality—all have combined to discourage [even] the greatest optimists. Many people maintain that we are lost, and that the nails of hunger will dig deep into all of us.—There have been cases of suicide recently. Of people throwing themselves out the fourth floor. Majer S. lib.[rary] worth 10,000 pounds was left behind on the Other Side. What will happen to it?—Someone from the Transfer Station fashioned an epigram: "If the Germans win the war, 25 per cent of the Jews will die; if the English win, 75 per cent" (that's how long the English victory will take).—The rabbis, it was pointed out during the discussion on Passover night, have shown no evidences of a martyr's spirit. Under compulsion, they have trod on Torah scrolls with their feet. This was defended on the ground that the Others apply the principle of collective responsibility. For an individual to disobey their commands would lead to tragic consequences for the rest of the Jews. Some questioned this argument, asserting that refusal would have led to the shooting of the rabbis, but would have had no consequences for the rest of the Jews.—During the days when the press gangs were most active, "the Thirteen" took 30 zlotys for permission to spend the night at their office.—The last few days (before the 10th of May) robberies have taken place in the Jewish quarter, as well as on the Other Side, but not on so dreadful a scale here as there. On Smocza, Gesia, Zamenhofa Streets, store windows were broken and produce removed. Of the more than seven thousand men sent to the work camps as of May 6th, one thousand were returned, too sick and weak to work. Death lies in every street. The children are no longer afraid of death. In one courtyard, the children played a game tickling a corpse. In Rawamazowiecka, it is said, there are 4,500 persons who have fled from Warsaw; in Mordi [and] Lublin, the large-scale emigration from Warsaw has contributed to a rise in the cost of living.—Some Jews have continued to work with

Christians. In Zarnow and Opoczno the peasants brought produce. If they hadn't helped, there'd be no Jews left there. The same true of Kalisz. Homeless folk from Mlawa have said that they would have died if the peasants had not helped them. Some of the rich in Warsaw lock their doors when they sit down to eat. Still others hide pastries in a table drawer, which they unlock when they sit down to eat—so that outsiders won't see the delicacy.

"Organist" is the name popularly given to a man who is heavily bribed; "musical" is the name for the man who takes a bribe from time to time.—Lajf[uner] and Wigder are writing memoirs. A number of important manuscripts have remained in Shur's possession: two volumes of *Das Kapital,* Kant's *Prolegomena* and *Critique of Pure Reason.* Goebbels' [?] secretary was in the work camp at Falenti, was enthusiastic at the Jews' work, became convinced that if you treat Jewish workers right, they can do good work.—The demoralization of the Jews of Warsaw is frightful. It has reached the point where, when two Jews meet, one says to the other: "One of us must be serving the Gestapo!" Recently, there was an instance of one woman giving another her jacket to hold. The latter had a suspicion that there was something valuable or contraband sewed in the lining. The next day there was a visit from the Gestapo. Still another instance: Someone from the Gestapo came and asked to see a table where something was supposed to be hidden. Of course, only the people of the house could have known about it. These are facts. The Others take every opportunity to declare that they owe all their information about the Jews to the Jews themselves.—The prices are rising like yeast. It's all tied up with the political situation. The posters about black-outs, and, perhaps, the military transports arriving in Warsaw have contributed to the rise of the price on potatoes to 5 zlotys on May 11th.—The Russian news agency Tass's denial of a break in German-Russian relations has influenced the fall of the price of potatoes to 3.50 zlotys. Prices can vary between the morning and the afternoon of the same day. In Otwock 100 Jewish Council officials were taken away to work camps because the Council didn't meet its quota of forced workers.—"Every people has the police it deserves," Szerynski, the chief of Jewish police is supposed to have said. —The roads are said to be full of Jews wandering on foot from place to place. Passover time They examined the packages of matzoth for propaganda. One hundred Jews were threatened with execution.—Mr. Mendel has discovered three places in the Ghetto where passes are manufactured.—The Jewish police uses the principle of collective responsibility, imitating the Germans. They close the gates of courtyards because all the tenants have not paid the police tax—30 groschen per capita. They take members of the House Committee as hostages if one of the tenants in a particular courtyard doesn't present himself for forced labor service at a camp.—People are said to have already seen the name of the director selected for a sugar refinery in the Ukraine where Jews are to be forced to work. Other people say that Ukrainian money was being printed (as of the 1st of April). Saw the Lodz Ghetto newspaper in Yiddish, containing a notice from the Jewish Special Court stating that persons accepting bribes would be sentenced to five months at hard labor, and persons breaking up attics for fuel would be subject to arrest.—Ludwig Berenson's opinion [of the lack of moral standards]: a deep man Berenson. He mentions a scene: A woman tears a bagel away from a woman bagel peddler. The latter beats her, tears the thief's hair. It doesn't bother her, she doesn't feel the blows, she is too intent on quieting her hunger.—The seventeen corpses brought to Warsaw from work camp on May 7th make a dreadful impression: earless, arms and other limbs twisted, the tortures inflicted by the Ukrainian camp guards clearly discernible. A medical commission of Theirs established exhaustion as the cause of death.—Rembertow, a Jewish Council that looks after its poor. The mortality lower than before the war. Of the 1,500 inhabitants of R., 300 are refugees from Lodz, Kaluszyn. Those who refuse to pay the community tax have their coats, produce, and the like taken from them. There's a free kitchen that dispenses 600 bowls of soup daily. There was one typhus case, so They published a decree stating than any Jew who tried to leave the Ghetto for the Aryan side faced the death penalty.—On the 9th of May prices began to rise again, because of the political news:* Stalin Premier bread went up to 12 zlotys, potatoes to 3.40 zlotys a kilo. Rubinstein's popularity is growing. A revue is being presented at Melody Palace, called "All Are Equal."†—The mortality is so high that the House Committees now have to worry as much about the dead as about the living. They have to find 15 zlotys for burial expenses for each corpse. Death in the street is becoming a mass phenomenon. In the courtyard at Leszno Street there lies a gallery of sick persons who haven't the strength to get up and beg. There were twenty-five typhus cases at 65 Pawia Street, of whom fifteen died. The "operators" are keenly interested in what Jews think of world events. They report to the Others about this. They inform at length in writing on individuals and institutions, among others on the Citizens' Committee founded by Berenson. They write the Others that everyone is stealing and committing crimes. Meanwhile, they're the chief source of evil themselves.— Heard this story: A confidence man took a large sum of money from an actor's family and kept milking them for a long time afterward on the pretext that he had news of the actor, and so forth. All this after the man was dead. The same confidence man is still fooling the actors' wife.—Heard this story about

* On May 6, Stalin replaced Molotov as chairman of the Council of People's Commissars.
† This was the Jewish Council slogan that Rubinstein was always mocking.

the Kohn–Heller firm. They got a permit from the monopoly for retailing fish in the Ghetto. Instead of charging 1.50 zlotys per kilo (the wholesaler charges them 1 zloty), they pay the monopoly 2–3 zlotys on condition that the latter permit them to sell the fish at 6–7. They rationalize the high price on the ground that three-fourths of the fish is spoiled.—The battle against black-market speculation supposedly waged by "the Thirteen" takes the form of demanding a rake-off from each shop. Besides, individuals from "the Thirteen" accept bribes, as well as bread and produce, at every step.

May 18

My dear:

On the 16th of May the news spread like lightning that the loud-speaker had broadcast at half past eleven that Goering* had been shot and had died of his wounds. Half the city is supposed to have heard the broadcast. But it was impossible to find a single person who had heard it with his own ears. There were reports of such people, but they all turned out to be false. Some people had heard the same news the day before, at greater length. There had been a sharp debate and deep differences of opinion at the Nazi Party convention, and after it was over Goering had attempted to escape and had been wounded. On this meager foundation, the Ghetto built complete castles in the air—about an armistice, peace being declared. People drank toasts to the new days coming, and, for a short time, breathed freely. There were even some people who wanted to cross over to the Other Side, for who was there to stop them? In their imagination they could see the Wall torn down, the Others walking with downcast heads. The rumor was said to have sprung from the news of the death of Pastor Gerling, or Gerlich. That afternoon and the

* Field Marshal Hermann Goering, German Minister of the Interior.

next day came the bitter, sober aftermath. The press did not confirm the news. This mass psychosis, during which a few people actually heard the Others' soldiers talking about Goering's death in the post office, reminds us of the Sabbataian psychosis of the seventeenth century, when Jews who believed that Sabbatai Zevi was really the Messiah sold all their possessions and prepared to journey to Palestine. They knew nothing of the Goering story on the Other Side. They learned about it from the Jews the next day.—"The Thirteen" has set up a relief society headed by Dr. Sirota (the son of cantor Sirota) which distributes bread and coffee daily. There's a long queue on Leszno Street; some of the people in line get pieces of bread. Today, the 18th, they distributed 110 loaves of bread requisitioned from bakers. A small expenditure and great publicity! It is said that "the Thirteen" is getting the concession for bringing potatoes and greens into the Ghetto. Kohn is getting the concession for a horse-driven streetcar.—During the Goering story, the value of hard dollars went up to 200 zlotys. The whole affair is said to have been fabricated by the bourse through a former journalist, a man called P., who makes a living out of such things. The next day the dollar fell to 150.—The cost of living keeps rising. Bread costs 14.50 zlotys per kilo again.—In Meissner's memorandum on the Gestapo, he demonstrates that the camp guard is constituted according to Rosenberg's* instructions. But it turned out that several dozen of the camp guards were listed in the German and Polish police criminal files. The memorandum notes that in some of the camps there was no food for the campers at all between the 4th and the 9th of May. In general, firms need permits for produce. There is simply a dearth of produce.—The dead campers are brought

* Alfred Rosenberg, propagandist of the Nazi regime, head of the Institute of Studies on Jewish Questions established at Frankfurt in March, 1941, and of a Special Staff (Einsatzstab) set up in January, 1940, for ideological activity.

back to Warsaw by Pinkiert, the undertaker. There is a constant flow of new victims, although the situation has improved in some of the camps.—In Lodz there are 20,000 registered lung patients.—True, Lodz being a factory city, there was a great deal of tuberculosis before the war, too, but the figure of 50 per cent of the population is terrifying. The mortality is even greater in Warsaw.—In connection with the visit of Rumkowski,* it is worth noting that three-quarters of a year ago, when a German commission visited Lodz, he represented the Lodz Ghetto as a paradise. This was said to have influenced the establishment of ghettos in other cities of the Government General of Poland. That is to say, Rumkowski proved that the Ghetto experiment was a success.— Jews have been deported from Mlawa twice already. Nevertheless, they are returning there again, because conditions in Mlawa are far better than in Warsaw.—A few workers were seized trying to cross the Reich frontier; when They found out that the prisoners were looking for work, They permitted them to go through.—The generosity of the rich, never too great, has recently grown even less. The reason: their fear lest the cost of living rise and their money hoards not last for the long run—or even for the short run.—It has been calculated that while a Jew daily receives produce to the value of 13 groschen at nominal prices, an Aryan receives produce to the value of 37 groschen.—The special operation to force donations through sanctions is called by the rich "the scoundrel operation." The best proof that the operation was correct.

May 20

My dear:

In the middle of May, hunger and mortality resulting from it were most important. Recently, people have been

* To engage doctors for the Lodz Ghetto.

dying at the rate of 150 a day (as of the 15th of May, there were 1,700 deaths) and the mortality keeps growing. The dead are buried at night between 1 and 5 A.M., without shrouds—in white paper, which is later removed—and in mass graves. At first they used to be buried close together in separate graves; now they are all buried in one. There's a shortage of burial ground now, because the corpses can't be buried too deep. You reach the water line, and there isn't enough earth to pile over the grave. Consequently, the German and Polish health authorities are considering a crematorium for the Jews.—Various groups of excursionists—military men, private visitors—keep visiting the graveyard. Most of them show no sympathy at all for the Jews. On the contrary, some of them maintain that the mortality among the Jews is too low. Others take all kinds of photographs. The shed where dozens of corpses lie during the day awaiting burial at night is particularly popular. Today I visited the shed. It is a macabre scene. Under black paper covers lie heaps of corpses, thrown together, clothes awry—it's like nothing more or less than a slaughterhouse. The corpses are mere skeletons, with a thin covering of skin over their bones.—Recently there's been an increase in the cases of suicide. For example, two refugees committed suicide at 28 Panska Street by taking strychnine.—Two or three members of the same family are being buried at the same time these days. With bread costing 15 zlotys a kilo, half to three-quarters of Warsaw must eventually starve to death.—The cost of living has recently stabilized at 15 zlotys a kilo for bread, 4 zlotys for potatoes, 18 zlotys for groats, and the like. The refugees are the first to die. The first third of May, of the 15,000 in the refugee centers, 147 died, i.e., as many as would normally have died in all of Warsaw during a similar period. In the work camp at Dobrowice, near Skierniewice, the camp guard was abolished and a Jewish Law and Order Service established instead. As a result, production rose 50 per cent. The German firm consequently raised the rations. Twenty-five per cent of the campers returned. Some of them were sick (with gangrene of the arms and legs from being beaten and working in water).—For more than two weeks, packages for campers who were seized for work have been lying on the Umschlagplatz (the neutral ground on Stawki Street between the Aryan and the Jewish part of Warsaw). The Transfer Station has refused to grant permission for the packages to be sent to the campers. In the meantime, there have been further seizures of men for work service from the 12th through the 15th of May. There was an order for 2,000 Jews outside of the normal quota to be sent to Krasne.—The whole length of Gesia Street has become a gigantic bazaar. Everything from the Jewish part of Warsaw is sold in that street. You can find linens, shirts, handkerchiefs, underwear, suits, shoes—principally linens. There are at least a thousand people standing around trading in it. Christians smuggle themselves past the Wall to get to the Gesia Street bazaar. There never was so great a market in Warsaw, not even in Karcelak Street.—The Jewish Gestapo agents have written up the Jewish theater, revues, how the Jews felt about the Iraq affair* for the Gestapo's information.—On the gates hang announcements that the military authorities are looking for people to work in the Lublin and Cracow areas for 4.20 zlotys a day.—A few days ago the watch at the corner of Leszno and Zelazna Streets had an impulse to order Jews to run to the street corner. The motive: They can't bear the sight of Jews.—The moral ruination of the Jewish Council is attested by this incident: The Council's work department allocated funds for the purchase of seventeen loaves of bread for returnees from work camps—so the Council officials took

* On May 12, German aircraft appeared in Iraq. Iraq's proximity to Palestine made the German presence in that country a matter of particular concern.

ten of the loaves from the campers, who were barely alive, and gave them only seven.—This incident caused as much consternation in the Ghetto as had the Yugoslav affair,* when people drank toasts to Allied victory. Considering the situation just described, the hunger and the work camps, one can understand why the Hess affair† has revived Jewish optimism, the belief—really a desperate hope—that peace is imminent, for it alone can save us all from death through hunger. Little by little, the populace has embellished the Hess flight to England. For example, there's a story about three generals, Milch, Moltke, and Hoffmann, who fled with Hess. The story runs that the flight is associated with a division of opinion among the Nazis revealed at the last Party conference. There is talk that Goering was killed, that Hess's flight was aimed at Russia, that he was trying to persuade the English that England and Germany should oppose Russia together. The populace has crowned the Hess affair the *Ness* [miracle] affair. They see it as a way out of their hopeless situation. People make puns: A *Ness* begins with Hess. In the morning Hess was a *Mess* [dead man]. (The first communiqué stated that he had flown to an unknown destination, and there was no news of his whereabouts); in the afternoon Hess was a *Ness;* in the evening Hess had performed a *Ness* and turned himself into a *Mess*. It was a *Hessliche* [ugly] affair. And the like.—The main currency-exchange dealer is Blond Solomon (from Pawia Street). All day he sits at his desk poring over the Talmud. Every once in a while, a Jewess enters with a greenback. He interrupts his study to exchange it for hard and soft currency. Incidentally, the dollar has risen significantly as a result of the Hess affair. The hard dollar has gone up from 128 to 170 zlotys. The soft has gone from 50 to 70.—. . . A few days

* On April 6, Germany had invaded Yugoslavia, overturning the revolution of March 27.

† The night of May 10, Rudolph Hess flew to Scotland; he said he had come on a private peace mission.

ago, about the 10th of May, news came of the evacuation of Jews from Siedlce by the military authorities. For the time being, 6,000 persons. Hess approached the microphone and said just two words: "Da Hess." ["Hess speaking."] Most of the corpses are anonymous, especially those found in the street, without identifying documents of any sort. It's rare for somebody from the family to turn up, and when he does, it's for the corpse's shirt.—The undertaker carts roam the streets all day, some drawn by horses, others by hand.

16/JUNE, 1941

Beginning of June

At the end of May a conference of sixty—merchants, journalists, doctors, engineers—was called under the auspices of "the Thirteen." . . . Some attended out of fear; others out of curiosity. Gancwajch, the head of "the Thirteen," speaks fairly well and won over some people who knew nothing of his scoundrelly deeds. They think he can really accomplish things, particularly after he asserts that he can help with the food supply. The only thing is he needs a citizens' committee to show he has some popular backing. He set up a food-supply commission, a children's-aid commission, headed by Dr. Korcszak, a cultural commission, and so forth. Lately he has achieved some cheap victories by arresting a couple of thieving Poles and ethnic Germans. . . .

[Another specimen of original cryptic notes which were never elaborated.]

Cultural activity in the Ghetto.—How it began.—The fear and terror of meetings.—The dangers associated with them.

—Until we were informed on, we talked about [conditions in] the Ghetto.—The false concept of a closed Ghetto.—Only two ghettos closed.—Lublin, Czestochowa open. The answer to the appeal in behalf of the orphan's home. . . . False reports. —Characteristic of *Gaz.*[etta] *Zhid.*[owska], the Jewish newspaper, that it serves all gods: Czerniakow, Gancwajch (endless announcements. . . .).—The Jewish newspaper prints boring lectures about the Hebrew language, calendar, communiqués from the front, articles on Hebrew literature. Compulsory Judaization.—Some [of the Jewish Council people] are delighted because of the "autonomy" of the Ghetto.— Dr. Feldschuh at the youth division of the Service. "Blockheads of all parties, unite!" Chairman of the Council refused to allocate 15,000 zlotys for antidysentery injections.—Cost of living somewhat stabilized.—Good lunches for the workers in the [large] shops, worth 3.80 zlotys.—A military auto distributed bread.—The prostitute serves everyone. Gancwajch's father died, G.'s sycophants buried him with funeral orations. Saw G.'s supporters and friends at the funeral.—The intelligentsia, assimilated Jews, attending Jewish concerts for the first time.—Goldfaden evening in honor of the Yiddish dramatist.—*Itzik-Shpitzik*—marionette show performed for children in Yiddish. Rubinstein's blackmail of the Jewish Council: He will shout, "Down with H[itler]!" if the Council doesn't give him special favors.—R. pretends to be a state official. He acts batty. "The following," says R., "will survive the war: the Council, 'the Thirteen,' and He."—To feed every house, every apartment, would require 100,000 free lunches.

"Rather sell your last vest than lie in a wooden chest [coffin]." "There is free money inside wood sabots, but they cost 9 zlotys—and that's a lot"—two of Rubinstein's sayings. After the priest of Kampinos delivered his sermon in behalf of the Jewish campers, everything changed: the camp guard, the farm

[?], the leaders. They set aside 50 zlotys each for the sick.—
The worst camp—Vilna.

The Aryan wife on the House Committee at 32 Swientojerska Street did not want to divorce her Jewish husband.
His first wife was one of the Others; his second wears a pious
Jewess's wig.—Packages get lost in the Ghetto—the man who
receives them is afraid to share.—"All equal," the Jewish
Council slogan, is the misfortune of the Ghetto. Instruction
in schools in Yiddish or Hebrew, not in Polish.

My dear:

Most of the work campers from the Warsaw district
have melted away. Of 7,000, 2,000 have remained in work
camp. Some of the camps have been dissolved, because there
was no food supply for them. Some of the campers escaped
and found work with the peasants, who used to visit the
camps frequently looking for persons considered unfit for
camp work. The peasants would feed the "unfit workers"
for a few days, and then employ them at field labor. In a number of villages the peasants displayed considerable humanity to the campers, to whom they threw loaves of bread and
other food.—The Toporol society did a lot this year. They
planted flowers and vegetables in 200 courtyards. Wherever
you go you see Toporol signs—indicating a planted area—e.g.,
"Do Not Walk on the Grass." But they weren't successful
everywhere. In some places there was so much traffic that
the seeded plots were trampled over, e.g., the Plaza of the
Three Walls. Seven hundred young people took courses spon-
sored by the Toporol at 2 Elektoralna Street.—Where the
Hospital of the Holy Spirit used to stand before it was burned
down, there is now a broad field sown with various vegetables. It was a hard job getting these clumps of grass set
aside for seeding. Now the places where the war ruins used

to be are blooming. They're even breeding hens in incubators. A row of plots where the prison used to stand has been seeded on Gesia Street. Twenty agronomists are employed. House gardens, balconies, have been seeded. But we've still a long ways to go before the Ghetto turns green.—Many courtyards have been converted into gardens. Some of the courtyard gardens have been rented out as children's playgrounds. Naturally, the children of the rich can enjoy them, because the charge is from 30–40 to 70 zlotys a month. The poor children never see a patch of grass. Traffic in fresh air!

[Notes taken at one of the conferences that Gancwajch held to present his work.]

G. is special deputy for Leszno Street. We are not to feel ourselves obligated by his talk.—We have come to ask him questions, not to give him anything. We ("the 13") represent no one but ourselves. "Who are you exactly?" "I have been given the concession to administer the houses on Leszno Street." He can offer employment for our department of the district. Has nothing against the Jewish Society for Social Aid.—He dare not criticize the Jewish Council, because it is under the Gestapo!—Has intervened with the authorities often—stopped the beating of Jews, had brutal watchmen removed. "Why doesn't he work with the JSSA?" He wants to be associated with them, but the Council won't talk to him. He came to the Council to offer his services as a humble soldier. He can import raw material, which the Council is afraid to do. He could have had the Ghetto put off. Had a conference with Leist, the Nazi commissar of Warsaw. A half million zlotys could have done it. He is to receive the concession to remove garbage. Wanted to be part of the Council, but autonomous—if the Occupying Power would permit him to join. He wants only to work on Leszno Street.

He doesn't want to distribute the produce himself, the society should distribute it. "He has undesirable people in his organization." "Where do his finances come from?"—For all the money on Nowolipki Street, he wouldn't devour Leszno Street! His income—from administering houses. Has engaged in interventions, has led delegations from the provinces to ask to have the resettlement deadline postponed. Sent Them memoranda about the work camps. Would introduce forced labor [inside the Ghetto], employ people in factories here. Shows that there's almost no raw material for tanneries. Would begin a Jewish newspaper, a daily. "What does he intend to do on Leszno Street?" He doesn't want to set up a state of his own, only to add to what already exists. Would form a special commission for Leszno. He'll support the commission. "What about his 'Office to Combat Speculation'?" They check on bakeries. A loaf of bread should weigh 82 dekos. Aims to requisition sugar and flour. Not to ship it over to the Other Side, but to keep it in the Ghetto. "What about the raids on apartments?" For 30,000 zlotys a month (18,000 from the house administration), he'll see to it that there are fewer "interventions." Wants to form a circle of the friends of Leszno Street. Will take over the factories in the Ghetto.

My dear:

The Special Ambulance Service of "the Thirteen"—the Rapid Aid—wear a red Star of David and blue-striped caps.— The poor are terribly lousy. They don't have half a cake of soap among them, live in fearful conditions, crowded, filthy. The nurses of the TOZ—Society for the Protection of the Health of the Jews—found complete nests of lice under the bandages of the poor. Heller and Kohn are exempt from wearing arm bands. Three people in the Jewish Council have this privilege.—The beggars really get to work after nine o'clock at night. They're afraid of no one, and walk in the middle of the street yelling for a piece of bread.—The coal department of the Council perpetrates this swindle: Their representatives approach institutions with the proposition that they'll furnish the institutions with coal on condition that they keep three-fourths of the coal themselves.—Services were held in the Tlomackie Place synagogue for the first time on Shevuot, the Feast of Weeks. Czerniakow came to the synagogue with his adjutants Zabludowski and Lichtenbojm. An honor watch of Jewish police standing in front of the synagogue defiled before him.—On the Feast of Weeks, Gancwajch's son was bar mitzvahed at the Azazel Theater.* The boy was nominated a petty officer at this occasion.—A wooden bridge was put up across Przebieg Street, because there is a Christian old-age home at the end of the street, and They wished to isolate that house from the Ghetto. The bridge affords a view of the Vistula River and Zholibozh. Jews stand there in crowds all day looking at the Other Free World. The black-out tests have posed a hard problem for the poor, who haven't the money to buy black-out paper. Its cost has gone up dreadfully.—"When will the war end?" a German was asked in a shop. "When we eat once a day, you Jews once a week."—Until the 1st of January [1941], all those Others who were younger than thirty-five believed in Germany's victory; until the 1st of May (before the Hess affair), those who were under thirty; after the Hess affair, those who were under twenty.—Ashkenazy's wife died some time ago; she was living in the Aryan part of Warsaw, because she was a baptized Jew. She was buried under a false name, because, as a convert, her body would have had to be transferred to the Ghetto for burial.—Jewish children are now learning about Warsaw from pictures—the walls prevent them from seeing the original.—They're showing propaganda films

* Ironically, Azazel is by some regarded as the devil in the Bible whom the sacrificial scapegoat was sent to.

against Jews in movie houses again, under the title, "Jews, Lice, Typhus." They exhibit whole reels filmed in the Ghetto describing the lousy condition of the Jews. There are films taken in the work camps designed to prove that Jews are lazy. Their production in the camps is 10 per cent that of the Poles, but after six weeks their production rises to 60 per cent. But you can see in the pictures that the Jews are exhausted and are working barefoot, while the Poles are wearing boots.—It is forbidden to write letters abroad, only post cards. This does not apply to Aryans.—The migration from Warsaw is continuing. People are leaving by car and wagon. Some of them travel to the Reich, to Ciechanow, for example, where they can live well and even save some of the 3 marks a day they earn. They get papers in the Ghetto certifying that they are exempt from work-camp service, and then return to their new homes in the Reich.—Typhus is spreading very fast—280 houses have been closed because of it. This produces great difficulties. A number of bureaus were the first places to be closed, and when they moved to new buildings typhus broke out there, too. The baker Gefen fed the typhus patient in his home well, to get him cured as soon as possible.—An illustration of the Jewish Council's corruption: Even beggars have to pay. They have to bribe the Council in order to get relief.—To fix a hall at 12 Elektoralna Street for the Toporol Society, the economic section of the Council calculated the fee would be 6,000 zlotys. Actually, it would cost less than 200.—The free oatmeal lunches (that the Council announced in posters) have somewhat altered the popular mood for the better. All the refugees in the refugee centers are to receive one meal a day, the children twice a day. The workers in the shops are also to receive lunches, as are employees of the Jewish Council and Jewish community institutions. The reason for this sudden generosity is the colossal mortality, and, even more, the disreputable look of the Jewish streets. It is the beggars and the corpses who have won us this small concession. Besides, typhus has done its part.

June 10

"*Canailles* [scum] of all groups and levels, unite"—under the wing of "the Thirteen"! They are forming a religious section, headed by those well-known thieves, Rabbis Blumenfeld and Glicensztajn (incidentally, never a rabbi). It collaborates with the post-office censor.—Something odd has happened to the means-of-subsistence ration cards. You get supplies for ten coupons when there are fifteen of them. The reason: 10 per cent goes off for relief. Until the 1st of May, the magistracy recognized 400,000 bread ration cards. It refused to recognize some additional tens of thousands as properly registered (an average of 460,000). After a long time and great effort, the authorities recognized the cards of 16,000 persons who had been resettled—although they had resettled 50,000 persons themselves. As a result, 420,000 bread cards have to be distributed among 460,000 persons, and many people have none.—Kohn and Heller import vegetables into the Ghetto. They're doing wonderful business. Rhubarb costs almost twice as much in the Ghetto as it does on the Other Side.— Some people call "the Thirteen" crew "Zubatov men."[*] They conceal their ugly work behind a veil of decency, reminiscent of [the pander] Yankel Shapshovich in Sholem Asch's *God of Vengeance,* who builds a synagogue to cover up his ugly profession. This explains their zeal for cultural activity. When that didn't succeed (the populace wouldn't come to their affairs), they undertook a noisy program of charity (Special Service). Some honest people moved in their circle for longer

[*] After the Czarist police chief who offered Russian workers material advantages to wean them away from revolutionary activity.

or shorter periods. . . . There is such fear of "the Thirteen" that some honest people haven't the courage to refuse their invitations. Here is a characteristic incident to illustrate the extent of this terror: Gancwajch invited a Mr. S. P. to collaborate in the Special Service. The latter, having no alternative, took to bed, though he was perfectly well, called a doctor to visit him at home, and got an affidavit from the doctor certifying that Mr. S. P. was suffering from a heart condition and could not take part in any community activity.

Unfortunately, there are many people who allow themselves to fall under the spell of Gancwajch's sweet talk—his energetic demonstration of the great services he is capable of performing for the Jews, the evil decrees he has already averted, and the things he could do if he had the support of Jewish society. The persuasiveness of his speeches (he is a polished speaker in both Yiddish and Hebrew) quickly evaporates, however. People sober up; he leaves a bitter aftertaste in the mouth.—Recently, "the Thirteen" formed a youth section of the Special Service, headed by the . . . scoundrel Katz.—There are three currencies in the Ghetto: hard, soft, and Gancwajch.—I was informed that the overseer of the Kutno Ghetto had all the Jews stripped naked and collected a million and a half marks—a quarter of a million from one Jew.

17/AUGUST, 1941

There is a marked, remarkable indifference to death, which no longer impresses. One walks past corpses with indifference. It is rare for anyone to visit the hospital to inquire after a relative. Nor is there much interest in the dead at the graveyard.

Next to hunger, typhus is the question that is most generally absorbing for the Jewish populace. It has become the burning question of the hour. The graph line of typhus cases keeps climbing. For example, now, the middle of August, there are some six or seven thousand patients in [private] apartments, and about nine hundred in hospitals.

The disproportion between the number of patients at home and those treated in hospitals is to be explained by the fact that the hospitals have, for a thousand reasons, lost their therapeutic character. They have become "places of execution," as Dr. Milajkowski, director of the Ghetto Health Department, expressed it. The patients die from hunger in the hospital, because they get nothing to eat but a little soup and some other minor nourishment. The patients don't die from typhus, really, but because of their weakened condition.

Typhus is particularly dangerous for the so-called "better class of people," who can't resist it and die—while the common people, though more poorly nourished, survive. Some 8 per cent of the patients die. The phenomenon of high mortality among the professional class was also true during the First World War, especially in Russia, Serbia, etc. Actually, the professionals do everything to avoid the lice. Some of them smear oil and naphtha on their bodies, others carry [vials of] foul-smelling sabidilla around with them to drive off the lice. But the lice are omnipresent. They literally fly through the air, and it is almost impossible to avoid them. The so-called "disinfection columns" sent out by the Jewish Council health office actually spread lice. The same is true of the health-department doctors, who are fearfully corrupt. The "disinfection columns" extort money from the rich, whom they exempt from disinfection. The doctors cooperate. The disinfection steam bath organizations sell bath certificates, so that those who need to be disinfected buy the certificates and do not bathe. The sulphur used in the disinfection is so weak that the lice survive, so that the whole antiepidemic operation is, in fact, a swindle, perpetrated chiefly by the doctors and the "sanitation columns."—Inoculation against typhus is very expensive and [consequently] available only to a few. An injection costs 400–500 zlotys for two people. However, the rumor is spreading that Professor Hirszfeld has been placed at the head of the antiepidemic campaign.—Every house is supposed to have its own shower and disinfector. The House Committees are supposed to see to it. Equally ineffective is the quarantine, after which one comes back even lousier than before. The disinfectors have an effectiveness of 60 per cent; 40 per cent of those treated remain lousy. In all, 300 of the 1,400 houses in the Ghetto have suffered from typhus, i.e., some 150,000 people have had to take disinfection steam baths. But they've stopped closing the gates [to prevent epidemic], because it would have been necessary to keep all the houses closed, and the baths are in no position to bathe so many persons. It would be necessary to bathe 8,000 people a day, and only 2,000 can be handled. The figure 8,000 applies when there are about forty typhus cases a day. But, as the number of cases has gone up to seventy or eighty, it would seem that some 16,000 persons ought to be bathed daily. Typhus has latterly been spreading very fast among the personnel of the community organizations, particularly among the staff of the refugee centers, the community center workers, the help in the public kitchens, etc.—Recently, houses where there are cases of typhus are closed for one day, to allow all those whose apartments are dirty to go to the baths. Those who live in the apartment with a case of typhus have to go to the quarantine. But this happens very rarely, because they all run away, taking their things and the lice with them. In my house [at 18 Leszno Street] there was a typhus case. The residents of the house took all the invalid's identification papers away from him, put him in a ricksha, and bought off a Polish policeman. The patient pretended to be unconscious. He died in the hospital, and the house avoided disinfection. Taking all this into consideration, the prospects for the winter, when the epidemic will truly spread, are perilous indeed. The doctors calculate that every fifth Jew will be sick with typhus in the winter. Consequently, persistent rumors have spread about the possible resettlement [deportation] of the Jews from Warsaw. This is said to be considered as one possible way of removing the peril of typhus.—Doctors who illegally attend thousands of patients at home are doing wonderful business. They limit the number of home visits they make each day.—The problem of [disposing of] corpses is a pressing one in the houses of the poor. Not having the money to bury their dead, the poor often throw the corpses in the street. Some houses shut their gates and refuse to permit tenants [with a corpse at home] to leave until they have had the body buried. On the other hand, the police district chiefs, not wanting to bother with the formalities connected with [disposing of] corpses, simply throw the bodies from one streetcar to the next. The bodies are buried in mass graves at the graveyard, where there are tremendously high sand mounds in the old section. On hot summer days, the stench from these mass graves is so strong you have to hold your nose when you pass. It seems the graves were dug too shallow, and that is what is responsible for the smell.—The undertakers, particularly the brothers Pinkiert, are doing exceptionally good business; some of the undertakers have special carts for individual houses, which give them business every day. Corpses are carried. . . .*

August 30—Tragedy in Osowa, near Chelm, where there is a voluntary work camp. There were a few cases of typhus. The S.S. men took over, ordered the Jewish workers (around fifty of them) to line up. Five men dug a trench grave behind the line-up, another five were machine gunned [and fell into the trench], then still another five dug and were machine gunned, etc. Finally only five or six men were left of the whole camp—the Jewish policeman, the cook, the council representative. A terrible warning that if the epidemic doesn't subside. . . . Curiously enough, the typhus cases recovered and came here to the Ghetto from the hospital.

Characteristically, there has been but one case of murder in the Ghetto.

The 11th of July—The letter "V" for Victory, posted by the Germans, is flooding all of Warsaw. You see it everywhere—

* Manuscript breaks off.

in the streetcars, movie houses, on the walls, postmarks, and the like.

The populace keeps making up jokes—for example, the "V" stands for fifth-class state lottery. Everywhere on the Aryan Side, next to the "V" they wrote: *"Deutschland—Verloren, Verspielt, Verrat"* [Germany—Lost, Played Out, Betrayed]. Many of the streetcar conductors are said to have been put in prison for having allowed the "V" to be torn down or scratched out. There has been a series of German communiqués describing victories in Russia recently. However, after the German communiqué of the 12th of July announcing that They were at the gates of Kiev, the populace lost its confidence in the communiqués. The argument is that, since They cannot show any territorial gains, they are trying to impress us with numbers. The populace is confident of the eventual Soviet triumph, as of the triumph of the Allies in general. The Soviet Army's stand is amazing the Jewish populace. Now that the Russians have held out for seven weeks, the belief is growing from day to day that they will eventually liberate us from the German Occupation.—People are betting heavily on how the war will progress. Many people wagered that Kiev would fall by the 5th of July. When that did not happen, they moved the deadline back. There have been detailed reports describing how war-weary the Others are, and how they are beginning to fall apart. For example, in the 13th number of the Social Democrat organ, *The Hammer*, which was available in the Ghetto, too, there were reports of conversations with ethnic Germans who were disillusioned, pessimistic, sure They would lose the war. Heard of an instance where an ethnic German bought a place in his aunt's name— she was a Pole.

As usual at such times, people put their faith in all kinds of visionaries. Osowiecki, it is said, foresaw a very important event happening on the 17th of August. A Jewish soothsayer, a woman who, according to the statement of an acquaintance, foretold the [German] occupation of the neutral countries, is now predicting peace in three months. Incidentally, the general populace says the same thing—except that of late, seeing the Russian war being prolonged, they're beginning to think we'll be spending the winter with Them, and this thought casts terror into their hearts, for where are they to get coal for the winter, and how are they going to get food?—The fate of the refugees is horrifying; they are dying at a fearful rate. In the refugee center on Stawki Street 35 per cent of them died in five months' time.—Heard a heart-warming story descriptive of the attitude of the Christian workers to the Jews. There was a Jew who worked in the Alpha chocolate factory. When the Ghetto was closed, he was left with a wife and three children and no means of livelihood. He began to sell everything he had. His Polish fellow workers wrote him several times, but he didn't answer. One night, a Polish fellow worker came to his apartment and saw what was happening. A few days later, the men from the factory sent the Jewish worker a ricksha, together with 350 zlotys to buy what he needed. Thanks to his Polish friends, the man is now able to earn a living pedaling the ricksha.—Four theaters are active. Mark Arensztajn's production of *Mirele Efros*—in Polish—is worth mentioning. It's being played in the New Chamber Theater, a remodeled church on Nowolipki Street. The performance of this Yiddish play is in Polish because there are a large number of converts and assimilated Jews in the Ghetto. Besides, some of the actors, too, are converts.—"The Thirteen" has finally been dissolved. Some of them will become members of the Jewish police, where that infamous character, police officer Szternfeld, will verify "the boys'" qualifications. There is a well-grounded fear that any honest people still left in the Jewish police will [now be] completely demoralized. What are "the other Thirteen" boys who are now unemployed to do? It is said that some of them have begun openly to work for the Others. What will happen is that there will be a growth in the number of informers and blackmailers, and we won't be able to guard against them because they won't be wearing green caps any more.—It is said that Gancwajch has gone to Lemberg to do *business** there. Others of his gang are said to have gone to Bialystok, to work as informers and the like there. "The Thirteen's" Special Service† is nothing but bluff and swindle. You could get one of their caps if you paid them; but they did nothing constructive.—There are various inspiring stories about the Bolshevik prisoners of war. Their bearing inspires respect. To prove that the Bolshevik army is half-naked and barefoot. They took the prisoners' shoes away from them. The prisoners, however, keep shouting that the "Germantzies" have taken their shoes away. I saw the Polish populace throw them cigarettes. There are stories of their courageous attitude toward their guards. People say that the same party of prisoners of war is taken through the town any number of times, to give the impression of a large number of prisoners.—The story goes that the wounded soldiers in the military hospital at the corner of Leszno and Grodowa Streets stopped giving one another the Hitler salute one fine morning, as though by agreement. It is also related that every day those who have been released from the hospital to go to the front rebel. They are shot in the citadel for insubordination. Some of the patients in the hospital are said to have applauded two Jewish boys whom they watched through their windows clamber over the Wall. When a Polish policeman and two German gendarmes began to beat the children, the wounded soldiers shouted at them: *"Du ausgefressener Schweinehund!"* [You lousy pig!] There's a similar story of how soldiers threw bread over to Jewish children in Krasin-

* Word in English.
† Ostensibly a rapid-aid ambulance service.

ski park. When a gendarme began to beat the children, the soldiers are supposed to have cursed him: *"Du ausgefressener Chazer!"*

The Jews are tireless. They run their own politics, their own strategy. According to them, you would think that Turkey would have entered the war long ago. Every day it seems as though the rumor spreads that Turkey has declared war on Germany—at any rate, it has spread several times, the last time in the middle of August.

Heard that the [German] soldiers are badly demoralized. Near the main railroad station, there's a whole market for all kinds of things bought from soldiers—sheets, conserves, anything that can be carried out of the barracks. From time to time, an auto appears with. . . . Gestapo . . . raid the soldiers. Someone yells: *"Die Schweine kommen!"* [The pigs are coming!]. A mob of soldiers goes running off to disappear inside houses, where they hide out in private apartments. A soldier once ran into an apartment on Chmielna Street of a Jewish woman whose sister, a convert, lived with her Christian husband [in the Ghetto?]. The soldier told her that he stole something from the barracks every day and sold it. He made a living from doing that. He had been told three times to appear before the commission that decides who is to go to the front. But he won't appear. Why fight for the black marketeers to to have more to eat and grow fat on? He's against the war with Russia in general. People who are in contact with the Others say that this is a widespread attitude among the Germans, the war against Russia being very unpopular. The Others know there is no retreat from Russia; hence this attitude.

The director of the public kitchen at 40 Leszno Street, Rachel Auerbach, told me that there's a pot in use there that is now serving the third generation of one family—the first two generations have died out. This happens often in families who get all their food from the public kitchens.—The lunches served at the public kitchens have deteriorated badly. The oats that used to be milled on the Other Side are now milled in the Ghetto. They're more expensive here than on the Other Side, and poorer in quality. Why was the milling transferred to the Ghetto? There are two answers. The official answer: The mills on the Other Side have to work for the Others; they can't work for the Ghetto. And then, some people say, the real answer is that it's a typical swindle perpetrated by the food-supply office of the Jewish Council. Whatever the reason, the fact is that oats are more expensive and poorer in quality.— The loud-speaker continually campaigns against the Jews. Pictures of vicious-looking Jews are distributed in the streets bearing the legend, "Bolshevik Antichrist."

The question of what to do with the beggars remains the order of the day, despite the 120,000 free lunches—despite the Council's efforts and the welfare fund drive of CENTOS [the children's welfare organization]. The number of beggars increases daily. Although the police waged an energetic campaign against the beggars a few months ago, at a directive from the authorities, there are more beggars than ever on the streets nowadays. A large number of them consists of children. I saw a band of four or five children who eke out an existence by playing in the street some child's game they have probably learned in school. Another beggar, who is a former work-camp inmate, carries everywhere with him for exhibition purposes a photograph from happier days, to show how handsome he once looked, he who is now a ragged wreck of a man. This display of photographs has become the latest mode of begging. Apparently it is effective and wins sympathy.

Some of the Jewish beggars have moved over to the Other

Side of Warsaw. This was a widespread phenomenon a month ago. Hundreds of beggars, including women and children, smuggled themselves out of the Ghetto to beg on the Other Side, where they were well received, well fed, and often given food to take back to the Ghetto with them. Although universally recognized as Jews from the Ghetto, perhaps they were given alms for that very reason. This was an interesting symptom of a deep transformation in Polish society. Recently, however, the authorities have been waging a bitter campaign against Jewish beggars on the Other Side. The police arrest them, assemble them all in one place, beat them up, and then shove them back into the Ghetto. The Polish police show no mercy to women and children. As a whole, the Polish police are a disgusting lot. With the recent disappearance of "the Thirteen," the Polish police have taken their place. They block your way in the street until you pay up. They visit the unrationed bakeries and small shops and extort hundreds of zlotys—for purposes of "air defense." The illegal Polish newspapers have printed the names of those policemen who have beaten up women and children caught smuggling or begging [as a warning that they would be punished]. They treat the Jews with an arrogance often surpassing that of the Germans. When they are on guard duty, for example, they are often stricter than the Germans. The ethnic Germans enrolled in the Polish police are the worst of all.

Another plague is the streetcar conductors. The new order prescribing severe penalties for passengers without tickets has produced some melancholy consequences. The conductors are doing a lucrative business. People climb on the trolley from both sides at once—knowing this, the conductors approach passengers who have just climbed aboard and have not had a chance to buy a ticket, and fine them 5 zlotys each for having no ticket. If you haven't the money to pay the fine, or if you say a word of complaint to the conductor, they march you off to the guard. There have been cases of people being sent to Oswiecim for this crime—whence nothing more is heard of them. Others are thrown into the jail for Jews on Gesia Street. There's a German commissar there, a man called Schamme, and he and the conductors split what they make in fines from passengers. If you slip something into his hand you're let out very fast—otherwise you languish there for weeks on end. This jail is where the old army prison used to be.

There have been cases of Germans dropping bread out of their cars for beggars as they ride through the Ghetto, or stopping, calling a beggar boy over, and giving him a loaf. But these are isolated instances of humanity. For the most part, the beggar children stand near the hospital on Ogrodowa Street, near the telephone building on Leszno Street, and wait for someone to have pity and throw them a piece of bread.

A special class of beggars consists of those who beg after nine o'clock at night. You stand at your window, and suddenly see new faces, beggars you haven't seen all day. They walk out right into the middle of the street, begging for bread. Most of them are children. In the surrounding silence of night, the cries of the hungry beggar children are terribly insistent, and, however hard your heart, eventually you have to throw a piece of bread down to them—or else leave the house. These beggars are completely unconcerned about curfews, and you can hear their voices late at night, at eleven and even at twelve. They are afraid of nothing and of no one. There has been no case of the night patrol shooting at these beggars, although they move around the streets after curfew without passes. It's a common thing for beggar children like these to die on the sidewalk at night. I was told about one such horrible scene that took place in front of 24 Muranowska Street where a six-year-old beggar boy lay gasping all night, too weak to roll over to the piece of bread that had been thrown down to him from the balcony.

Lately, whole families have been out begging, sometimes even well-dressed people. Musicians and singers take their children along with them to "work." The father plays an instrument, while his child or children put out their caps for a coin. There's one singer who stands outside with his young wife, who is dressed with real elegance. As he sings his wife collects alms. Near by, stands a cradle with a small child in it— the parents have no one to leave the child with. The child is being trained to be a beggar, literally in the cradle. Generally speaking, family begging has become the mode. Some parents do it because children attract attention, others because they can't leave the children alone at home. Incidentally, the beggars' practice of falling to the ground and lying there has stopped. Those who lay down because they were really too weak to stand have all died out; the simulators have apparently concluded that it's not a very profitable tactic. Some of the beggars have taken to singing in the courtyards. There are a number of songs, particularly popular being one about Bialystok.

They use horse-drawn wagons, pull handcarts, rubber-wheeled carriages, litters, etc. The horse-drawn wagons are loaded with bodies. The coffins of the poor are piled on top of one another. In some of the houses in the poorer section (e.g., in Wolynska Street), whole families die out. There are cases where the body of the last of the family to die lies untended for days until neighbors smell the odor of death. One mother hid her dead child so as to be able to enjoy his ration card as long as possible. There have been cases in some of the houses on Wolynska Street of rats gnawing at corpses that have been allowed to lie untended for several days. Ten houses are empty in 7 Wolynska Street. All the residents have died out. In general, this death of entire families in the course of one or two days is a very common occurrence. There has been an enormous increase in the number of orphans, since the grown-ups die first, particularly the men. [But] there are practically no children under two, simply because there's no milk at all, either for the infants or the nursing mothers. If things continue this way, the "Jewish question" will soon be resolved very quickly in Warsaw.

I heard about a social worker connected with YYGA [Jewish Social Self-Aid Society] who fasts once a week, and contributes his rations to the poor.

A very interesting question is that of the passivity of the Jewish masses, who expire with no more than a slight sigh. Why are they all so quiet? Why does the father die, and the mother, and each of the children, without a single protest? Why haven't we done the things we threatened the world with a year ago—robbery and theft—those things whose threat forced the House Committees to buy up food for the poorer tenants? There are a great many possible answers to these questions. One is that the [German] occupation forces have so terrorized the Jewish populace that people are afraid to raise their heads. The fear that mass reprisals would be the reply to any outbreak from the hungry masses has forced the more sensitive elements into a passivity designed not to provoke any commotion in the Ghetto. Still another reason is that the more active element among the poor has settled down one way or another. Smuggling offers a means of livelihood for thousands of porters, who, beside the portage fee, take another 10 zlotys per load smuggled in to keep quiet. The shops and the orders from the German jobbers give employment to a large number of other factory workers and artisans.

Some enterprising workers have turned to street peddling (bread, for instance, on which they make 25 groschen a kilo). The result is that it is the inert, unenterprising poor people who are dying in silence. Another factor in keeping the populace in check is the Jewish police who have learned how to beat up people, how to "keep order," how to send folk to work camps. Significantly, it is the refugees from the provinces who are dying of hunger, those who feel lost, helpless, in these alien surroundings. Their protest is converted into a beggarly cry of woe, an energetic demand from the passerby for alms, a protest of sorts to their own *landsmannshaften*, a demand for a piece of bread—from a Jewish institution or House Committee. However, the aid given them is not sufficient, especially when whole neighborhoods consist of nothing but poor people. And, after a few cries, they turn quiet, resign themselves to their fate and wait—in fact ask—for Death, the Resolver of all evil, to hurry. I had a talk with one refugee who had been hungry for a long time. All his thoughts were occupied with food. Everywhere he went, he dreamed of nothing but bread. He stopped at every store window where food was on display. But at the same time, he had grown apathetic, nothing mattered to him any more. It was hard for him to bring himself to wash, and he did so only because of his childhood training. Perhaps this physical passiveness, a direct result of hunger, is a factor in the silent, unprotesting wasting away of the Jewish populace.

A few days ago, about the 25th or 26th of August, Engineer Luft was shot to death. His death was very characteristic of a certain kind of Jew. Luft had been an Austrian officer, and had been decorated with the Iron Cross. He was proud of his Jewishness. An argument arose between Luft and a uniformed Ukrainian over a ricksha. The Ukrainian ordered Luft to show his papers. Luft had a pass but categorically refused to show it. The Ukrainian prodded him with his bayonet; Luft still refused. Finally, the Ukrainian took out his revolver and shot Luft dead.

The bakers are making very good money. So are the bakery workers, some of whom are doing quite well—i.e., about 500 zlotys for a five-day work week. The union (which is very active, illegally, of course) sees to it that the unemployed bakery workers work the remaining two days of the week. The union delegates work only late afternoons, going halves with the workers who take their places the rest of the time. I'm told that this system pays off well for the union delegates. But I have not checked this information.

A German refugee beggar survived a bout of typhus out on the open street. One day he suddenly appeared walking the streets wrapped in a blanket. A physician took his temperature and found it to be 39 degrees Centigrade [102.2 Fahrenheit]. But apparently his attack was a minor one. Now he's walking the streets coatless again.

A beggar boy has been singing sweetly in Polish:
"I'm not giving up my ration card,
There are better times a-coming."
His voice is listened to with pleasure, and the audience throws him coins. Rubinstein's phrase about giving up the ration card to death has made a tremendous hit. My son said that he was afraid that [St.] Petersburg was going to give up the ration card [i.e., fall into the hands of the German army].

The children are speedily becoming demoralized. Illustrative of this tendency are the pitched battles between children's gangs, in which prisoners are taken. One gang—

Kutzik's—is notorious for thrashing girls at night on Tlomackie Place. The gangsters don't give a damn for the Jewish police. Following scene: A platoon from the Jewish Council's health department is performing its exercises. A gang ridicules them loudly, yelling: "One, two, three, four, grind the organ!" I saw a dignified gentleman standing in front of the Sholem Aleichem Academy put out his hand for alms.

18/SEPTEMBER, 1941

During the month of September, packages for the Ghetto —received through the mail—have been confiscated on several occasions. The excuse: smuggling. Jews are receiving large numbers of packages from the provinces. In one instance They took away 4,000 packages from abroad (Portugal)— certainly there was no smuggling involved in that.

Heard about this dramatic scene that took place in one of work camps last year. From the Warsaw neighborhood, a few tortured campers, beaten, bloody, were being transported in one of Pinkiert's funeral wagons. They passed, going the opposite way, peasant wagons loaded with injured, exhausted new campers. The new board of candidates looked out the window—they were on the way to the same camp. Seeing what the returnees looked like, they held a conference among themselves, shouted out: "You can kill us, but we won't go!" and began jumping out the windows. The director of the Jewish Council labor office, Ziegler, lost his head and began shooting the soldiers who were transporting the corpses.

In November army clothing returned to the shops. Rejected because the buttons were missewn—deliberately out of line, and the like.

At the gate of the Ghetto, a sign in four languages.

Ziegler, an Austrian first lieutenant, worked in the Council's labor office, was killed last year in Oswiecim. The reason: He discovered in the Ghetto the violation of five Jewish girls by officers. He was supposedly thanked for his discovery; later, when the opportunity offered itself, arrested and sent to Oswiecim.

Dr. Hagen delivered a lecture to Jewish doctors in the Council hall. Appealed for a stronger fight against typhus. New decrees for this being prepared: severe punishment, up to death, for not reporting cases. For leaving the Ghetto, drastic penalties. He knew of a case in which a Jew from Warsaw infected seven people outside the city. Said that typhus was beginning to decline at the end of 1940, and almost stopped. And that the impressing of new refugees had brought a new epidemic wave. Jews, he declared, must remember that they had been saved from the chief enemy, Bolshevism.

The files of "the Thirteen" were burned by the gang and Gestapo agents just before they were liquidated. So no one will ever know their secrets—unless one of them talks up after the war.

The Kohn and Heller horse trolleys connect the Small Ghetto with the Ghetto proper (run from Leszno Street to Solna Street), cost 60 groschen a ride. They're always crowded, and, inevitably, perfect for spreading epidemics.

Terrible atrocities in the graveyard. The mass graves; the mean way of burying the poor, throwing them into graves like dogs—that isn't enough. Now it turns out that graves are dug up at night, gold teeth extracted, even the shrouds stolen. Recently, a disciplinary hearing held for Jewish policemen caught doing this. In a word—the deepest pit of degradation.

Beginning the second half of July, repeated rumors that Jews are to be expelled from Warsaw. Various versions. One, that only some of the Jews will be expelled—namely, the refugees. Even the numbers involved have been cited, estimates ranging from 150 to 300,000. Another version, on the other hand, has *all* Jews expelled from Warsaw, with no exceptions. The reason—the fearful spread of typhus and other communicable diseases. The rumors so widespread that Czerniakow found it possible to ask the Gestapo. They denied it categorically. Some people insist that the Jewish Council will handle the operation, so as to make something out of it for themselves at the same time, namely, collect ransom from those permitted to remain. Typical of what the populace thinks of the Council—considered capable of perpetrating so evil an act. The best testimony to the Council's reputation.

Heard something at the end of August from Gancwajch that the Germans are readying a project that will call for the resettlement of all the Jews now in the G[overnment] G[eneral], etc., in the East, somewhere in Polesia. One of these days, he says, the project will be all set.

Kohn and Heller are busy importing thieves from the occupied areas.* They pull in thousands of zlotys at it. It's said they're making a fortune from the horse trolleys. Some time ago they got permission to import twenty wagons of potatoes, which they bought [on the Other Side] for 40 groschen and sold at 2 zlotys in the Ghetto. Gancwajch is opening a market fair at 44 Leszno Street. Will be another good piece of business. It's also reported that he is making efforts to move to Lemberg to begin a new career.

There was an advisory meeting a short time ago of the landsman society of people from Kalisz. The report of what

* The German-occupied areas of Poland were Ostland or East Prussia, and the western part of Poland, which was incorporated into Germany.

had happened to the Kalisz refugees was horrible—30 per cent of the refugees had died. For the rest, this is a general phenomenon. The refugees are dying in the refugee centers. . . .— The Pomiechowek affair, in which 800 people were exterminated because they were sick, caused the Jewish populace of the Ghetto to tremble, because it demonstrates what can be expected to happen here if the attempt to arrest the spread of disease inside the Ghetto should fail. There is also talk about a drastic resettlement of Jews from the Ghetto because of the epidemics here. In general, They blame the Jewish populace for spreading typhus in the provinces, claiming that the Jews who flee Warsaw carry typhus with them everywhere they go.

Mid-September

The English communiqués have recently been full of descriptions of sabotage in various countries occupied by the German army. There is no large [munitions] industry in the Ghetto, but the Jewish tailors working in the German commissary shops, wishing to do their part for the sab.[otage], have sent off a transport of military uniforms with trousers sewed together, buttons on backwards, pockets upside down, sleeves reversed (the left sleeve where the right should be). The transport was returned from Berlin, and now the Production Department is all agog. There are threats of drastic punishment.

Schools have become a current issue again. There are to be three languages of instruction—Yiddish, Polish, and Hebrew. But there are many difficulties in the way of finding school space, because [available] rooms have been turned into soup kitchens and the like. The converts are to have a separate school of their own. There was a big controversy over this school. Gepner maintained that, for political considerations, the baptized Jews ought to attend the common schools. The only thing is, they should have special religious instruction. But the baptized Jews don't want that. They want schools of their own, and they'll get them, because they get whatever they demand.

The converts get as many free lunches as they ask for. Even those who have means get free lunches, though they have recently done us a big favor, and their Caritas kitchens feed Jews. The baptized Jews also get produce like everyone else. Recently, they have been getting 4 or 6 kilos of sugar per person. They occupy the most important posts in the Jewish Council, the police, and similar institutions. They look after one another. They push their way into every situation, and are very successful. Some of the rabbis and nationalist Jewish elements have begun to put up a fight, have called meetings, but so far without results. Incidentally, heard about a baptized Jew, who, when asked why he had converted during the war, said, "To get a bigger loaf of bread." Even now the rumors are making the rounds that cases of conversion to Christianity are taking place in the Ghetto. How much truth there is in this cannot be ascertained.

At the end of August and during September, there were frequent instances of people being seized to work loading barrels of benzine onto train cars, etc. The seizures took place in the morning, principally on Karmelicka Street. They also enter private apartments to seize workers. The specialists in working with Jews and organizing ghettos have recently been called to newly occupied cities—Lomsza, Bialystok.

At the beginning of September '41, Dr. Morgenstern, the director of the former Hebrew Immigrant Aid Society [HIAS], was arrested. The organization was liquidated, its functions taken over by the Relatives Aid. But Dr. Morgenstern continued to correspond with [the American directors of HIAS] abroad on subjects of emigration and used the HIAS stationery. Mendes of the Gestapo, who had ordered HIAS liquidated, is now threatening to send Morgenstern to a concentration camp, or CC as they call it for short, for his audacity.—A few months back, 100 Jews (or perhaps it was 50) were seized by the watch for carrying false passes. Actually, the passes were legitimate, only they had not been registered. The people carrying them were arrested, sent to Oswiecim, and the familiar telegram came back from there with news of their death. The worse things become—and they really are becoming worse—the greater the hopes people place on the war's ending. . . . But there are differences of opinion about when that date is to be. Some people maintain the war will continue until next spring, others that the end will come as early as October or November of this year.

Heard of a woman who foretold to a great many people what was going to happen to them in the near future. As Mr. Menachem [Kohn] tells it, she predicted the whole course of the war, ending with the prophecy that the war will end in November of this year ('41). The Jews reason that the war must end this year, because the numerical value of the new Hebrew year 5702 is the same as that of the word Sabbath [meaning "rest," or "stop"]. The populace is fearfully weary and can bear the war no longer.

On Sienna Street, where the Jewish aristocracy lives—particularly the baptized Jews—fashion is in full swing again. Smartly dressed women promenade up and down Sienna. Lately they've taken to appearing in long boots, like men. Of course, a pair of boots like that costs at least 450 zlotys.

The brethren Kohn and Heller, who are very active and doing tremendous business, have recently opened a magnificent market of their own at 44 Leszno Street. Guards stand at the market door to keep beggars out. The Kohn and Heller horse-drawn streetcars, connecting streets that have no electric streetcar service, are a huge success. They're packed to overflowing. The populace calls them "Uncle Kohn's Cabin—Lousy Cabin." The common people say, "I'm taking a Kohn-Heller." Now, they have gone into still another business. They import [customers'] relatives from the occupied areas. This is enormously important for many people who have secured official positions and are in danger of arrest—it's literally a matter of life and death to be able to prove one has a family to support. It costs 1,500–2,000 zlotys to have a relative imported from Bialystok. One man paid 50,000 zlotys to have his wife brought into the Ghetto. This was right after the [Russian] occupation of the eastern areas [of Poland].

A joke is making the rounds. Germany has waged a total war in Poland, a *momental* ["momentary"] war in France, a *ratal* ["installment"] war in England, and a fatal war in Russia. H.[itler] is trying to imitate Napoleon. He began the war with Russia on the 22d of July,* the same day Napoleon invaded Russia. But H. is already late, because Napoleon was in Moscow by the 14th or 15th of September. They say that at the beginning of his Russian campaign Napoleon put on a red shirt, to hide the blood if he should be wounded. H. put on a pair of brown drawers.

Characteristic of the amount of smuggling in the Ghetto is the fact that several weeks ago (the early part of August, 1941) bread became dearer on the Other Side than it was in the Ghetto (i.e., so much bread was smuggled into the Ghetto from the Other Side that there was an actual shortage of it there). Most of the smuggling is during the early evening and

* June, actually.

after five o'clock, although there's smuggling at night too, particularly in certain places where the Wall runs through a courtyard, as on 5 and 7 Swientojerska Street. The same is true for Kozla Street. As a matter of fact, most of the smuggling there is via a gate on Nalewki Street, through which a German post wagon drives. The merchandise is immediately loaded onto rickshas and dispatched. Once a wagon drove up from the Frederik Puls [soap factory] with contraband. There are Christian houses on Kozla Street with latticed windows. The Christians have bored holes under the windows, through which they pass large amounts of merchandise to the Jews. When they catch sight of Germans, they shout, "Joe's coming!" and the street empties out. Another smuggling route is via the hole connecting the former post-office building on Leszno Street with the finance-ministry building. The hole is regularly walled up by the Germans. But before the day is over the hole, the immortal hole, is open again. At 12 Rymarska Street, in the building that houses the Melody Palace, goods are smuggled across the adjacent rooftops. The man who makes the first approach to [a guard] and proposes that he go into smuggling is called a "musician" after the locale— Melody Palace. The guards don't take money; mostly they prefer "gifts," particularly gloves, socks, linen, etc. But they're not too proud to take money. However, money is taken as prepayment for a whole job, not for each wagon separately.

Mid-September

The mood in the city is terrible. Again there's the danger that the Ghetto will be cut 40 per cent. They are about to liquidate the Small Ghetto, i.e., the area from Zaluta Street to Chlodna Street. The reason is that 1.5 mil. soldiers are supposedly coming to Warsaw, and there is no place to put them. Other people say that the Small Ghetto is to be closed because it is on the route taken by the German army going west. They don't want to have Jews living on the route. Nor will They accept the Jewish Council's proposal that a bridge be built connecting the Small Ghetto with the Large.—The last few days the question of evacuation of the Small Ghetto has become a pressing one for people living on Sienna and Sliska Streets (the part of Sliska that borders on Sienna Street). This is supposed to be the area of the Small Ghetto that will be the first to be liquidated. At stake is the fate of more than 100,000 souls who would have to pack up next winter and move into the already overcrowded Large Ghetto. In general, the populace recalls that the Jews get a special bonus every year at around the time of the High Holy Days: Two years ago, September, 1939, it was the famous [German] bombardment directed exclusively at the Jewish quarter; a year ago, it was the establishment of the Ghetto, and this year, it's the evacuation of the Small Ghetto. It seems that when winter approaches the scoundrels become restless. The whole German health department is against the plan of liquidating the Small Ghetto, eventually to be recompensed by apportioning Powanzki town [to the Large Ghetto?]. They are against it principally because the terrible pressure of population will lead to a spread of epidemic. The Governor General himself is the initiator of the plan. The popular unrest is dreadful. The populace has lost its head.

Another subject, one which has been absorbing our attention for a long time, is that of the epidemics, particularly typhus. The doctors are fearful that next winter every fifth person—and some maintain that the figure will be as high as every other person—will be sick with typhus. All the disinfection techniques are of no avail. Instead of combatting typhus, the "sanitation columns" spread it, because they blackmail the homes where the rich live, where there really is no need for any disinfection, with the threat of ruining their linen, clothes, and the like. On the other hand, the filthy houses that really require disinfection are let off if the residents pay the columns. So the lice move freely all through the Ghetto. The overwhelming majority of typhus cases (some people maintain that there are about four or five thousand such) are concealed. The German health department speaks in terms of some 14,000 cases. The houses [where the typhus cases are concealed], are not disinfected; the lice carry the typhus from there all over Warsaw. The doctors are making a fortune out of treating people secretly, taking 50 and 100 zlotys for a visit. At the same time they decide in advance how many visits they will pay each day. It is worth mentioning at this point that the "sanitation columns" are so busy blackmailing the rich that they haven't the time to board up properly the windows of houses where typhus is discovered, to make them something like gas chambers; the result is that the lice survive and even increase.—The populace resorts to all kinds of measures to avoid the lice, but if one has to go through Karmelicka Street, which is crowded whichever way one turns, or through the bazaar at 40 Leszno Street, or through Walicow Street, or if one has to take the streetcar, or visit the public kitchen, one is bound to become infected sooner or later. The employees at the community institutions, such as the Joint Distribution Committee, or CENTOS children's aid, and particularly at TOZ medical aid, are particularly subject to infection. These officials have no money to have themselves inoculated (nor have the common people), and the serum is very expensive—one injection costs 400–500, and even as high as 600 zlotys. It is typical that all the serum comes from the hospitals of the Others or is imported from Wajgel's Institute in Lemberg. The cost is high, because in the first place the labor involved in making the serum is difficult (the internal parts of at least 150 lice have to be extracted by hand). In the second place, the serum has to pass through a number of hands, being contraband, and the price increases with each agent. People carry around all kinds of camphor and other noisome chemicals which are supposed to repel lice. Some people smear their bodies with lysol and other disinfectants. The poor people are not permitted to enter the houses of those who are better off, because they are carriers of lice. The disease has a mild course. Some 8 per cent of the patients die, many of them during the period of convalescence when a hearty diet is needed and the patients have no food.

The course of typhus is mild among the poor. On the other hand, for those better off there are often complications.

19/OCTOBER, 1941

The latest victories of the Germans—the encirclement of Moscow, the defeat of Timoshenko's army—have called forth a huge wave of pessimism among the Jews. They ask themselves: "From whence shall our help come?" Everyone is very bitter at England for having stopped its aerial bombardments of Germany during the past two weeks, although it was clearly the function of the English to raise a diversionary offensive against Germany. The average man maintains that England would like to see both Germany and Russia defeated, so that England and America might emerge from the war the real victors. But—the average man reasons—having annihilated Russia, Germany would be in a position to hurl its armies at England with increased vigor—so the English tactics are hard to fathom. I know of one household where every morning the wife makes life miserable for her husband because of England's inactivity. The husband proves beyond the shadow of a doubt that he is not personally responsible for the British policy. But that does not help him in the slightest; his wife continues to belabor him. Although everyone, optimist and pessimist alike, is convinced that Germany will lose in the end, some people are beginning to speculate as to whether

Germany, by taking possession of the industrial centers of Europe, might not gain temporary control of the world. But there are very few people who really go that far, for to allow oneself to believe this would mean to have to draw the necessary conclusion: collective suicide.

What was the motive for liquidating the Small Ghetto? First, the matter of smuggling. They want the Jewish areas to touch Christian areas only in the middle of the street, not through adjacent houses, as for example on the famous Kozla Street, because such direct contact makes smuggling possible. An even stronger motive is to isolate [further] the Jews from the Aryans. The only part of this great danger (the liquidation of the Small Ghetto) that has so far been realized has been the evacuation of Sienna Street. That street was threatened with evacuation last year, too. At that time it was possible to buy off evacuation through the "donation" of the large sum of 4 kilos of gold, worth 200,000 zlotys, to the [German] Winter Aid. * Everybody contributed—both tenants and boarders. But this year it proved impossible to buy the Others off. Neophyte Avenue at Sienna Street, with its row of fine modern houses with central heating, was excluded from the Ghetto. In general, Sienna was the street where the Jewish aristocracy lived. A broad street, with good air, little poverty, few beggars, kept clean—literally, an island [of elegance] in the Ghetto. In the evening you could see well-dressed women, wearing lipstick and rouge, strolling calmly down the street with their dogs, as though there was no war. There was none of the confinement, hullabaloo, or nervousness of the Ghetto here. An isle of repose. A survival of the expansiveness of pre-war life in the middle of the Ghetto. The Others left [the residents of Sienna Street] a very short deadline—the 5th of October—to move into the Ghetto. These 6,000 inhabitants of the other side of Sienna Street had no new houses set aside

* The Nazi party relief organization.

for them to move into. They were permitted to take all their things along with them. Help for those who had to move was organized. The Jewish Council and the Sienna Street [House Committees?] distributed 27,000 zlotys (left over from last year's "donation" to Winter Relief) for the support of the poorest people among those who had to move. Anyone who applied for relief received it. The typhus patients represented a difficult problem. It was a hard job moving them over; there were also a few cases of suicide, because some of those who had to move lost their source of livelihood by leaving.

The danger of liquidation of the entire Small Ghetto has not disappeared however with the evacuation of Sienna Street, and now there is talk of new changes being imminent. The other side of Elektoralna, all streets on the west side of Zelazna, this side of Chlodna, all the streets from Bonifraterska up, Tlomackie—all are to be excluded from the Ghetto, and housing capable of accommodating 8,000 is proposed to take care of 45,000 residents. . . .

The Warsaw Jews viciously exploited the dilemma of those who were forced to move from Sienna Street. They demanded as high as 150 and 200 zlotys for one room. And payment for months in advance. The Quartering Office of the Jewish Council moved a number of families from Sienna Street into certain apartments.

Two beggar children sat in the street holding up a sign that read S.O.S. One is forced to concede that this is the simplest and truest statement of our predicament—and our only slogan. The commerce in ration cards is one of the most melancholy developments in the Ghetto. The officials and shopkeepers are leeches who exploit the predicament of the poor who lack money even for a piece of bread; the former buy up the bread and sugar ration cards of the poor. In general, this trafficking in the ration cards of the dead, of the missing, is a very lucrative business for certain elements in the Ghetto, particularly officials. They are hyenas of the worst sort. Since not all of the poor people are able to get free meal tickets, some of them sell their ration cards for free meal tickets—exactly the way a poor peasant sells the harvest of his future crop.

On the 23d of October [1941] died Samuel Lehmann. Worked to the last moment. Collected a great deal of folklore having to do with the war. The representatives of the real Jewish Warsaw met at his funeral. Characteristic that his funeral coincided with that of one of his heroes, Berel the Pig, who told him many stories. But Berel's funeral was much bigger than Lehmann's. Czerniakow, the president of the Jewish Council, when asked for a free burial plot, didn't know who Lehmann was (poor fellow!). He is lying in the literary men's section of the graveyard, near J. M. Weissenberg.

The Lublin Jewish Council asked for permission to conduct a social affair. The Occupation Powers refused; so the Jewish Council complained that social affairs are permitted in Warsaw. The authorities replied, "Very well, we can grant you permission, on condition that Lublin's Ghetto be closed like the one in Warsaw." Naturally, the permission was respectfully refused. Better an open Ghetto without social affairs than a closed Ghetto with them.

This Rosh Hashana, people were seized for forced labor. Jewish informers took soldiers along with them to the prayer quorums during services, and there—in the prayer rooms—people were able to buy their way out of forced labor service.

Mr. Isaac's 25th wedding anniversary was celebrated with a party where wine and tarts were served. He attributed his development to the *Sturm und Drang* [youthful rebellion] period of his life. From his father, he inherited vigor and health. He reminisced about his youth and told some stories that sounded fantastic—one about how he and some other fellows carried off a peasant woman who slept over her stall in the market place and deposited her in a puddle of water, and how he and the boys had hidden behind some bushes to see what would happen when the peasant women awoke from her bad dream.

Heard from a reliable source that "the Thirteen" were in Germany's espionage service before the war with Russia began. That may be the explanation for the Gestapo's favoring them. There is an evident and terrible slackening of the sentiment of compassion. Walking through the streets, one passes children as emaciated as skeletons, barefoot and naked, who put out frozen-blue hands for alms—in vain. People have grown as hard and unfeeling as stones. A Jew who was on the Other Side told me how complete strangers stopped him in the street and plied him with unanswerable questions: Why did the Jews allow thin, barefoot children to go over to the Other Side and beg? "Aren't you Jews ashamed to permit it?"

. . . The university professors Hirszfeld and Zwajbojm are giving medical courses in the Ghetto, on a university level. The students work in an anatomical laboratory.

Here's a joke that's making the rounds: A woman was having a difficult labor. Nothing anyone did could help her. But the moment her friends left the house, the infant came crawling out of the womb to ask his mother: "Mama, can I come out now, have all the *shleppers** gone?"

A great many cases of conversion. At Hoshana Raba time more than fifty Jews were converted (data from the Council).

* Literally, one who pulls or drags something. Also used in the Ghetto as a term for "strong-arm" squads.

The reason being that the Catholics look after their converts. Hope that the converts would be able to leave the Ghetto—there was even some talk of a converts' Ghetto in Zholiboz. Nevertheless, this is a psychopathological phenomenon. As the saying goes: "You want a job in the Jewish Council? Convert!"

Illegal Polish literature is distributed in the Ghetto a little at a time. The importers are, partly, Polish policemen, street cleaners.—It's said that the P.O.W. [Polish Military Organization] has its members in the Ghetto, who are doing some work, but only among a limited number of people. The Polish tax collectors are of different types. Some of them are hoodlums, do anything they please when they get into a Jew's house. They have the right to make a search of the person and confiscate whatever money they find. They make no distinction between a tenant and a subtenant. Everyone found in the apartment is responsible for the common tax. Objects are removed; people are beaten and injured. There are some houses where the tax collectors simply wreak pogroms. On the other hand, some of the tax collectors are noble patriots and advise the tenants how to avoid payment, so as not to increase Germany's income. On Pawia Street there's a gang of swindlers that get weekly salaries from the exchange brokers that come to 50, 100, and even as high as 200 zlotys a week. The swindlers are partners with the Germans, who go over and demand the money from the people avoiding payment.

Heard from someone returned from Ostrowiec that the Jews there are employed by the Germans in large factories. There are 600 Jews working in the Starachowice munition works, who get meals besides pay. The same for Ostrowiec. The month of October fell under the zodiacal sign of further resettlement. This time it was the turn of the part of Krochmalna Street where the poor people lived (all but a small part of the street). This included the big folk school at 36 Kroch-malna, as well as the last numbered houses on Ogrodowa Street and all of Chlodna Street. The purpose: The borders [between the Christian part of Warsaw and the Ghetto] are to run through the streets, and not a single Jewish house is to have a common border with a Christian one. Some 18,000 persons were encompassed in the resettlement. It took place without any trouble. There were no particular obstacles. The populace sold all their things and moved over into the [Large] Ghetto. The poor people of the Large Ghetto received their brethren from Krochmalna hospitably, so that the Jewish Council and the YYGA, which undertook to provide relief, had little to do. In all, only some 200–300 people went to the social-aid centers for relief. The cost of transporting goods was high. A moving cart cost 80 or 100 zlotys.

A characteristic recent development in the Ghetto is wagons to which human beings are harnessed. The practice is based on a simple calculation: It costs 80 zlotys a day to maintain a horse, only 20 zlotys to maintain a human being. Besides, during the "resettlement," one saw many wagons loaded with furniture that were being drawn by human beings. The thieves wreaked frightful damage during that period. . . .

The Germans entered Baranowice on the fifth day of the war [with Russia], i.e., the 27th of June, 1941. There was no defense of the city. The first few days, when only the military administration was there, things were bearable. But as early as the beginning of July, the situation became very difficult —like everywhere else. At the beginning of August, the army veterinarian asked (the Jewish Council apparently) for thirty-two Jews to convoy horses to Radom. It appears there's a horse hospital there. The thirty-two Jews were each put in charge of a certain number of horses; they were all loaded onto animal wagons and transported to Radom. En route they (i.e., the Jews) were given fairly good food and were subjected to no special indignities.

When they arrived in Radom, they presented the horses in good condition, a fact that the veterinarian lieutenant who had traveled with them explicitly underscored. He accompanied the thirty-two men to the Jewish Council in Radom, and, in recognition of their good work, ordered passes made out to enable them to go wherever they wanted.

The Radom Council generally takes . . . zlotys for preparing a transit permit. But in this case, of course, no money was to be gotten. The thirty-two insisted that the officer's order be honored. Possibly there was a sharp verbal exchange between the Baranowice Jews and the Jewish Council. For the record, it must be noted that the Council president, (Lazar? Wasser?) happened at that time to be in Otwock at his summer villa. What we are about to describe consequently took place with the knowledge and perhaps on the initiative of the vice president (name unknown).

They—the Jewish Council of Radom—got in touch with the Yellow police force, and reported that there were thirty-two out-of-town Jews in Radom for whom the Jewish Council was not responsible. The Others came, arrested all thirty-two, took them to a village behind Radom, ordered them to dig a large grave, and shot them. Only two of the thirty-two managed to escape.

20/NOVEMBER, 1941

Nov. 1–10

During the first third of November, 1941, a decree was published threatening Jews with the death penalty if they left the Ghetto without a pass. This is a little present Governor General Frank left for us after his last visit to Warsaw. The decree had some effect on the pattern of prices, but not much. —On the 3d of November (it is said) two Jews were shot in the street, without a hearing—because they left the Ghetto without a pass. One of them is the well-known movie-house owner, Lehmann (shot at Theater Place); the other Jew was shot at the train station. And now there are eight Jews, six women among them, who have been handed over to the Jewish police for execution. Auerswald, the Ghetto commissar, insists that the Jewish police constitute their own execution squad to carry out the sentence in the Jewish prison on Zamenhofa Street—corner of Gesia Street. The chief of the Jewish police, Szerynski, a convert who goes to church every Sunday and is known to be a grafter of the first water, has agreed to it under threat of being shot himself if he refused. It will be a terrible thing if Jews have to be their own hangmen! Incidentally, some one hundred Jews are in jail for the same crime, a death sentence hanging over their heads.

The typhus epidemic has diminished somewhat—just in the winter, when it generally gets worse. The epidemic rate has fallen some 40 per cent. I heard this from the apothecaries, and the same thing from the doctors and the hospitals. This is really an irrational phenomenon; there's no explaining it rationally. The only possible explanation is that most of the people in the refugee centers, which are the chief centers of epidemic, have already had the disease. Another explanation is that poor people wear heavy clothing in the winter, so the lice can't get at them easily. At any rate, the epidemic has lessened.

Here's an example of how the Warsaw Jews are exploiting those resettled in the Ghetto: A man sublet an apartment. He is paying the electricity bill for himself, his landlord, and a neighbor who has the same electric meter. Jalowecki, the representative of the Polish Self-Aid Society, was amazed at the activity of our House Committees. It takes the Poles several months to deal with an applicant; applications move very fast with us.

A child took lunch in two separate public kitchens. When discovered, the child begged with tears in his eyes to be allowed to have two lunches, because he did not want to die like his little sister.

The bare Jewish graveyard, next to the Evangelical and Catholic ones, which still have their trees, is a symbol of Jewish woe. Living and dead, the Jewish populace suffers evil. —The beginning of November '41, news from Lodz that the Lodz Jews had been prohibited from marrying and having children. Women pregnant up to three months have to have an abortion. In a word—Pharaoh's laws revived by the Prussians.

The House Committee of one of the houses on Mylna

Street decided that no new tenant could move in until he had paid an extra 20 zlotys. The money is a kind of insurance in case of death, so that the H.C. will have no difficulty disposing of the body.

This is supposed to have happened the second half of October. Six Jews came to the director of the Polish-language theater at 52 Nowolipki Street. (He's supposed to be a baptized Jew, name unknown. The star of the theater is the popular Michael Znicz, also a convert.) They identified themselves as official colleagues of the Yellow police force of "the Thirteen" and demanded 1,000 zlotys, or they would have him sent away to prison or work camp. After a greal deal of bargaining, they came to an agreement and decided to go into a bar and have a drink on it.

Soon afterward, an auto carrying policemen in yellow uniforms rode up to the bar. Before they could move, the six blackmailers were in handcuffs. Then the Yellow police had a few drinks with the theater director and drove off with their prisoners. It turned out the director was no fool. Unobserved, he had put in a telephone call, and the Yellow police had come at once.

The way it's told, the six blackmailers were held in the Pawia Street prison for two months and then sent to Oswiecim. "To be killed"—those are the exact words in which the wife of one of them was told of her husband's destination.

Yussele Ehrlich is the commandant of the Jewish prison on Zamenhofa and Gesia Streets. Before the war, he was a confidence man and strong-arm guy, worked at counterfeiting until 1936 (possibly was in the stock market—this has to be investigated). When the Germans took Warsaw and the police began to liquidate the criminal elements, particularly among the Jews, Yussele Ehrlich was arrested and sent to Oswiecim. Apparently, he assumed certain duties of a despicable character, because he was released rather quickly. He then went off to the provinces, where he organized three or four factories (one of them near Warsaw), for counterfeiting money, which he later issued.

Since June (or July) of this year, he has been the commandant of the Jewish prison, where people in the know say that he is the complete opposite of men of this type—actually, really, a man with an explicitly evil character, with despotic tendencies. His underlings tremble in fear of him.

The 28th of October, 1941, a Jewish policeman went through every apartment in both courtyards at 93 Dzielna Street (about 2,000 tenants) and handed out tickets, supposedly for showing light during an air raid. What it was all about he wouldn't say. No remonstrances availed that: (1) there's been no electricity for a week so no one could have put on a light; (2) most of the houses never put on the lights at all; and (3) all the windows are covered with heavy drapes or plastered with black paper, etc. All who refused to stick a couple of gold pieces in his palm (he was willing to take a fiver, too) got tickets for keeping the light on. However, the majority of the tenants gave him no money.

The fine for breaking black-out regulations is 55 zlotys. Nobody made a note of the policeman's number.

The popular collaborators with the Yellow police include: Anders (his family name—address unknown) and Milek (his surname—his family name unknown). Anders was a popular boxer before the war (at the Maccabee Star club), the son of a well-known porter—latterly one of the leaders of the [reactionary] union of porters. Milek lives at 52 Panska Street, is on the House Committee there.

Neither of them wears a badge.

At the end of 1940, they were both sent to Oswiecim, but there they "rehabilitated" themselves and promised to accomplish great things. They operate exclusively in political matters, informing on political agitators alone.

Anders has a brother-in-law called Pfefferman, a Jewish policeman in the second district (32 Krochmalna Street). The agreement in the district is that Pfefferman gets sent to the jobs where the pickings are ripest. There is a band in Pfefferman's cap (i.e., he's an educated man of the second rank). He is said to have been a tremendous failure and awful blockhead before the war. But now he's very well off, because he's been given the most lucrative posts. Wherever he goes, he holds the common funds. The chief of the second police district at 32 Krochmalna Street is a certain . . .eischman from Galicia, a convert. He insists on being addressed as Elder, or Captain. His subordinates describe him as a fearful disciplinarian, holds the reins very tight on all of them. He had four policemen sent to Oswiecim.

Mid-November, 1941. The first frosts have already appeared, and the populace is trembling at the prospect of cold weather. The most fearful sight is that of freezing children. Little children with bare feet, bare knees, and torn clothing, stand dumbly in the street weeping. Tonight, the 14th [of November], I heard a tot of three or four yammering. The child will probably be found frozen to death tomorrow morning, a few hours off. Early October, when the first snows fell, some seventy children were found frozen to death on the steps of ruined houses. Frozen children are becoming a general phenomenon. The police are supposed to open a special institution for street children at 20 Nowolipie Street; meanwhile, children's bodies and crying serve as a persistent background for the Ghetto. People cover the dead bodies of frozen children with the handsome posters designed for Children's Month, bearing the legend, "Our Children, Our Children Must Live—A Child Is the Holiest Thing." That's how people express their protest against the failure of CENTOS to collect these children in a center and save them from certain death in the street. Especially when it is known that CENTOS has collected almost a million zlotys from taxes (postal payments, bread ration cards, etc.). Children's Month is a grand success—posters (every two or three days a new one), a fortune expended in money, well-attended concerts and affairs. But it did not make an impression on the large part of Jewish society. The House Committees were not deeply touched, and they actually gave the ridiculous sum of 50,000 zlotys. The expenditures came to practically that much. Another ostentatious feature of the operation was the disgraceful subservience to the big money givers, to people like the president of the Jewish Council, who was crowned First Citizen of the Jewish Quarter by Dr. Wielikowski at the opening meeting. To crown such an incompetent as Czerniakow first citizen publicly requires vast courage and subservience. The same ceremony was performed at other occasions, all to find favor in the eyes of the Council president.

The YYGA [Jewish Social Self-Aid Society] is another matter. Built up by the House Committees, it has aroused all of Jewish society in Warsaw to relief work and is a thorn in the side of the Council power-holders, who are trying to strangle it. The YYGA, declare the Jewish Councilmen, is the forge of opposition to the Council. The fact is, it is true that the activities of the Council are sharply criticized at meetings of the House Committees, but that is the Council's own fault: its blatantly class character; its tendency to throw the whole tax burden on the shoulders of the poor and to exempt the rich entirely. The YYGA is the only institution where there is freedom of thought in the Ghetto, where an honest criticism of the Council and its machinations prevails.—The winter that is now upon us is hitting the Jewish populace hard. There is a shortage of three items: coal, gas, and electricity. Coal is distributed by the Heating Commission of the Jewish Council, of infamous reputation, and of course it goes only to Councilmen and their people. Converts like Kramszczik are running things. They never even thought to provide each house with at least enough coal to heat one apartment. For the rest, there's the fear of epidemic; they'd rather the poor died of the cold. For several weeks there has been neither gas nor electricity in the apartments, except for certain hours— from ten at night till seven in the morning. The result is that most of the populace, and not the poorest people either, don't have enough hot water for a glass of tea. Consequently, the question of the distribution of available hot water has become a pressing one. The shortage of electricity during the daylight hours has compelled most of the Jewish enterprises to go over to night work. Places like barber shops have had to close down completely. Some confidence men have exploited the electricity shortage by promising for a consideration to be paid the electric company to get enough power for light. This happened, for example, at 24 Leszno Street, only after a day or two the light disappeared again. The money paid in was not returned, of course. The shortage of current produced sundry facile explanations, which turned out to be incorrect. At first, people believed the shortage was aimed exclusively at the Ghetto. But then it turned out that some Aryan districts were affected too. Another explanation was that the shortage was sabotage. Still a third opinion imaginatively [!] attributed it to large-scale thefts of current, amounting to a million kilowatts. But, in the end, it turned out the reason was a simple one: saving.

For a few hours during the 11th of November, Polish flags flew over the freedom memorials. A flag even flew over the memorial at Poniatowski for a few hours, though there is a guard there. The same was true at the memorial to the flyers at the Plaza of the Lublin Union.

Nov. 22

The execution of eight Jews, including six women, has set all Warsaw trembling. We've gone through all kinds of experiences here in Warsaw, and in other cities, as well, particularly in Lithuania, where mass executions are common. But all past experience pales in the face of the fact that eight people were shot to death for crossing the threshold of the Ghetto. This sentence was said to be a pet project of Auerswald—a man the Jews thought at first was a friend of theirs and an honest man. The death sentence was carried out in the Jewish prison at 24 Gesia Street. At first They insisted that the Jewish police execute the sentence, and that the "city fathers" be present. It is told that Szerynski declared to Przhewarski, the Polish police chief, that he would carry out the sentence; but fifteen minutes later he would commit suicide. Another report would have it that Szerynski declared that even if he were threatened with death for failure to carry out the sentence, he would not do it. The fact is that the Polish police were the execution squad. Some people say that there were volunteers. However, all the preparations had to be made by the Jewish police, the Law and Order Service. The Law and Order men led each of the doomed persons from his cell, one at a time, tied him to a post, and afterward bound his eyes. Auerswald was late to the execution. He said: "A shame, too late." A few S.S. officers attended, calmly smoking cigarettes and behaving cynically all throughout the execution. Of the Jews, Szerynski, Lehrmann, and Lejkin were there. The latter was supposed to have distinguished himself with his zeal in dragging the condemned from their cells. The proctor read the sentence, and then the execution took place. The street in front of the prison was black with people. The screaming of relatives was heard. The sentence was executed at half past seven in the morning on Tuesday. Among the six women were a beggar, a mother of three, a sixteen-year-old, fearfully hysterical before the execution. Rabbi Wajnberg was also present, with evidence from one of the sentenced men. It is said that the prisoners bore themselves calmly. At night red posters appeared, signed by Auerswald, notifying the Ghetto that the death sentence had been carried out. It was typical that all eight had been arrested by Polish policemen. One woman lost her life over 100 zlotys. She offered a policeman only 50 zlotys to let her go; he insisted on 150 zlotys. One of the two men was a glazier who supported his family by working on the Other Side. Another 400 Jews have since been arrested, of whom 20 have already been sentenced to death by the court. It is said that the severity of the sentence has caused great agitation among the Germans, too. At any rate, the death penalty for leaving the Ghetto is completely unprecedented. This is the first instance.

But the whole affair—and the death sentence in general—has had very little deterring effect on smuggling, which continues with undiminished vigor. Jewish smugglers continue to scale the Wall, because, as they put it, if they can't smuggle they are sentenced to death anyway. Consequently, there has been no marked rise in prices as a result of the death sentence. Smuggling flourishes, and will continue to flourish, so long as the Germans have an interest in abetting it.

The first cold spell has had very bad effects. On the streets one regularly comes across children frozen to death. One sees barefoot children walking outside on frozen legs. Today, 22 November, saw a boy dancing barefoot with the cold on Nowolipki Street. The sight of barefoot children and grownups makes you shudder. And yet, outside of one shelter for children, nothing has been done to provide lodgings for the poor.

Why was the Winter Relief late? One of the reasons was, indeed, the resettlement. But the more important reason is that the Jewish Council is trying to liquidate the Jewish Social Self-Aid Society at any cost, and it won't let the YYGA have anything whatsoever to do with relief. So meanwhile nothing is being done, and here it is the end of November.

21/DECEMBER, 1941

On the 15th of December, 1941, a death sentence was carried out on fifteen Jews who left the Ghetto without a permit. Among those in prison awaiting judgment by the Special Court (whose judgments are confirmed by Governor General Frank) is a young woman who was caught in this way: She had to take care of something on the Other Side. So she was standing on the Jewish side of the Wall gate talking with the police about how to get past. Then a civilian came over and proposed that he get her past. He really did get her over to the Other Side. There he demanded payment. The young woman (very beautiful, it so happened) offered him money. But he demanded that she sleep with him. When she would not consent, he arrested her.

In the beginning of December, I heard about a gang of Jewish scoundrels who removed teeth from corpses' skulls, working at night. Word of the matter reached the Occupying Power, which conducted an investigation and put the guilty men in prison. As I heard it, the Germans filmed scenes of Jews pulling teeth from corpses.

The 14th of December a horrible thing happened at the

funeral of a couple who died of gas poisoning. The policemen suddenly, without warning, began shooting at the funeral procession. Two persons fell dead on the spot: Mrs. Runda, the director of the old-age home, and a Jew from Franciszkanska Street. Five persons, including a child of ten, were wounded. Jews have no peace, even when accompanying the dead to their eternal rest.

The elect.[ricity] affair made a strong impression on the Jewish populace during November and December. One fine morning, without notice, the current failed throughout the Ghetto—at first it stopped from seven in the morning until ten at night; afterward it stopped completely. The only exceptions were the rich h[ouses] which paid various confidence men and got current immediately. Sometimes they had to pay a second and a third time. The fee varied, from 1,000 zlotys up. It is simply incomprehensible how it all happens, but there are a great many incomprehensible things in the Ghetto. The shortage of electricity ruined complete sections of the economy, such as the grain mills, small factories, and the like.

Carbide has gone up fearfully—costs as high as 9 zlotys a kilo, naphtha has gone up to 24 zlotys a kilo; the same is true of candles—27 zlotys a kilo. Carbide is the most popular fuel. The lack of light has ruined all community activity. Meetings of House Committees are very hard to call together; the same is true of district meetings of H.C.'s.

In December the Jews received some of the Aryan houses on Chlodna, Zelazna, Nowolipie, and other streets for the Ghetto. The Christians left their apartments in a terrible state. They took out the window panes, locks, frames, even floors and gas meters. Simply a complete demolition. On the doors of some apartments hang notices from various German institutions that have appropriated the apartments for *their* Jews. In general, Germans are constantly intervening for particular Jews. Of course, these interventions are effective.

On the 22d of December, Jews were suddenly forbidden to move from Sienna Street, except for the part of Sliska Street that borders Sienna. But it wasn't possible for everyone on Sienna to have an exit on Sliska, because they would have had to knock down walls to make such exits. So some people had to crawl through holes, cellars, and the like [to exit via Sliska Street].

People are entertaining themselves in the Ghetto, not only in public places, increasingly notorious, but also at [private] card clubs that are springing up in every house and. . . .

A terrifying, simply monstrous impression is made . . . [by] the wailing of children who . . . beg for alms, or whine that they have nowhere to sleep. At the corner of Leszno and Karmelicka Streets, children weep bitterly at night. Although I hear this weeping every night, I cannot fall asleep until late. The couple of groschen I give them nightly cannot ease my conscience.

Notable among the crew that has been enriched by the war, whose only interest is gorging and reveling (they sometimes run up bills of thousands of zlotys), are the Messrs. Emil Wajc and Jacob Zilberstajn. Both are from Torun, where they live to this day. They only visit Warsaw occasionally for business purposes. They produce brushes for the German army and make millions, literally. A short time ago their monthly sales reached 2 million zlotys. They perform miracles of ingenuity. They are able to make brushes out of sticks, reeds, pillow beaters, and similar items.

After the Russian victory at Rostov,* the Jews began to call the city "*Rosh-tov*"—meaning, "a good beginning" in pidgin Hebrew.

The plan of organizing ghettos in Poland comes from before the war. Isaac [Giterman?] was shown by a high German official a hectographed work, dated June, 1939, in which four [places where there were to be] ghettos in Poland were designated.

At the shops military uniforms arrive, precut, as well as the proper number of spools of thread. You can only earn money if you work.

According to calculations, 45 million neutrals died during the other [First World] War. Who knows how many will die now, at a time when hunger has all the occupied countries in its grasp.

The Jewish Culture Organization has organized a whole courtyard for a pilot experiment. Yiddish is used all the time there. A fine exception from the general run of the rich Warsaw pigs is H. Bregman, who has been giving forty-two people free lunches daily for months.

From the 6 zlotys the workers in the shops earn daily, the Jewish Council deducts 5 per cent, the Transfer Station 10 per cent.

The refugees are boiling potato skins at their centers. Eating them leads to swelling of the belly.—Heard that those who have fled from Warsaw are wandering from place to

* On November 28, 1941.

place, because the cost of living has become very high everywhere. In Lublin a kilo of groats costs up to 20 zlotys.

What is Gancwajch after? One thing is known, that he writes weekly reports about the Ghetto. One such report was even read [by an informant]. It described political attitudes in the Ghetto. It also reported on the activity of the Polish parties here; G. mentioned, for example, that the Aguda is conducting illegal schoolrooms for traditional Jewish instruction, and the like. It is not known what the report says about the parties of the left. Gancwajch is also known to have written a book called *A Year in the Ghetto*. But the text is unknown.

If Gancwajch is trying to save his soul through literature and art, Kohn and Heller are trying to achieve the same result via piety. They frequently donate schoolrooms and Talmudic academies, support rabbis and other "sacred vessels." They are also trying to save their souls by becoming patrons of children's homes and like institutions, to which they throw several hundred zlotys every once in a while. Sometimes as much as a thousand. But perhaps the blessings of the pious will help them—if not on this sinful earth, maybe in the Hereafter. Kohn and Heller are doing excellent business. They have their own markets on Leszno Street, horse-drawn streetcars, various concessions, and the like. Besides, they have made millions importing hundreds of refugees from Lodz, taking 3,000–5,000 zlotys a head. Kohn and Heller are said to be very solid. If they tell a man that they will get him out of prison for a certain fee, they only take the money if they succeed. Honor among thieves.

22/JANUARY, 1942

The Jewish book stores are no more. The stores were closed down, the books removed. The remnants of those books that were salvaged from Swientojerska Street, where Jewish book dealers were active for generations, are now being sold out in the street. The central book exchange is now Leszno Street, where the best works by the modern authors are sold by the basketful. Nor is there any lack of forbidden merchandise— e.g., the works of Feuchtwanger, Zweig, Kautsky, Lenin, Marx, Werfel, et al., or out-and-out anti-Hitler literature in plain view (*The False Nero*) [by Feuchtwanger].... Foreign-language books are very popular, especially those in English, since every one is assiduously studying English, in preparation for emigrating after the war (Penguin Books). Most of the book sellers are the former proprietors of big book stores on Swientojerska Street—a street famous for the annual attacks by the anti-Semitic National Democratic hoodlums before the war. . . . Polish books are being sold on Leszno Street, Yiddish and Hebrew books on Nowolipki and Zamen-hofa Streets, and elsewhere. Of late, one notices the sale of Talmudic volumes—completely unprecedented. Such volumes used formerly to be regarded as holy and transmitted as a family inheritance from generation to generation. The sale of such volumes by the basketful is a sacrilege that is the best evidence of the level we have descended to.

One of the book sellers is the well-known Hebrew author Czudner. However, he has the nasty habit of hiding the best books and keeping them for himself. Once a literary man, always a literary man. . . .

January, 1942

Periods of break-up have the virtue of illuminating like a giant searchlight evils that have previously been concealed. During these days of hunger, the inhumanity of the Jewish upper class has clearly shown itself. The entire work of the Jewish Council is an evil perpetrated against the poor that cries to the very heaven. If there were a God in the world, he would have long ago flung his thunderbolts and leveled that whole den of wickedness and hypocrisy of those who flay the hide of the poor. The finance politics of the Council is one great scandal. "Equal Treatment for All" is the miserable slogan of the finance ministry. In its name, indirect taxes are levied that fall heaviest on the poor. When a group of men in the resettlement committee demanded that the rich pay a proportionately higher tax, and applied sanctions to those who would not pay up, everything in the world was done by the Council to cover up this incident. The poor people have to meet the costs of their own relief. Adults, for example, pay 70 groschen for a lunch, when it costs only 50, so as to cover with the extra 20 groschen the deficit created because the children only pay 25 for the same lunch. The same is true of the 10 per cent the Council takes from sales of produce. It is taken impartially from the millionaire and the poorest beggar. The same goes for the work battalions.

Here, again, the upper class pays groschen, while the impoverished middle class and the poor, who suffer the most, pay proportionately higher taxes. Those who suffer most are the poor, who are the sickest and have to sell all their possessions to buy medicine. During Children's Month (October), there was another sales tax that fell on all consumers alike. The same for postage, and the like. If funds are needed to combat epidemics, there is a general levy of 2 zlotys on such items as bread rations. Similar examples run into the dozens. The Council's budget is covered by the poor. The rich, on the other hand, do a thriving business on which there is no tax at all. Ours is the only Jewish Council that practices so criminal a policy.

[Telephone code for smuggling goods past the] Wall. "A," [telephone message] at five o'clock, for example, means that the goods can be moved through that night. "B" means it's dangerous. There's one spot where they've set up a crane to hurl sacks of flour, sugar, and the like, over the Wall. At that point the Wall dividing the Ghetto from the outside world is low.—Bread is said to cost 8 marks in Lodz. Coal is unobtainable. A pot of hot water costs a fortune. Five thousand Jews volunteered and went to work in Germany. Ten thousand voluntarily reported for work [in Poland].—In Warsaw last week (the beginning of January), three Jews were killed in one day while smuggling goods past the Wall at Zamenhofa and Stawki Streets, one of them a refugee who was the father of eight children. The smuggling goes on. Thanks to it, we have sufficient means of subsistence and the price differential isn't too high.—There has been a lot of talk about Gancwajch recently. He used to edit a weekly in Sosnowiec. Once was a Communist, a Zionist, speaks Hebrew well (he speaks Hebrew with Warszawiak), Polish, and Yiddish. Very talented, but ready for anything. He refers to his cousin Merin,* but there is doubt as to whether the latter is really supporting him. He says he [will] follow in Merin's footsteps. He is supported by the political department of the Others. His bureau is called the Lodz G.[estapo]., or the Jewish G. He says he has broad shoulders, and wants to take over the Jewish Council. He is now trying to build up a following and sympathizers in Jewish society, J. Warszawiak, known for his social-climbing, is helpful to him in this respect. The latter writes letters daily to journalists, writers, and to anyone with a reputation. Every day he [Gancwajch], in speaking to people who are dubious about working with him, mentions the name of an important new adherent. He says these people are all ready to work with him and give lectures. It is said they are supposed to form a cultural federation. Dr. Schubert, of the district office,† who supports G., is said to have expressed surprise at the failure of Czerniakow to turn to him in cultural matters. They'll give you as much culture as you wish; bread is something else altogether. The man on the street says that there are nightly orgies in Gancwajch's night spot. How much truth there is in this, I have not been able to establish. Gancwajch promises to set up public kitchens for the Jews of Leszno Street, where he is the administrator of the houses. It was because of him, he stated at a meeting of the House Committees of Leszno Street, that [Janusz] Korcszak was set free, as well as the brother of the rabbi of Ger, and that the ghetto in Minsk-Mazow was disestablished. [He was] also responsible for saving Sienna Street [for the Ghetto], also Grzybowska Street (he thought up the idea that the apostates needed the church on G. Street). Heard this opinion of him: three-fourths scoundrel, one-fourth romantic. People know what he is very well, but they stream into

* See p. 155.
† See p. 131.

his night spot. His aides are one Kohn, Kamersztajn, Szternfeld, Adv.[ocate] Glajchweksler, Adv. Kremensohn, Adv.
Zajdler—most of them from Lodz. There is talk (apparently
baseless) that a meeting was held in the Coliseum Cinema,
where the slogan [on the wall] read: "Warsaw without Jews
and without Walls." Bands have been formed on the Other
Side to confiscate bread and other produce bought from
Jews. In Lodz hundreds of people are said to be dying daily
from cold and hunger.—The inmates of Oswiecim wear
wooden clogs on their bare feet. This wounds [their feet],
which don't heal. Blood poisoning sets in, and death follows.
Other inmates are sent out from a hot house to a room where
they are forced to take a cold shower—lung inflammation,
then death. Dr. Rubinsztajn and . . . were killed in the Pawia
Street prison for wearing a red sweater and white shirt
—a patriotic demonstration.—From some provincial cities,
packages are arriving in Warsaw via post. It is said that this
is only from the Kielce area. The Radom and Lublin area are
forbidden to use the mail for such purposes. The question of
who is worse off now, the Jews or the Poles, is often discussed.
A curse: "Your mother's a whore!" sworn at the Jewish Council. The other day Jewish merchandise was confiscated in
the innkeepers' division in the Ghetto, this . . . commerce.
Jews have sold a great deal of merchandise on the Other
Side, receiving raw material in exchange.—At the beginning
of January, eighty people were forced to do calisthenics on
Chlodna Street, typically, on the very same spot where three
people had been killed an hour before. A new watch, and
smuggling resumes. *Men of valor* appear at the graveyard;
hats have to be removed in salute—an act that desecrates the
holy place. A rumor, not checked, that in Lodz the dead cannot be buried in the local graveyard. They have to be sent
away. Reason unknown.—Coal costs 700–800 zlotys here.
On the Other Side, it costs 400 zlotys. The hungry tear the

bread out of your hands. Exile demoralizes; hence so many refugees from Lodz in "the Thirteen." The door of every apartment has to bear a sign listing all the residents.—The game They play at the Pawia Street prison: They pretend to be freeing prisoners, who get ready. Their clothes are disinfected, but then they remain. Happens a number of times. —The treatment of slaves in antiquity was better than the treatment of Jews in the work camps. All of the fifteen weeks the campers were there they never took off their clothing. Their shoes had to be cut open when they returned.—A doctor of the Others said: "Why don't you take care of your garbage? The stench can be smelled on the Other Side of the Wall."—Heard that many Jews have burned their sacred volumes, fearful they may be accused of keeping copies of the Talmud. Somebody high up said that there are people in the Warsaw Jewish Council who know all about how to run a ghetto. He'll take them over to London when they set up a ghetto there. A night spot has been opened in the cellar of Hotel Britannia at 18 Nowolipie Street. It's open until seven in the morning (apparently for loose purposes)—"The Thirteen" owns it. Revelry unconfined there. The first day they made 10,000 zlotys; the second, 2,000. A kilo of wine costs 25 zlotys there; checks run from 500 zlotys up. . . . Four instances of bread-snatching. Hunger is growing. Near almost every house and courtyard gate men, women, and children lie on the ground begging for help.—On the Other Side they say: "You want to have a good time—go to the Ghetto." Warsaw is having a good time. Every Sabbath hundreds of affairs are run for the benefit of the House Committees. Heard a few instances of extortion. This is how it works: The Others detain a Jew. Then somebody from "the Thirteen" communicates that the man can be let go for a large sum of money. They hold the money on deposit. To the joke about why there are no crèches at Christmas time this year [?], you

can add: "Because the Three Wise Kings are in London."*
—According to himself, Gancwajch was a right Labor Zionist
before the war. Some six years ago, he was supposed to have
been in Germany, where he is said to have formed a Nazi
youth organization. The other week all the Jewish book dealers were closed down—such as Kozak, etc. Also public and
private libraries. The Poles are said to have killed Ziambo,
editor of the *Warsaw Courier*, for revelations about the former Pol.[ish] men in power. Near his body a note was said
to have been found declaring this to be the work of the illegal Polish underground organization. As a result, several
dozen Poles are said to have been shot. Another version
reports several hundreds shot and thousands imprisoned.—
Mr. Majer Balaban says that lectures will be given at the people's university that Warszawiak is organizing for "the
Thirteen." Dr. Lajpunger has also promised to lecture. Gancwajch is reported to be convoking meetings of the intelligentsia where the Jewish Council is criticized. Saw a little
girl begging at Panska Street, singing the familiar song:
"Winter is come, winter is here." Last Friday ninety bodies
were discovered, sixteen of them from the refugee centers.
In the foundling home (previously at Wolska Street) a child
froze to death. Heard on the 16th of January that the Ghetto
is to be completely closed on the 7th of February. Heard
that one diamond broker had several hundred thousand
zlotys' worth of diamonds for sale to Christians. A *German*
snapped them up for 20,000 zlotys, sold them in Lodz, and
with the 20,000 marks he got there bought noodles [gold dol-
lars]. The currency exchanges and diamond merchants have
recently been raided. At the Melody Palace, They took away
the musical instruments for 40,000 zlotys.† The same at Dick-

---

* The mocking reference is to three kings who had lost their thrones
through German conquest of their countries: Zog of Albania, Peter of Yugoslavia, and George the Second, of Greece.

† A reference to smuggling.

stein's. A man from "the Thirteen" came into a shop, bought real coffee; an hour later came back, took 10 kilos of coffee, arrested the owner, but for 1,000 zlotys was willing to let him go.

The plight of the refugees in their centers is simply intolerable. They are freezing to death for lack of coal. During the month, 22 per cent of over a thousand refugees died in the center at 9 Stawki Street. There is no coal to be had for the refugee centers, but there's plenty for the coffee houses. The number of those who have frozen to death grows daily; it is literally a commonplace matter.—The populace was just bursting with jokes about the new year. One of them was that 1942 would be called 1941, because H. had promised his people he would end the war in 1941.

January was the month of the fur-coat decree, which affected the whole of the Government General of Poland. This decree ordering Jews to surrender their fur coats was a severe blow to the poorer people, who sometimes had nothing but an old tattered fur coat to wear. The decree made the whole Ghetto poorer by tens of millions of zlotys (the estimate is 30 or 40 million zlotys). Nothing was received in return here.—Last year in Lodz, people were able to sell their fur coats for large sums and received means of subsistence in exchange. The first deadline, three days' time, was so short deliberately, to prevent the populace from evading the intent of the decree. Nevertheless, one way or another, people did manage. Thousands of fur coats were smuggled over to the Other Side to Christian friends. Many fur coats were concealed inside the Ghetto itself, many persons destroyed their fur coats, rather than hand them over to the enemy. The majority, however, gave up their coats, fearful of their neighbors' informing on them, or of being asked to show papers certifying they had given the coats up. The "hand organ" ground powerfully all the while. Business was wonderful. The Jewish Council officials sold as many fur-coat certifications as requested. Naturally, people sold the fur coats for groschen, literally. But when the deadline was extended, the prices rose. The Warsaw Ghetto looked odd during this period. For the streets were packed with Christians, particularly Christian policemen, who detained Jews on their way to the Jewish Council with their furs and offered to buy them. The transactions were completed out in the street or behind a gate. There were instances of beggar children being given odd pieces of fur, which they used to keep their hands or feet warm. A rich folklore developed around the subject of the fur coats. The popular fantasy is rich and quickly reacts to everything that happens in the street.

The Russian victories at Mozhaisk and the breakthrough at Kholm in January produced the street saying: "Jews, have no fear! Poles, rejoice! Germans, go packing!"

Last year's Polish calendar printed the national holidays blank.

At the beginning of January, the legend "1812" [date of Napoleon's defeat in Russia] was written on all the posters in the Ghetto. On the Aryan side of Warsaw, on the 8th of January, the legend: "For Germans Only" appeared on every scaffolding.

At 14 Ostrowska Street is a house where there are only women and children. All the menfolk have died. In general, men have a markedly higher mortality—the reason being that men have less endurance, work harder, and so forth.—A new society has been formed, called Strength through Malicious Joy.*

There was a sequel to the fur-coat affair. The second half of January, the question arose of how to free those Jews who

* Paraphrasing the Nazi slogan, Strength through Joy.

had been sentenced to death by the Special Court for leaving the Ghetto without a permit. They were willing to set the prisoners free for 1,500 furs to be bought by the Jewish Council. The same was also supposed to apply to the several hundred Jews imprisoned for the same offense. The Jewish Council, in its usual fashion, wanted to lay the whole burden of payment on the shoulders of the poor, with the cooperation of the House Committees. But the [final] decision was to include the rich, as well, in this operation. The rich were handled ruthlessly. Those who did not voluntarily appear at the Council offices to contribute were dragged out of their beds at night and held until they did pay up. There was a discussion in community circles as to whether the House Committees should cooperate in this operation. Some people held that we ought not to, because that would be helping the enemy win the war; other people maintained that we Jews have been forced to sacrifice so many victims that, if we have a chance of saving a few hundred Jews from death by buying off the Germans, we ought to do so. Especially since the 1,500 fur coats were not really a voluntary offering, but a forced contribution. The House Committee meetings held on this question were a huge success. The halls and corridors were overflowing; more than a million zlotys had to be raised to cover the cost of the 1,500 fur coats.

"*German General Woes!*" some of the news vendors shout —instead of *German General News,*—"*Cracow News,* Pack o' Lies!" There's even one daring newsboy who yells: "Big Fire on Praga Street" (where the army stores are), "Thousands Arrested!" and the like.

The 26th of January, the Jewish police raided all the card clubs. They confiscated all the money they found. There are several hundred card clubs in Warsaw. Some of them are the only support of the House Committees in the houses where they meet.—A Jew received the following authentic letter in code from an acquaintance in Switzerland: "Mr. Yekl [Germany] has suffered some very bad attacks. It would be better for him to die soon, so he wouldn't have to suffer. Mr. Shalom [peace] will soon be here. We are waiting for him." Since the Germans took so long to take Mozhaisk, the Germans called it Nie Mozhaisk.*

"Komm herunter, grosser Reiter—der Gefreiter kann nicht weiter!" they said at the Friedrich the Great Memorial in Berlin ["Come down, great knight—the nation you liberated can go no further!"]—Besides the information they glean from accurate radio news broadcasts, ex-newspapermen are spreading reports of exaggerated communiqués. They're always far in advance of Russian army movements—a couple of hundred kilometers. After the breakthrough at Kholm, they advanced as far as Vilna; after the victory at Mozhaisk, they sped past Smolensk, Vitebsk, Minsk, and the like. Stalin telegraphed them: "God, not so fast. I can't keep up with you!" On the 2d of January, Jews were talking about the Russian occupation of Vilna, the German evacuation from Kiev.

The Quartering Office of the Jewish Council is a nest of corruption. If you do manage to pass through all seven hells of the Inferno and get an apartment, it may turn out you've not paid enough graft. The apartment will be without water and gas and a fifth-floor walk-up. Besides, the gangsters working in the house administration office have sometimes (as in the case of 18 Chlodna Street) changed the apartment numbers. You may find you have paid extra for some room in a garret.

Christmas Eve, the White House, or the Castle (that's what they call 20 Chlodna Street where Czerniakow and the Jewish Council big shots live), threw a party. [Benjamin] Zabludowski danced like a Cossack, got drunk, and gorged himself.

* *"Nie"* means "never" in German.

The next day he died. The city received the news of the death of Czerniakow's right-hand man with joy. Zabl. was an evil person, and besides there had been doubts recently as to his honesty.

CENTOS [the Children's Welfare Organization] is only taking on officials who have already had the typhus, so great is the danger of being infected with typhus in the public institutions, the street children being particularly dangerous.

People are buying books cheap, in order to trade in them after the war. The affair of the extra bread ration cards—for the police, 12 kilos of bread; for the Jewish Council and other officials, 4 kilos; for workers, 6 kilos (30,000 cards)—evoked tremendous bitterness among the populace. This has all been at the expense of the poorest people, half a kilo of bread per person being subtracted. It is not known whose idea this is—whether it really is the commissar Auerswald's, or whether the Jews thought it up themselves. At any rate, it is seen as a dangerous precedent. The fear is that this may mean the first step in depriving people of the right to live; that it may lead to further [discriminatory] limitations. Some officials have thought of refusing the "gift," but they are afraid such a refusal might have dire consequences. Consequently, some of the officials have agreed to do without 1–2 kilos of bread, to which the new ration cards entitle them, for the benefit of those in the refugee centers [whom they donate the bread to]. However, not all the officials are in agreement with this plan—for example, the Jewish Council officials.

23/APRIL, 1942

April 10

Here is what happened tonight: In the famous night spot at 5 Leszno Street (formerly a post-office building), where there used to be the most smuggling at night, a policeman shot a smuggler. The policeman went to the hospital, taking with him a doctor and a nurse, to save the injured man. But meanwhile the smuggler had died. Incidentally, the famous hole—the immortal hole, immortal because They were forever walling it up and the smugglers were forever breaking it open again—was finally (after what happened to Junka, who was shot by a policeman while smuggling on Rymarska Street) really walled up, and so tight that it can't be broken through.

On April 12 rumors were thick that an extermination squad had come to Warsaw and had begged permission to go on a rampage through the Ghetto for just two hours. But permission was not granted. Auerswald wouldn't agree. Some people say that when the extermination squad arrived in Warsaw from the provinces it found orders to move on to the front. This rumor is associated with the fact that there are various foreign contingents in Warsaw, such as Lithuanians and Ukrainians, and they're just waiting for the right moment to start a pogrom. Besides, one is always hearing reports about extermination squads that are wiping complete Jewish settlements off the face of the earth.

One hundred sixty-four of the German Jews who came to Warsaw a few days ago, the cream of the young people, including a large number of *chalutzim* preparing to migrate to Palestine, were sent to the penal camp at Treblinki, near Sokolow, where most of them were exterminated in a short time. In three weeks, out of 160 Jewish young people from Otwock only 38 were left.

24/MAY, 1942

May 7

[Original notes of a report to Ringelblum on conditions in the Vilna Ghetto and others.]

Commandant of Vilna, Herring [says]: "I am for the Jews, who are better than I am. Whatever has been done has been by command from Berlin."

Jews were burned in the streets: in all Lithuanian towns. There is still a grave in the middle of the city.—Kovno—Ghetto, last month there was a new operation—economic—German police in the Ghetto, bad economically—threat of death from hunger. Shavli—4,000 Jews working in factories, very good.

Riga—4,000 Jews—in Minsk 900 Jews—very bad situation. Jews [working?] in the peat bogs, Vilna area.

In Vilna, 20,000 Jews, 50,000 Jews arrived from the surrounding area. Horribly expensive—43 rubles for a kilo of bread—10 marks a week, laborer's wages.—In Bialystok a kilo of bread 13 rubles, cost of living high.

Community life flourishing in Vilna—evening concerts—teachers' federation formed.

In Vilna high school established, lyceums, Hebrew-speak-

ing groups every Friday night, literary lectures twice a week
—things very free in the Ghetto. Cesler, a Jewish *provocateur*,
walks around without the [yellow] patch—a patch on both
sides—chest and back—the Jewish badge in Vilna, like the
arm band in Warsaw—[he talks about a] Jewish state. . . .
YIVO [Yiddish Scientific Institute] c.[ommittee] of twenty
—YIVO archive segregated—Straszun libr.[ary] is [incorpo-
rated] in the University library.

Teachers—Herzl manuscript found—many valuable things
concealed in the Ghetto.—Found the archives of the lab.[or]
movement.—No sky to be seen in the Ghetto, save a narrow
strip; a sport department was established, a courtyard made
available—there is not a single tree—a courtyard was cleaned
up and is to be transformed into a warehouse [?].—Jaszunski
at the head of the Jewish Council—rivalry between the Council and the Jewish police.

Some 2,000 Jews work at furs, live on Slowacki Street outside the Ghetto.

Bialystok—G.[estapo] demanded a list of persons who
had arrived in Bialystok from Pruzhany (more than 2,000
Jews)—they're expecting roundups.—Those who have come
to Bialystok from Vilna are in danger: The Council asked to
have 35,000 Jews officially legitimatized; unofficially there
are 40,000. From Vilna there have arrived in Bialystok some
200–300 persons, work intensively in munitions: textiles,
leather, furniture, barrels. The Council devotes all its energy
to having the textile factories employ Jews, push the Poles
out. Many Germans arrive with propositions for factories. The
Jews are the organizers and administrators of the whole war
industry. Some 2,000 Jews or more leave the Ghetto to work
outside. They've begun getting winter clothing ready, ceaselessly sewing. An exhibit outside the Ghetto of all the things
the Jews are making. People not permitted to walk in the
street, considered not politic to thrust oneself in Their eyes.

Food supply good; 25 dekos of bread, horsemeat, olive oil, potatoes. Those who work get a bonus of .5 of a kilo of bread; every working man gets 50 kilos of potatoes. There's no hunger. Everything is cheaper than in the Warsaw Ghetto. Bread, 13 rubles a kilo. Butter, 200 rubles. They have the sense of security: "It can't happen here."—Someone said that the schools are mixed: both Yiddish—and Hebrew—[speaking].

May 8—The Ghetto has calmed down somewhat since the massacre of April 18 (when fifty-two people were shot down in the street). People have become a little more optimistic. They've begun to believe again that the war will be over in a few months and life will return to normal. This good mood has been aided by false communiqués that have become widespread with the cessation of true accounts after Friday's massacre. What is in these communiqués? Well, first we learn that Smolensk has been retaken through an airdrop of 60,000 soldiers who joined forces with the Russian Army camped west of Smolensk. The same communiqué has taken Kharkov. Another communiqué disembarked a whole army in Murmansk, borne by 160 ships, not one of which was sunk en route. Of course, when Hitler heard this news (this was *after* his May 1 speech), he collapsed. Then, the Allies won a great victory on Lake Ilmen, where the communiqué killed 43,000 Germans and took more than 80,000 captive. This was the Nineteenth Army; the captives included two German generals. As though this were not enough, a communiqué has deposed Mussolini and made a revolution in Italy. Add to all this an ultimatum from Roosevelt to the German people giving them until May 15 to surrender. In a word, the Jews in the Warsaw Ghetto aren't content merely to recite Psalms and leave the rest in God's hands; they labor day and night to lay their enemy low and bring an early peace. . . . When will the war really end?

The Ghetto Jews can't bear it any longer, that's why we try our utmost to see the war's end as imminent. There are people who seriously believe that the situation in Germany at this time parallels that of the year 1918. They cite statements by well-known Germans and reports from German Jews who have been driven into Warsaw to the effect that Germany has been recently flooded with illegal leaflets, so-called "circulars," inciting soldiers, workers, and intellectuals to rebel against the regime. Other evidence cited for the imminent downfall of Hitler is the four or five illegal radio stations and the very bad food situation. Letters from Germany (in code, of course) describe vast popular dissatisfaction. The final, conclusive argument for an early conclusion to the war has come from a Jew whose last name is Czerwiec [June], and from the fortuneteller, Madame M.

Czerwiec is the Jew from Nalewki Street who predicted the German attack on Russia in June. When asked what was to happen afterwards, he prophesied that the Germans would be halted in November and unable to advance a foot. So he was nicknamed Listopad [November]. Later they called him Luty [February] because he predicted that the Germans would be in dire straits in February. Now they call him Czerwiec again, because he predicts the war will be over the middle of *this* June.

Madame M. was a law student who lost her husband (a Warsaw lawyer) during the war. She knew about it eleven months in advance, but one can't avoid his fate—says she. A few months before the war began she dictated to one of her followers (another lawyer's wife) a detailed account of how the war would break out (with exact dates), and a description of the bombardment of Warsaw, the razing of the power-house, the failure of gas, water, and electricity. She is said to have foreseen later developments, as well. I know that two or three months before November, 1941, she prophesied that the German Army would be defeated in Russia in the second half of November and be unable to make any further advances. Later she predicted terrible times coming for the Jews. Now she says that in June there will be no walls left standing in Warsaw, but the Jews will be here. We will not be deported. Still, she expects very bad times. The Germans will incite the Poles against the Jews. There will be a three-day pogrom. But those who survive will be saved.

A slaughter like that of Friday, the 18th of April [1942], took place in a number of towns in the Government General. There is news of slaughters of this kind in Cracow, Tarnow, Czestochowa, Radom, Kielce, Ostrowiec, etc. In each place there were about fifty dead. The killings took place in the street at night there too. Those killed were a varied lot. In some cities it was the returnees from Russia, who were considered Communists; everywhere the local [Jewish] authorities declared they didn't know anything about it, they hadn't prepared any lists for the Others, and so on. In some cities, at the same time as the killings took place, there were arrests of persons who were sent nobody knows whither to this day. Those arrested included Diamond, the president of the Radom Jewish Council, and his representative, Merin. It was part of a general operation. During his last visit, Himmler must have issued an order for massacres to be perpetrated everywhere in the Government General of Poland in order to terrorize the Jewish populace. Probably this is in connection with the spring campaigns. They want their rear to be secure.

They threw a little fright into the Jews, so the Jews would keep their heads down.

The end of April and beginning of May we lived in terror of deportation. Where this rumor emanated from no one knows. One opinion has it that the Polish merchants spread the rumor in order to persuade the Jewish populace to sell their possessions. There was even some talk of the number of deportees being from 150,000 to 200,000, the country of destination Rumania. There were rumors emanating from the Kitchen Department of the Jewish Council that "non-productive" elements would be deported, and only workers would be able to enjoy the benefits of the kitchen. This was regarded as a grave omen. However, Council circles have assured us that the danger of deportation that has been hanging over our heads has been avoided, thanks to the presence of factories in the Ghetto that are supplying the needs of the German Army. This is a tragic paradox. Only those Jews have the right to live who work to supply the German Army. The same was true in Vilna, Rovno, and dozens of other cities where there were mass slaughters of Jews. The only Jews left alive were those who directly or indirectly worked for the Germans. Never in history has there been a national tragedy of these dimensions. A people that hates the Germans with every fiber of its being can purchase its life only at the price of helping its foe to victory—the very victory that means the complete annihilation of Jewry from the face of Europe, if not of the whole world.

The Warsaw Ghetto is hard at work for the Germans. They're repairing clothing stripped from soldiers killed in battle, and are beginning to prepare such winter items as quilted trousers, vests, and overcoats. Also straw shoes, furniture, etc. The center of all this activity is the firm of Toebbens at 12 Prosta Street, where more than 1,000 workers are busy. It's typical that in the waiting room outside the office of Bauch, the man in charge of work, a number of pointed rods of various size and thickness hang. These, it would seem, are implements that no German can get along without. They're the symbols of bloodthirsty Hitlerism that one finds everywhere—in concentration camps, in work camps, in prison, and even at places of work.

The following is typical of the present attitude of Polish Jewry to philanthropy. Two years ago the Chassidic rabbi of Ruzyn wrote his disciples in Lublin to sell their furniture and give the proceeds to charity. It was his understanding that they were not doing any business and had no ready cash. His disciples disobeyed him and did not sell their furniture. Then the Germans confiscated almost all the furniture in every Jewish home in Lublin. Later, the rabbi wrote his disciples to sell their furs and give the proceeds to charity. Again, his Chassidim disobeyed him. And again the Germans came, this time to confiscate the furs. Finally, the rabbi wrote his disciples to sell their Sabbath clothes and give the proceeds to charity. His disciples disobeyed him once more, and the Jews were deported from Lublin.

Two days ago (May 5–6) a characteristic smuggling incident took place. The corner house at 21 Franciszkanska Street that is next to the Wall is a hotbed of smuggling. A ladder is thrown over the Wall and smuggling goes on all night. But this night the smugglers quarrel among themselves, and one of them informs where it will do the most good. The police come at once and catch a whole crowd in the middle of operations. Machine guns begin shooting, one smuggler is shot dead on the spot, one or two others wounded. Then they search every apartment in the building, take away a great deal of goods, and arrest forty smugglers. For 40,000 zlotys, they return the goods and set the smugglers free. That is the sum that the police claim to have lost because the smugglers used the Wall to bring goods in, rather than taking them through the watch at the Ghetto gate, where the police get a cut. Most of the smuggling goes through the watch. It costs 100 zlotys per wagon. The driver has to know the password, or else he can't get through.

There are policemen who make 2,000 zlotys in an hour or two. The smuggling of goods past the Wall continues, resulting every day in the sacrifice of a large number of wounded and dead. Often minors and children are among the victims. There is one policeman who is renowned as a model German. Nicknamed "the gentleman," he is the soul of honesty. He permits wagons through the gates of the Wall, refusing to take a bribe. He also permits Jewish children to pass to the Other Side by the dozen to buy food, for the most part potatoes and other vegetables. Examples of his wondrous decency and honesty are recounted daily. He plays all sorts of games with the smuggler children. He lines them up, commands them to sing, and marches them through the gates.

The inspection guards can be bought, too. A short time ago, a whole wagon of contraband was "burned" (i.e., confiscated). But 200 zlotys were sufficient to persuade the inspection guards to let the wagon into the Ghetto. There is good reason for the proverb that three things are indomitable: the German Army, the British Isles, and Jewish smuggling.

They tell this story: Churchill invited the Chassidic rabbi of Ger to come to see and advise him how to bring about Germany's downfall. The rabbi gave the following reply: "There are two possible ways, one involving natural means, the other supernatural. The natural means would be if a million angels with flaming swords were to descend on Germany and destroy it. The supernatural would be if a million Englishmen parachuted down on Germany and destroyed it."

They are now filming the Ghetto. They spent two days

shooting the Jewish prison and the Council. They drove a crowd of Jews together on Smocza Street, then ordered the Jewish policemen to disperse them. At another place They shot a scene showing a Jewish policeman about to beat a Jew when a German comes along and saves the fallen Jew.

There is a big sign in German in the cemetery ordering Germans not to visit the Jewish graveyard. Supposedly, the grounds for this ban are sanitation, but in actual fact, the reason is quite different. Crowds of Germans used to visit the cemetery to stare at the famous shed where daily the skeletons of the corpses of poor people who had starved to death in the street were heaped—candidates for mass graves. Standing there, the Germans used to discuss the "Jewish question" among themselves. Some of the Germans enjoyed the sight of the victims of Hitler's extermination policy; others, however, expressed their revulsion at the consequences of what they named "German culture." Apparently, these graveyard excursions left a strong imprint on the excursionists; consequently, they were halted.

Tonight, the night of May 12, 1942, there occurred an event similar to that which took place on Friday, April 18. During the course of the night four Jews were shot: Sklar,* Feist, Zaks (a sportsman), and Tenenbaum. Apparently these men were associated with the liberation movement. At night they were taken out of the Pawia Street prison and shot outdoors, each in a different street. This shooting of people in the streets has become a deliberate tactic since April. The aim: to terrify the populace, to terrorize them.

Two hundred thousand uniforms stripped from the bodies of dead German soldiers were brought into the Warsaw Ghetto. The uniforms were horribly lousy and blood drenched. From the number of them, one can imagine how

* Sklar was an important Bundist, head of the Bundist kitchen located at 2 Orla Street. No exact information is available about the other three men.

many hundreds of thousands and millions of men fell on the Eastern front during the winter. Many of the blouse pockets contained surrender appeals dropped from Soviet airplanes that constituted a kind of safe-transit pass, identifying the bearer as a Soviet friend. Although the concealment of such appeals was subject to heavy punishment, they were discovered in a great many officers' pockets. The pockets contained, in addition, letters from friends and family that give a glimpse into the moods of both the soldiers and those they had left behind in the hinterland. The general impression was of a terrible depression among the soldiers.

The Praga cemetery, which is more than 150 years old, is being leveled. The devils won't even let the dead rest. They've done the same sort of thing elsewhere in Poland and Germany. So unimportant a thing as the antiquity of a cemetery, its cultural and historical significance, is of no importance whatsoever to them.

The South American citizens living in the Ghetto were called to the Pawia Street prison. There they were informed that they would have to leave Warsaw by the 18th inst. for Switzerland, where they will be exchanged for German citizens. But there is still a question as to whether the newly created citizens, i.e., those who bought their citizenship for a price during the war, will be allowed to benefit from this exchange.

Here's a mystery for you: Surov, a Soviet citizen who once shared a Pawia Street prison cell with all the other Russian citizens, now moves about as free as a lark, lives on the Other Side without a special permit, is in business. How has he managed all this? What price has he paid—does he pay—for his hard-won freedom?

Often the Ghetto serves as an intermediary between two Christian merchants. This sounds paradoxical, but it is a fact. Christian merchants are fearful of dealing directly with one another, because the office of price inspection can shut down their stores. But if they buy and sell in the Ghetto, where there is no office of price inspection, they can charge whatever they want. A short time ago, I heard a story about a firm that bought 1,000 carbide lamps. These lamps were smuggled into the Ghetto and then smuggled out again to another Christian firm. Have heard the same thing about other firms. Recently, the value of hard currency [dollars] rose from 150 to 186 zlotys. The reason is said to be that since merchandise is being confiscated, the Polish merchants have decided to exchange all their money for foreign currency, which is then sent to the Other Side.

The demoralization of the Polish police and Polish secret agents is indescribable. They do nothing in the Ghetto but move about detaining wagons full of merchandise and extorting protection money. The populace shivers at the sight of them and gives them whatever they ask. They get monthly payments from each of the merchants—the secret agents from the crowd that hangs around Franciszkanska Street get 200 zlotys from every leather merchant. One of the merchants collects the protection money and brings each of the eight agents in the district his share. Anyone who wants to open up a secret grain mill has first to report to the agents and pay them off. If he doesn't, they threaten to nab him at work and fine him 2,000 zlotys. The number of grain mills is very large. There is one in almost every house where there is electricity.

They are still filming the Ghetto. Every scene is directed. E.g., yesterday they ordered a child to run outside the Ghetto Wall at the corner of Leszno and Zelazna Streets, and to buy potatoes there. A Polish policeman catches the boy and raises his arm to beat him. At that moment who should come along but a German policeman: He grabs the Pole's arm—children are not to be beaten!

The period ending that fateful Friday, April 18, may be termed "the period of legal conspiracy." All the political parties in the Ghetto conducted activities that were practically semilegal. Political publications sprouted like mushrooms after rain. If *you* publish your paper once a month, *I'll* publish mine twice a month; if *you* print twice a month, *I'll* print weekly; it finally reached the point where the bulletin of one of the parties was appearing twice a week. These publications were distributed openly, "in full view of the people and the congregation." The political leaflets and communiqués used to be read in offices, factories, and similar public places.

The various parties used to hold their meetings practically in the open in public halls. They even had big public celebrations. At one such meeting, a speaker addressing an audience of 150 preached active resistance. I was myself present at a celebration along with 500 young people who all belonged to the same party. The names of the authors of the anonymous articles that appeared in the party newspapers were common knowledge.

We had even begun to debate and insult one another, as in the good old prewar days. We imagined that anything went. Even such illegal Polish publications as *Barykada Wolnosci* [Barricade of Freedom] used to be printed and distributed in the Ghetto. (I haven't checked this fact.) Everybody imagined that the Germans were indifferent to what the Jews were thinking and doing in their Ghetto. We thought that all that the Germans were concerned about was ferreting out Jewish merchandise, money, currency—that they were uninterested in intellectual matters. We turned out to be sadly mistaken. That bloody Friday, when the publishers and distributors of illegal publications were executed, proved that our political constellation is not a subject of indifference to Them, particularly when it has some connection with what is happening in the Polish, non-Jewish part of Warsaw.

The Jewish Council people have tried to exploit the bloody Friday for their own purposes: to repress completely the social and political life of the Ghetto. First they spread the rumor that Friday's massacre was attributable to the illegal publications. And then they warned the people of the Ghetto that if these [illegal publications] were to be repeated, the fate of Lublin would be visited on Warsaw—i.e., the deportation of the Jewish population. The only question that rises in one's mind is: Why were there similar massacres (courtyard executions by gunfire) in Radom and other places where there were no illegal publications? One body of opinion would have it that Friday's massacre has "rehabilitated" the Ghetto [morally]. This is the first time that Jewish blood has been spilled for reasons of political—not purely personal—activity.

Bloody Friday has had strong repercussions. The illegal press has stopped publishing. There has been a significant weakening of political activity. The interest in social undertakings has slackened. It was a hard blow to people's spirits; half the city spends the night away from home these days. Anyone who had anything at all to do with any kind of community work is terrified. Since the slaughter was the result of tattling by Jewish informers (apparently, from the Kohn and Heller firm), people tremble to speak a word. The English communiqués, which used to be so widely disseminated (some people actually made a living out of them!), have ceased appearing. However, since people are hungry for every tidbit of news, lies are fabricated out of whole cloth.

Every day we have another batch of lies. After Friday's slaughter, a crew of swindlers turned up who persuaded people to part with money for the privilege of having their names removed from new lists of those doomed to slaughter. The example of Blajman, who during the weeks before the slaughter was blackmailed for 5,000 zlotys ransom money, has made people mortally fearful of blackmailers. But gradually, little by little, people are beginning to straighten up again. The only thing is that what used to be a kind of "legitimate" conspiracy is now being transformed into the real thing and is going deep underground.

The Pawia Street prison has become a center of persecution, outside as well as in. Inside, the prisoners are tortured ceaselessly—a new prison guard has taken over recently. But whether the guard be old or new, prisoners are tortured. The Pawia Street prison has become the point of departure for Oswiecim. Also, a number of people have been taken from the prison and shot outside, right in the street. Lately, the prison has also become a source of misery for those on the outside—for its neighbors and those who pass by on either side of Pawia Street. The neighbors have had to cover their windows with thick black paper or black wooden slats. Night and day, windows have to be closed.

The Jewish Gestapoists are now busy looking for an alibi. They are desperately trying to look good, so as to prove that they, at any rate, are real Jews, true Jews, Jews with a sense of public interest. Gancwajch, e.g., is turning into a regular Maecenas, supporting Jewish literature, art, theater. He arranges "receptions" for Jewish writers and artists, where there is plenty of food—nowadays the important thing. A short time ago he threw an all-night party at the El Dorado night spot. . . . The party was opened with the dedication of an ambulance, named Miriam (after Gancwajch's wife at home). Gancwajch's business interests are flourishing. He has the administration of 100 buildings, which brings him in a pretty penny. Beside, he issues thirty certificates a month, at the rate of several thousand zlotys per certificate; he's also a partner in various businesses. In a word, he's thriving. Gancwajch's function in the Gestapo is not completely clear. But one thing is certain: He gets nothing for nothing. He has to pay for every favor. To help them meet their Passover needs, Gancwajch sent the Jewish writers 6,000 zlotys.

One can judge the depths of poverty in the Ghetto from the fact that there are houses where everything has been sold—even pillow cases and sheets, so that people are sleeping right on the feathers of their pillows and beds. You come across beggars who are covered all over with feathers. These have sunk below the threshold of hope.

Death lurks in every chink, every little crack. There have been cases of everyone living in an apartment being fearfully tortured because someone opened a shutter. One of the tortures is to have the culprit strip naked and then roll down a pile of coke. The pain is excruciating, and every part of the body bleeds. Besides, every now and then, Jews who just happen to be passing by the Pawia Street prison are seized, tortured, and beaten. The Germans driving prisoners in trucks to the Pawia Street prison beat the passers-by on the street mercilessly. The Gestapo agent sitting in the back of the car leans out the window, reaches along the narrow Karmelicka Street, and slashes at passers-by with a long, lead-tipped stick. He overturns rickshas, and beats the ricksha drivers. At sight of the truck, people run into the nearest courtyard to hide. Often the Gestapo agents shoot. Many a man has been killed or wounded by one of these wild street shootings, which have become the thing since the 18th of April, bloody Friday.

The heroic girls, Chajke and Frumke—they are a theme that calls for the pen of a great writer. Boldly they travel back and forth through the cities and towns of Poland. They carry "Aryan" papers identifying them as Poles or Ukrainians. One of them even wears a cross, which she never parts with except when in the Ghetto. They are in mortal danger every day. They rely entirely on their "Aryan" faces and on the peasant kerchiefs that cover their heads. Without a murmur, without a second's hesitation, they accept and carry out the most dangerous missions. Is someone needed to travel to Vilna, Bialystok, Lemberg, Kowel, Lublin, Czestochowa, or Radom to smuggle in contraband such as illegal publications, goods, money? The girls volunteer as though it were the most natural thing in the world. Are there comrades who have to be rescued from Vilna, Lublin, or some other city?— They undertake the mission. Nothing stands in their way, nothing deters them. Is it necessary to become friendly with engineers of German trains, so as to be able to travel beyond the frontiers of the Government General of Poland, where people can move about with special papers? They are the ones to do it, simply, without fuss, as though it was their profession. They have traveled from city to city, to places no delegate or Jewish institution had ever reached, such as Wolhynia, Lithuania. They were the first to bring back the tidings about the tragedy of Vilna.* They were the first to offer words of encouragement and moral support to the surviving remnant of that city. How many times have they looked death in the eyes? How many times have they been arrested and searched? Fortune has smiled on them. They are, in the classic idiom, "emissaries of the community to whom no harm can come." With what simplicity and modesty

---

* There were more than 60,000 Jews in the Vilna Ghetto when Germany invaded the Soviet Union in June, 1941. Most of them were massacred at that time.

have they reported what they accomplished on their journeys, on the trains bearing Polish Christians who have been pressed to work in Germany! The story of the Jewish woman will be a glorious page in the history of Jewry during the present war. And the Chajkes and Frumkes will be the leading figures in this story. For these girls are indefatigable. Just back from Czestochowa, where they imported contraband, in a few hours they'll be on the move again. And they're off without a moment's hesitation, without a minute of rest.

May 22

Friday, the whole police force was called out. There was a big disturbance in the street. Some people were talking loudly about an imminent resettlement of the old, the sick, the unemployed. Others said that people were being impressed for the camps. It turned out that what was happening was that people with specialties were being impressed for the work camps. Specialists such as locksmiths, rugweavers, and the like were picked up at their addresses. If the person in question was not at home, his father was taken, or the nearest of kin at home at the time. Those picked up were sent to Zembrow. The misfortune is that many of those who declared themselves to be specialists during the registration are not such in reality; they purported to be craftsmen rather than figure as unemployed. Friday's pick-up is said to be the beginning of a big operation, the aim being to pull the Jewish populace into the factories where Poles have been working until now. If this turns out to be true, the Warsaw Ghetto can be saved for the time being.

"Jews won't work." That's what the German newspapers say. As an illustration of the contrary, I offer the following scene: 103 Plaza Zelazna is the place where those who work for the Germans outside the Ghetto change shifts. A truck arrives, and Jews throw themselves at it from all sides. They climb all over it. The soldiers can't handle the mob. They beat at those nearest with their rifles, but it does no good; the mob won't retreat. They want to get up into the truck at any cost, and there are many more than the outside work can use. The soldiers shoot in the air—but that does no good, either; the mob won't leave. Finally, the driver backs up, the mob disperses, but not before one person is badly injured. That, finally, restores order. But why do they mob the truck? The answer is simple. People working outside the Ghetto are given two good soups and half a kilo of bread a day. That's the reason for the mob.

May 23

The Gestapo men in the Pawia Street prison have to have their daily victims. Just the way a pious Jew feels bad if he misses prayers one day, the Gestapo men have to pick up a few Jews every day and break a few arms and legs. Since the street in front of the prison empties out when the Gestapo auto drives up, and since passers-by avoid the streets around the prison, yesterday They stopped the streetcar that runs through Smocza Street near the prison, and dragged a few Jews out of the car.

The O.S. has passed from "poor" work (October, 1939, to May, 1940) to "good" work; since Friday, April 18th, we're back to poor work. It is necessary to save the information we have. The method: Sit down with the informant over a glass of tea, and write up the information afterward. Our luck that the O.S. work has been kept dark.

The Gesia Street jail now contains more than 1,300 prisoners, over 500 of them being children. Some are to be tried in the Special Court (*Sondergericht*), the rest in the Auerswald Court. The Special Court has already pronounced more than 200 death sentences, not yet executed. The posts where the condemned will be bound before execution are located in the same yard where they take their daily exercise. The conditions in the jail are indescribably crowded; the jail can accommodate 300 to 500 prisoners, and there are something like four times that number there now. The cells are terribly filthy. The professionals are confined under better conditions. The mortality in jail is very high. Nevertheless, the prisoners have succeeded in doing wonderful things for the children, who run about half-naked and tanned in the fresh air all day. The children perform calisthenics, sing Yiddish and Polish songs. Mothers come begging to have their children, who have been freed, put back in jail [!]. By the way, I saw a nine-year-old child who had been arrested. Among those imprisoned were some Gypsies, whom Auerswald terms "Gypsy-Jews." Some of the Rumanian citizens were set free. The Gypsy women are confined in a special cell of their own. The Gypsy men are in cells with Jews. We were met with hysterical weeping in the cell of the condemned. They begged us to secure better food for them, so that their nerves would be able to hold out. Shops, tailor shops, brush factories are being set up to give work to several hundred persons—this may be able to save the condemned. A delegation from abroad that visited the jail was unable to comprehend how people could receive death sentences merely for crossing over to the Aryan side of Warsaw. This, they declared, is inconceivable. These people must have committed some crime on the Other Side. The jail was ideally clean (for the delegation!). [They were shown] a special bathroom where the prisoners were bathed and disinfected twice weekly. Most of those who were arrested were beggar children who had sneaked out to the Other Side; a number were smugglers. These were the chief criminals. The plaza that used to be covered with tile has been transformed into a flourishing garden whose fruits will bring in more than 200,-000 zlotys. The garden is tended by prisoner gardeners.

May 25

This is a night that will remain in the memory of the Jews of Warsaw. Tonight the wild grass of the Ghetto was cleaned out. The biggest wheels of "the Thirteen," Levin, Mandel, Szymo[nowicz] (Gancwajch's relative) and Hurwic; they couldn't find Gancwajch at home. Szternfeld also managed to escape. It is said that the other lepers met the same fate. There are a number of reasons why "the Thirteen" was liquidated. A section of the Gestapo that used to work with Gancwajch is passing out of the picture, and it doesn't want to leave behind any of its former Jewish partners. Another surmise is that the clean-up affected the German partners of the gang, and the Germans dragged their Jewish colleagues down with them. Still a third account has it that one of the gang was imprisoned, and now he's tattling. He's telling everything, including how they blackmailed people with radios, and the like. And still other rumors would have it that they were offered the opportunity to do political espionage and refused. Naturally, that's just foolish talk. This is really just a continuation of the general program of getting rid of the undesirable Gestapo agents.—It's a program that's been carried out for several months, beginning with Anders, Milek, and others. One of the stories they tell is that, a few weeks ago, Szymonowicz threw a party for Gestapo officers that cost more than 25,000 zlotys. This is supposed to have been the last straw.

The Jewish gangster police exploit every situation to make money. Recently they invented a new swindle. The Germans are making a motion picture these days, so the police go to restaurant owners and demand food for a ball that's being filmed much bigger than necessary. A short time ago the police went to an apartment at 37 Leszno Street and stated that, since the place was going to be filmed, everyone had to leave the apartment at once. However, for 50 gold pieces they would take care of the matter. While they were at it, one of them picked up a gold watch that happened to be lying on the table.

They steal everything in the Ghetto, even telephones. The telephone men, for a consideration, will install a telephone whose number has been stolen from someone else who already has a phone. This happened, for example, in a house at 18 Leszno Street. Dr. Mesz's phone stopped ringing; it turned out that a shopkeeper on the same street had paid the telephone men to install a phone for him with the same number.

The Gestapo men today discovered a new game. They drag the Jewish musicians out of all the café houses, gardens, etc., and pull them over to the Pawia Street prison, where they are forced to entertain the company all night. They did that last night, and they're doing the same thing tonight. There is a theory that the reason why [some of] "the Thirteen" were shot was because they smuggled products worth large sums of money into the Ghetto.

Agents from the Transfer Station dressed in civilian clothing have been added to the police [stationed at the Ghetto gates]; their assignment is to watch the police. But nothing helps. They too are taken care of. They're bribed. As a result, a smuggler has to buy off four parties: Polish, Jewish, and German policemen, and now civilian agents as well. Even Napoleon wasn't able to handle smuggling, nor will the modern dictator be any more successful. The profits in smuggling are enormous. I heard about a partnership of four smugglers that made 35,000 zlotys in one week, but had to spend 19,000. The rest was profit. But the smugglers have all sorts of unforeseeable expenses. For example, if a wagon is "burned" [confiscated] and the driver is sent to prison, the smugglers maintain his family, sending it packages; they have to buy the prisoner's freedom, pay the lawyer, and so on. Besides, the smugglers support the families of smugglers who have been killed. As a rule, the smugglers are free and easy with their money. It's easy come, easy go. The smugglers' parties are famous in the Ghetto for the huge amount of food served. Smugglers love a good time, since they are never sure how tomorrow will end (with a bullet, an informer, arrest)—so it's eat, drink, and be merry. Anyway, profiteers are always free with money and food—sometimes handing them out to poor relatives, too. Smugglers come from the lowest classes— fences, thieves, porters, pimps, and the underworld in general. There are often Polish and German guests at their parties —they're the ones the smugglers work with.

Interestingly enough, the wagons that are smuggled into the Ghetto are insured. There's a special Jewish company that insures wagons against being "burned" "as of 70 Nalewki Street"—i.e., there's a base price for insurance against the merchandise being "burned" by the guards up to that point— additional insurance costs more. Keep in mind, that the so-called *Yunakes*—i.e., the uniformed ethnic Germans in the service of the Commissar—have a free hand in the Ghetto itself. They pursue the wagons of contraband and confiscate the contents if they can catch them. Furst, from the Jewish Council (a "big operator," the chief of the Council's economic department) got the contraband for the Council cooperative.

A large crowd daily assembles around the loud-speakers located in the Ghetto (at the corners of Mila and Zamenhofa

Streets, Gesia and Zamenhofa Streets, and Nalewki and Nowolipki Streets). The loud-speakers have been given several nicknames: Purim Noisemaker [Grager], Bonnet [Kapelush—after the shape].

The Gestapo beast devours its own progeny. There are beasts that devour their young. Why they do so is not the subject under discussion here. But the fact is that it is a natural phenomenon. The Gestapo is destroying its Jewish agents one after another. The consequence is that the chief Jewish agents, men like Gancwajch, Kohn and Heller, and Ehrlich live in constant dread, in anticipation of the mortal blow. The reasons for this [liquidation of Jewish agents] is probably the following: First of all, the Jewish agents know too much, many "businesses" being partnerships [between the Gestapo and Jews]; the Gestapo are fearful lest the Jewish partner blab to another German, and the Gestapo lose out in a profitable undertaking. Secondly, there are rival Gestapo apparatuses. Every chief, every Gestapo department, has its own Jewish agents. When the Gestapo chiefs quarrel, each kills the other's agents. Each of the three big Jewish operators mentioned above represents a rival Gestapo apparatus. Incidentally, Kohn and Heller refer to Gancwajch as Azef.*

Currently Kohn and Heller are the most influential, which is why Gancwajch and Ehrlich, the agents of the rival Gestapo apparatus, were caught on that calamitous Friday. Ehrlich's partner Gurman (nicknamed "Young") was shot, as well as Gancwajch's close friends, shot the same night in the notorious night club Arizona, at 18 Mila Street. Before that, the well-known Gestapo agent Milek Tine was shot

* Azef achieved notoriety in Russia at the beginning of the twentieth century for being simultaneously the leader of the terrorist Social Revolutionary Party and a police spy.

(there was a legend on the wall near his body that read: *Psu, psia smierc, zdech Milek Tine* [Milek Tine was a dog, and a dog's death he died]. The same thing happened to Anders. Now in prison are the Gestapo agents Swieca and Esterowicz, who were the first to inform the Gestapo about the illegal Jewish organizations and publications. It is reported that they were shot in the Pawia Street prison ten days ago, i.e., about May 8.

At this point, it may be in order to take up the question as to whether we have more Gestapo agents than other groups [under the Nazi heel]. There are said to be about four hundred informers. But my private opinion is that the activity in the Ghetto of hundreds of illegal operations—dairies, flour warehouses, bakeries, factories, transactions in leather and anything that's illegal—all this illegal activity could not be possible if there were that many informers. Consequently, we probably do not have more informers than any other group. For those who have been sent into the Ghetto from Eastern Europe are less fearful of every house porter [generally, in the employ of the police], of every stranger, than are those on the Other Side. My feeling is that the claim that we are more demoralized than other groups is an exaggeration, particularly when you consider the straits we are in, and that we face to a considerable degree the choice between evasion of unjust laws or death from hunger. So let us not make the picture darker than it is—particularly as it is dark enough.

The informer problem, so common in Jewish history, is with us again. Unfortunately, we are afraid to resort to terrorism, lest the Occupying Forces take a bloody revenge. Perhaps the most tragic thing is that a man like Josek Ehrlich (nicknamed "Frockcoat") goes around scot free. He gets special favors from the Food Bureau, intervenes in various Jewish Council offices on behalf of his men, and everybody does whatever he wants—all out of fear that he might inform, or take revenge in some other fashion. Or take a person like Judtowa. Her claim to fame rests on the fact that during World War I she lived with a German officer who is now the commandant of Warsaw. This whore exploited her former friendship to obtain all kinds of concessions and special favors. She had the concession of the Jewish theater and was the co-owner of a couple of theaters. She was given a concession for a bakery, and, beside everything else, received several hundred zlotys from the Social Welfare Department associated with the Council. Then, she was a big shot in various Jewish Council offices, where everybody was afraid of her, apparently because of her work [for the Nazis]. But it turned out that she went too far, and one fine morning Czerniakow sent a memorandom around to all the departments of the Council notifying them that Judtowa's representations were no longer to be accepted. Now she is trying to live off blackmail—e.g., she'll assert that the person she is trying to blackmail is on one police death list or another, and if he won't pay her, she'll call the police.

The beggars crowding the streets nowadays are different from last year's crop. Most of the beggars from the provinces have died out. The newcomers are a better class of people, their breeding being obvious in their faces and manner. They speak a good, sometimes even an excellent Polish:"*Droozy panstwo, jeszcze dzis nic nie jadlem*" ["Ladies and gentlemen, I haven't had a bite to eat today"]. Sometimes one comes across former students from the Institute of Judaic Studies, who ask for help in Hebrew. Some of the beggars are well dressed. If they didn't silently put out their hands, or ask for alms in a low voice, you would never imagine that they were beggars. On Karmelicka Street, near the Evangelical Hospital, stands a beggar whose clothes are impeccable; he has a pretty child with him who is clean and spotless; he begs not with outstretched hand but with his eyes alone. The children constitute the majority of the beggars, despite all the institutions maintained by CENTOS. Whole choirs of children sing in the street to large audiences. In general, groups of musicians giving real concerts in the street to large, appreciative crowds are a common sight.

The thing we were so afraid of during the winter, that it would be impossible to walk through the streets because of the filth, has been luckily avoided. We—the House Committees—got after the janitors, and the pavements were cleaned up, the courtyards, the stairs, and even the apartments themselves. The only trouble is that people have no handkerchiefs, or maybe it's become dearer to wash them, because you see more and more people, even so-called "cultured people," blowing their snot into the street, and then wiping their noses with a handkerchief. Wherever you go, on the steps of houses, in courtyards, and in the streets, you come across traces of snot.

May 30

Last week was a bloody one. Almost every day saw smugglers shot. Particularly around the Small Ghetto, where a policeman who has been dubbed "Frankenstein" is on service. He was given this nickname because he looks and acts like the monster in the film of that name. He's a bloodthirsty dog who kills one or two smugglers every day. He just can't eat his breakfast until he has spilled the blood of a Jew.

Friday night, some eight or nine people were killed, *a la* Friday, the 18th of April. One of them was a man called Wilner (from 11 Mylna Street) who lay sick in bed. He could barely crawl out of bed at the command of the hangmen; he sat down on a chair, unable to move any further. So they threw him out of the second-floor window, together with the chair, shooting after him as he fell. In the same apartment three other men were shot (a brother-in-law of his called Rudnicki, his son, and another person). Reason unknown. Besides, three people from "the Thirteen's" Special Service were shot to death. This is all supposed to be a continuation of the clean-up of "the Thirteen." A few days ago, all Jews were informed via the House Committees that Gancwajch, Szternfeld, and both brothers Zachariajch were sought by the security police. Anyone found guilty of concealing them would be held fully responsible—together with all the residents of the house where he lived. Those shot to death yesterday (29th of May) include the notorious Judtowa.

Yesterday also saw a big raid in the streets. People were picked up to work, ostensibly in labor camps, but actually in the German Todt* organization at Bobruisk. The wagons were set aside for workers from there. Of course, it was the poor people, who didn't have the money to bribe the police, who went. The price was 5–10 zlotys, if you paid when you were picked up on the street. By the time you reached the district assembly point, the price had gone up to 100 zlotys. At the central assembly point, it was 500 zlotys. It was terrible in the street. Thousands of people stood about at the central assembly point on 19 Zamenhofa Street with packages for those who had been pressed for service. A medical commission examined those who had been picked up and on the spot decided who was to go to work.

* The Todt was a German military organization that did heavy construction work, such as laying railroad tracks, using conscripted native labor.

Relief doesn't solve the problem; it only keeps people going a little longer. But they have to die in the end anyway. Relief only lengthens the period of suffering, but is no solution; for in order really to accomplish anything, the relief organization would have to have millions of zlotys a month at its disposal —and it has no such sums. The well-established fact is that the people who are fed in the public kitchens are all dying out, subsisting as they do only on soup and dry rationed bread. So the question arises whether it might not be more rational to set aside the money that is available for the sole use of certain select individuals, those who are socially productive, the intellectual élite, and the like. However, the situation is that, in the first place, the élite themselves constitute a considerable group and there wouldn't be enough to go around even for them; and, in the second place, why should laborers and artisans, perfectly deserving people, who were productive in their home towns, and whom only the war and the Ghetto existence have deprived of their productive capacity—why should they be judged worthless, the dregs of society, candidates for mass graves? One is left with the tragic dilemma: What are we to do? Are we to dole out spoonfuls to everyone, the result being that no one will survive? Or are we to give full measure to a few—with only a handful having enough to survive?

Another factor contributes to the failure of relief to solve the situation. Auerswald, the commissar in charge of the Ghetto of Warsaw, has recently taken to mixing in the internal affairs of the Ghetto. He regards the refugees as nothing more than sere leaves, bound to fall from the tree sooner or latter; he maintains that such people must not be supported by public funds. His general position is that only those who work should receive community help. He keeps diminishing the number of items of produce available for relief and is responsible for the fact that soups have recently been limited to three times a week; at the same time, the price of lunch had to be raised from 70 to 90 groschen.

Still another element in the Ghetto is opposed to relief for adults—Abraham Gepner, the president of the former Merchants' Association. Now he's responsible for food supply, and in this role can dispose of significant sums of money. Gepner is a fine man, but a capricious one. His is a dictatorial nature, one which can suffer no opposition toward either his person or his opinions. The policies of Gepner's Food Supply Agency are scandalous and deserve special treatment. But Gepner, who is now childless (his children have left the country), pours out all his fatherly feelings on other children. He has become the great patron of children in the Ghetto—not of all children, however, but only of those who are lucky enough to be sheltered in the home whose patronage he has taken over. These children live, literally, in luxury—all the others may perish. His children are provided with the best of clothing, shoes, entertainment—on the other hand, the children in the refugee centers haven't the barest necessities. They die from hunger under squalid conditions. "Our children must live" is Gepner's slogan; but "our children" means only the children of his homes. Gepner is one-sided; he places every means of the FSA at the disposal of the children—though their parents may die. It does not matter if there isn't enough money for soup for the grownups—so long as everything goes to the children. He forgets that, in the best interest of the children themselves, we must see to it first and foremost that the parents live, for the worst parents are better than the best home. Certainly the children should be given priority when it comes to relief. But this can't mean the kind of travesty that's common in the Ghetto nowadays, when Gepner's satellites, who make fortunes at the expense of the common man through the FSA, curry favor with Gepner by contributing a couple of thousand zlotys to *his* homes. It's self-evident that when everything is run according to the caprice of an old gentleman, there can't be any normal relief. Let me mention still another illustration of Gepner's one-sidedness and capriciousness. Gepner, that fine and noble gentleman, who impresses many people with his civic-mindedness, his proud bearing, is typically upper middle class when it comes to taxes. He maintains that everybody must be taxed equally, so he levies taxes on ration cards for bread, sugar, and honey. However, he is categorically opposed to forcing those manufacturers and merchants who are doing wonderful business now, even better than before the war, to pay larger taxes than the rest. To apply sanctions to such people, to take them out of their beds at night and drag them off to work in the refugee centers—he regards this as an unwarranted limitation of personal freedom. Those who apply such sanctions are modern-day Robespierres, terrorists. Gepner's is a typical attitude of the Jewish Councilmen.

The children's Lag b'Omer celebrations were very impressive this year. A large children's program was presented in the big Femina Theater hall. Children from all the schools performed. They were rewarded with sweets. Procession after procession of school children marched through the streets toward the Femina.

The Toporol* has introduced a good practice. All the available free space has been distributed, each individual getting a ticket entitling him to use of a certain area.

The 12th of May, there was a big raid on the Poles at

* Voluntary Ghetto institution that planted vegetables, gardens, trees, and made small parks in an attempt to improve the health conditions in the crowded Ghetto.

Kercelak Street [on the Other Side] and the surrounding market places. A large amount of manufactured goods was confiscated, [especially] leather, and thousands of Poles were seized for forced labor. The Jews lost a substantial sum through the raid, because most of the merchandise confiscated consisted of things that the Jews had given Christians on commission to sell on the Other Side.

The German Jews, deported here from Hanover, Berlin, etc., have brought a number of jokes with them. One of them is that they explain the emblem *Jude* [Jew] that they have to wear on their chest as being the initials of the words: *Italiens Und Deutschlands Ende* [The end of Italy and Germany]. Despite all they went through in Germany, they still talk about *"unser Fuehrer"* ["our leader Hitler"] and still believe in German victory. They are certain, despite everything, that they will return to Germany. Although it has been some time since they came to Warsaw (more than a month), they are still kept separate from the rest of the Jews. They live outside the Ghetto in special quarantine quarters. Some three hundred of them work in various outside work details. They have to wear the *Jude* emblem even when they secure permission to live in the Ghetto. The first thing they touched upon was the question of work. They were all working in Germany. The old folks can't get used to the new situation. The result is they're dying in large numbers. They're treated much better than the other refugees. There simply is no comparison between the way the Jewish Council treats the Polish refugees and its attitude to the German Jews. The latter get a quarter of a kilo of bread, soup, coffee [daily]. True, that's much worse than what they got in Germany, but compared with the usual conditions in the Ghetto, it's paradise. Demoralization is spreading rapidly through the Ghetto. While the poor become ever poorer and dress in rags, the girls are dressing up as though the war were nonexistent. There have been many cases of girls stealing from their parents, taking things from home to sell or barter for ornaments, or a hair wave—in a word, for luxury items.

In April or March Jews were forbidden to use German marks that bore the likeness of H. [Hitler]. Apparently they're afraid Jews might give him the Evil Eye!

Jonas Turkow acted this season in a Polish repertoire. The reason: There are no good plays in Yiddish. Besides, this is evidence of the marked assimilation so discernible in the Ghetto. The Jews love to speak Polish. There is very little Yiddish heard in the streets. We have had some heated discussions on this question. One explanation advanced is that speaking Polish is a psychological protest against the Ghetto —*you* have thrown us into a Jewish Ghetto, but *we'll* show you that it really is a Polish street. To spite you, we'll hold on to the very thing you are trying to separate us from—the Polish language and the culture it represents. But my personal opinion is that what we see in the Ghetto today is only a continuation of the powerful linguistic assimilation that was marked even before the war and has become more noticeable in the Ghetto. So long as Warsaw was mixed, with Jews and Poles living side by side, one did not notice it so acutely; but now that the streets are completely Jewish, the extent of this calamity forces itself upon one's attention.

25/JUNE, 1942

Collective responsibility is the principle the Occupying Power practices at every step. And the same principle has been adopted by public services, such as the gas and electricity companies. If a tenant doesn't pay his gas bill, the rest of the tenants in the house have to pay it. Otherwise, the gas is shut off—not in the apartment concerned, but throughout the whole house. Willy-nilly, the House Committee has to get busy collecting the hundreds of zlotys sometimes needed to pay the bill.

The German attitude to the Jews is best illustrated by this folk tale: Once there was a landed gentleman who was living high. He kept borrowing money on interest from his banker Shlomo, until finally the Jew collected his debts by auctioning off the gentry's property. Foaming at the lips, the impoverished nobleman cursed the Jew who had made him poor. In revenge, he called his dog "Shlomo" and beat it. The same thing, people say, is happening to the Germans. They are being defeated, their cities are being destroyed,* so they take

* On the night of May 30–31, 1942, the British R.A.F. made its first 1,000-bomber raid on Cologne. Other targets in Germany during May included Stuttgart, Warnemunde, and Mannheim. At the beginning of June, the R.A.F. carried out two 1,000-bomber raids on Essen and the Ruhr.

their revenge on the Jews by beating them three times a day.

A small group of people discussed the question of what would be the best thing to do if it were possible to send somebody from the Ghetto out into the world. Everybody agreed that the most important thing was to arouse the world to the horror of the organized extermination we are now suffering. There was no point in even considering the question as to whether or not this would worsen our condition. We have nothing to lose. The extermination is being executed according to a plan and schedule prepared in advance. Only a miracle can save us: the sudden end of the war. Otherwise, we are lost. Ought we to demand retribution? Some of the company held we ought. The several score thousand Germans in America ought to be collected and locked up in concentration camps—stick them behind barbed wire, put them on a diet of water, and let them perish of hunger (that's what is happening to us in Poland). Others of the company held that, if we were to demand retribution, this would incite the Germans even further, and lead to the complete extermination of the Jews. Another question the company discussed was whether it was right to send abroad a list of important persons so they could get visas and be rescued. Some of the company argued that the élite ought to remain with the common people and perish with them. A few people, on the other hand, referred to Jewish history and tradition, which calls for saving even one soul in Israel—all being equally precious. The consensus was that each special group ought to try to save its own important individuals, but that the group as a whole should make no such attempt. Another point emphasized was that the German people must be told about the plan to exterminate the Jewish population, because, though H. [Hitler] promised on several occasions to exterminate the Jewish people, they're doing everything in the world now to keep the Germans from finding out what is happening to the Jews. At the beginning, thousands of Jews were shot in the middle of the city, or right outside it; but lately, They're following this plan: The "non-productive elements," children up to the age of ten and old people over sixty, are locked in sealed railroad cars, which are guarded by a German detail and transported to an unknown destination. Generally, the transport goes toward Belzec, where every trace of the "resettled" Jews disappears. The fact that no one has so far succeeded in escaping from the death camp in Belzec, that up till now not a single Jewish or Polish witness of the extermination operation in Belzec has survived, is the clearest indication of how careful They are that the news not be published among their own people. Proving that if the German populace knew about it, They would probably not be able to execute the mass murder.

The malevolence of the Polish tax officials is indescribable. What they engage in is robbery, pure and simple. Their standard procedure is to enter a shop whose proprietor owes taxes, detain all the customers, search them, and take away all the ready cash they can find, *on account, for future taxes*. That is what happened the other week, and it's the usual practice. If a subtenant can't pay his tax, it's collected from the tenant, and vice versa. The Polish police behave the same way. Robbers, that's all. A policeman need only see a wagon of merchandise to become partners with the merchant. At the very least, he demands a huge sum of money, and his demand must be met, or he takes away the merchandise. Recently, they've been arresting Jews in the police stations (the one on Niska Street, for example) for no rhyme or reason. The police demand hundreds of zlotys to release these innocent prisoners.

The night of June 10, 1942, will be writ large, in bloody letters, in the history of the Warsaw Ghetto. Apparently, there was a decision to liquidate the smuggling of goods over the

Wall through mass terror, mass slaughter, at any cost. Dozens of smugglers were liquidated that night, in the usual way: They were hauled out of their apartments and shot to death in the street. Other smugglers were slaughtered at the Wall during the night and in the early morning hours. Frankenstein, disguised as a Jew, wearing a Jewish arm band, shot several Jews with a machine gun he had hidden in a sack. The same thing happened in the Small Ghetto, at Krochmalna and Czepla Streets. It would seem that the general plan is to exterminate the Jews in the larger cities of Poland through a policy of systematic starvation. This is being accomplished in Lodz; now it is also starting in Warsaw. By putting a halt to smuggling, They are forcing the Jewish populace to subsist on 7.5 dekos of bread daily. Incidentally, there was continued shooting at smugglers from hidden points on roof tops by camouflaged Germans, yesterday and early today. But the horde of smugglers don't panic at bullets. One of the smugglers told a friend that he would keep on smuggling, because if he didn't, he would starve to death. Rather die fast from a bullet than slow from hunger.

New reports are continually arriving about the program of systematic extermination of Jewish children and old people. The same thing that happened in the provinces is now going on in Biala Podloska, where sixty wagons of children under ten and old folks over sixty disappeared. Clearly, there's no camp involved, but simply annihilation of the very young and the very old. Jews who can't work to suit the German purpose are not needed. They are the first to be exterminated. Except for Pharaoh, who ordered the newborn Hebrew babes thrown into the river Nile, this is unprecedented in Jewish history. On the contrary: In the past, whatever was done with the grownups, the children were always permitted to live—so that they might be converted to the Christian faith. Even in the most barbaric times, a human spark glowed in the rudest heart, and children were spared. But the Hitlerian beast is quite different. It would devour the dearest of us, those who arouse the greatest compassion—our innocent children.

The historian of the future will have to devote a fitting chapter to the role of the Jewish woman during the war. It is thanks to the courage and endurance of our women that thousands of families have been able to endure these bitter times. Recently, there has been an interesting development: In some House Committees women are coming forward to replace the men, who fall out exhausted. There are some House Committees whose entire direction is in the hands of women. Relief particularly needs fresh, not worn-out personnel; it is very important there to have a strong reserve.

The Germans keep coming to the graveyard. Recently, there was a group of soldiers visiting. One of them wept, and said to a comrade: "The Fuehrer should see this!"

In the Ghetto (as well as outside it) Jewish physicians and professors are conducting scientific investigations. One of the most interesting subjects is hunger. Interesting, because it is the most widespread disease in the Ghetto and there's a simple remedy for it—just let the Germans leave Poland!

Here is something that happened during the filming of the Ghetto. A woman who was dragged to the Pawia Street prison from the famous ritual bathhouse at 38 Dzielna Street screamed and would on no account permit herself to be undressed. The soldier who was struggling with her gave her a blow and threw her out. But there was a Jewish policeman in the next room, and he demanded that she give him 50 zlotys for permission to leave, although the soldier had let her go. All the woman had was 30 zlotys. An argument broke out, which the soldier overheard. He opened the door and saw the woman still there, gave her a good beating, and threw her out of the room. There's another illustration of the fearful Ghetto anarchy and corruption. . . . One of the outside work details is the Powzki graveyard, where 700 Jewish workers, among other things, dig graves for German soldiers who have died in hospitals. A great many Jews would report for that work, if they had the chance—they would even pay for the pleasure.

Friday, June 26, has been a great day for O.S.* This morning, the English radio broadcast about the fate of Polish Jewry. They told about everything we know so well: about Slonim and Vilna, Lemberg and Chelmno, and so forth. For long months we had been suffering because the world was deaf and dumb to our unparalleled tragedy. We complained about Polish public opinion, about the liaison men in contact with the Polish government-in-exile. Why weren't they reporting to the world the story of the slaughter of Polish Jewry? We accused the Polish liaison men of deliberately keeping our tragedy quiet, so that *their* tragedy might not be thrown into the shade. But now it seems that all our interventions have finally achieved their purpose. There have been regular broadcasts over the English radio the last few weeks, treating of the cruelties perpetrated on the Polish Jews: Belzec and the like. Today there was a broadcast summarizing the situation: 700,000, the number of Jews killed in Poland, was mentioned. At the same time, the broadcast vowed revenge, a final accounting for all these deeds of violence.

The O.S. group has fulfilled a great historical mission. It has alarmed the world to our fate, and perhaps saved hundreds of thousands of Polish Jews from extermination. (Naturally, only the immediate future will prove whether or not this last is true.) I do not know who of our group will survive, who will be deemed worthy to work through our collected material. But one thing is clear to all of us. Our toils and tribulations, our devotion and constant terror, have not been in vain. We have struck the enemy a hard blow. It is not impor-

* *See* Introduction.

tant whether or not the revelation of the incredible slaughter of Jews will have the desired effect—whether or not the methodical liquidation of entire Jewish communities will stop. One thing we know—we have fulfilled our duty. We have overcome every obstacle to achieve our end. Nor will our deaths be meaningless, like the deaths of tens of thousands of Jews. We have struck the enemy a hard blow. We have revealed his Satanic plan to annihilate Polish Jewry, a plan he wished to complete in silence. We have run a line through his calculations and have exposed his cards. And if England keeps its word and turns to the formidable massive attacks that it has threatened—then perhaps we shall be saved. . . .

The last few days the Jewish populace has been agitated by the broadcast from London. The news that the world has finally been deeply stirred by the account of the massacres taking place in Poland has shaken us all to the very depths. For long, long months, we tormented ourselves in the midst of our suffering with the questions: Does the world know about our suffering? And if it knows, why is it silent? Why is the world not stirred when tens of thousands of Jews are shot in Fonari? Why is the world silent when tens of thousands of Jews are poisoned in Chelmno? Why is the world silent when hundreds of thousands of Jews are massacred in Galicia and other newly occupied areas? Having posed the questions, we answered them ourselves: Why should the world be shaken by the massacre in Vilna when the Germans slaughtered 180,000 in Rostov, a similar number of Ukrainians and Jews in Kiev? Why should the world be shaken by our suffering when rivers of blood are spilled daily on every battlefield? In what respect is our Jewish blood more precious than that of the Russian, Chinese, English soldiers? That is the classic answer; but we felt it did not suffice. Now for the first time we understood why they kept silent. London simply didn't know what was happening in detail; hence the silence. But another question [suggests itself]: Having their own radio station, how could the Polish government-in-exile not have known what was happening? Why did they know in London the very next day about 100 persons—political prisoners—executed in the Pawia Street jail, but months passed before London found out about the hundreds of thousands of murdered Jews? This is really a problem that no solution can satisfy.

The news that the interpellation of the Polish government-in-exile was radioed by all the British transmitters in all the languages of the United Nations, and several times in German, on Saturday (among others, by the German women's broadcaster)—and then the speeches delivered by the Archbishop of Canterbury, the Rev. Dr. Hertz,* the deputy Zygelbojm†— all this news excited Jewish public opinion in Warsaw. There was joy, mingled with fear as to how the Occupying Power would reply. The general feeling was that it was good for the world to know all about everything. Perhaps a way would be found of forcing the Occupying Power to stop the massacres. Zygelbojm's stand and speeches were cited for their talk about retributory acts of repression against Germans in America. . . . Let them [the United Nations] use force to stop the massacres in Poland. Another opinion held that the Allies, particularly democratic America, could not massacre Germans [in retribution], first, because they are American citizens, and second, because public opinion would not countenance it. But everyone held that it was most important for Germans to know about the extermination. Everyone in a position to meet Germans was aware that the Germans knew

* Joseph Hertz, Chief Rabbi of the British Empire.
† Artur Zygelbojm, representing the Jewish Socialist Bund in the Polish parliament, or Sejm.

nothing about the killings and massacres performed by special murder squads outside the cities or in murder camps such as that of Belzec. The Occupying Power is fearful lest the German populace, even the German soldiers, find out about the massacre of Jews, so it takes pains to see to it that the killings are secret. They use the Jews to bury their murdered brethren—in the end the gravediggers themselves are murdered. If the outside world contents itself with speeches and threats, perhaps the fear of German public opinion will save us. Individual Germans who found out about the Chelmno affair cried in agitation: "We'll pay for this with our necks—and our wives and children, too. They'll take bloody revenge on us for this!" . . . It's expected that the excitement in London and throughout the world will have some effect on the attitude of the Polish populace toward the Jews. . . . Meanwhile, the German press and radio are holding their tongue. What *can* they do? Confirming the news means alarming their own people; denying it means admitting that all their promises of putting an end to the Jews were mere words. People in the Warsaw Ghetto are awaiting the reaction of the German government with great interest, and laying great hopes on it. There are people who believe that the Germans will be afraid to perpetrate any new massacres from now on. Evidence is cited of Jews supposed to have been deported from Ostrowiec in sealed wagons being set free. If this is confirmed, it is really the beginning of a new era. The more sober among us, however, warn against having any illusions. No compassion can be expected from the Germans. Whether we live or die depends on how much time they have. If they have enough time, we are lost. If salvation comes soon, we are saved.

What are people reading? This is a subject of general interest; after the war, it will intrigue the world. What, the world will ask, did people think of on Musa Dagh or in the Warsaw Ghetto—people who knew for a certainty that death would no more skip over them than it had over the other large Jewish settlements and the small towns. Let it be said that though we have been sentenced to death and know it, we have not lost our human features; our minds are as active as they were before the war. The serious Jewish reader is fascinated by war writings. Lloyd George's memoirs are much read, novels from different countries dealing with the First World War, and the like. People particularly enjoy descriptions of the year 1918 and the downfall of the Germans. They attempt to draw analogies between 1918 and the present, looking for signs and omens to demonstrate that the defeat of the so-far-unconquerable German army is at hand. People delight in reading about the reception of the German armistice delegation at Compiègne. In fantasy, people see a new, more drastic Compiègne. I happened to read the great work by Maxence Van der Meersch, *Invasion: 1914,* the tale of German invasion of France and Belgium during the First World War. Every stage of that occupation simply begged for comparison with the present, far crueler war. But one thing was common to both wars: the cold, merciless pillage, robbing the civilian population of the occupied countries of all their possessions. One gathers from the very strong pages of Van der Meersch's novel that the previous world wars were total wars, exactly like the one we are in now. The occupied countries were completely devastated, their population enslaved and forced to work for the Germans. Having read this book through, one asks: "But what was done to avoid a new Hun mastery of Europe?"

There are people who relish reading about Napoleon. They draw parallels between the Cursed One [Hitler] and Napoleon—always to the latter's benefit. For, while there were rivers of blood spilled on every battlefield of Europe on Napoleon's conscience, he overturned the feudal world and introduced a new, revolutionary order. Whereas, after the Cursed One, nothing will remain but tens of millions of victims in every country of the world, and a Europe that, leveled and ravaged, will have been thrown back centuries by the war.

People love to read about Napoleon because his story proves that the star of the dictator, the so-called "invincible" man, fades inevitably, and much faster than anyone could ever imagine. The readers delight in the account of the march on Moscow, with its tragic culmination, that was to prove the beginning of Napoleon's end. Reading in the winter here about the severities of the Russian winter, we hope that history will again repeat itself and the end will be the downfall of the Cursed One. The winter this year (1942) did not conclude, as the winter of 1812 did, with the catastrophic defeat of a tyrant. But it is certain that H., like Napoleon, has committed the mortal blunder of tangling with the Russian colossus, with its enormous reserves of manpower and material. Tolstoy's *War and Peace* is enormously popular nowadays. Many people who had already read it several times are reading it all over again because of its portrayal of the Napoleonic disaster.

In a word, being unable to take revenge on the enemy in reality, we are seeking it in fantasy, in literature. This explains our preoccupation with books about previous wars, which we turn to for a solution to the tragic problems of the present war. To my mind, however, all this search for historical analogy is beside the point. History *does not* repeat itself. Especially now, now that we stand at the crossroads, witnessing the death pangs of an old world and the birth pangs of a new. How can our age be compared with any earlier one? Is there any comparison between the White Terror of the feudal world and the slaughter of Kiev, or Rostov, where hundreds of thousands of civilians were murdered? Hitler would physically extirpate millions of people, simply because they refuse to recognize his New Order in Europe. What is needed is a special research project to investigate the similarities and differences between the wars at the end of the feudal world and the end of the capitalistic one. But one thing is clear: A simple comparison of the two periods is impossible. They are two completely different periods, with other concepts entirely.

The bombardment of Cologne evoked great joy among the populace. In the first place, it was regarded as the beginning of a new English strategy. The English had seemed to be asleep. It was considered the beginning of a new period, almost the beginning of a Second Front in Europe—especially as the bombing was accompanied by a barrage of English propaganda, the threat to annihilate systematically all the industrial cities of Germany. However, the Jewish jubilation was quite different from the general one. Day in, day out, in hundreds of cities throughout Poland and Russia, thousands upon thousands of Jews are being systematically murdered according to a preconceived plan, and no one seems to take our part. The bombing of Cologne, the destruction of thousands of buildings, the thousands of civilian victims, have slaked our thirst for revenge somewhat. Cologne was an advance payment on the vengeance that must and shall be taken on Hitler's Germany for the millions of Jews they have killed. So the Jewish population of tortured Europe considered Cologne its personal act of vengeance. After the Cologne affair, I walked around in a good mood, feeling that, even if I should perish at their hands, my death is prepaid!

A new Jewish police squad, appropriately named the Border Patrol—after the former infamous Polish Border Patrol—is now being formed. Its duty will be to patrol the Ghetto walls, to prevent smuggling. They've already begun painting huge white numbers on the Ghetto walls (every 50 meters). Each policeman is to have a numbered area to patrol, and they are to be paid at a special rate—10 zlotys a day, and a larger quota of bread and other produce.

Lejkin, the captain of the Jewish police, called the force together and appealed for volunteers. However, since only a small number volunteered, policemen were assigned the dangerous job (every policeman will be responsible for the smuggling in his numbered area). It's the devil's own plan, this attempt to use the Jews themselves to starve the Ghetto to death. For the rest, this isn't the first time that the Occupying Power has compelled the Jewish populace to dig its own grave. They do it at every step. It is very painful to have to admit that the Others always find people to do the dirty work with relish, sometimes even with exaggerated zeal.

The German soldiers' willful treatment of the Jews is beyond description. As an illustration, let me tell you something that happened a week ago. An officer and a common soldier came to a Jewish mechanic and demanded an air pump and a new tire. The Jew explained he had none; they searched his shop and couldn't find any, but they took him away anyhow and insisted that he take them to another mechanic, threatening to shoot him afterward. They could not find what they wanted at the second shop, either, so they all went to a third shop. A whole cavalade of mechanics following in the wake of the officer and the common soldier were threatened with execution. Luckily, the Germans changed their minds at the last minute, and the Jews were saved.—There was a project to have the Jews in the Government General of Poland wear yellow badges instead of arm bands. Czerniakow advised a representative of the authorities not to do this for economic reasons. Too much wool would have to be used. Malnutrition has become a widespread disease. In the Lodz Ghetto a famous doctor from Prague has discovered a good antidote to swelling [of the belly] caused by malnutrition. It's really a simple remedy—eat potatoes. But where are they to be gotten, when a kilo of potatoes costs only (!) 4 zlotys a kilo? The rumor about Judtowa's death unfortunately turned out to be unfounded.

THE GHETTO BREAKS | UP

The end came with tremendous speed. By September, 1942, the Ghetto had been in existence almost two years. But in the last two months of that period, it lost more than three-fourths of its inhabitants.

On July 22, 1942, the Jewish Council published a German notice to the Ghetto that all but a necessary few were to be deported "to the East," regardless of age or sex. Only Jews working in German industries or employees of the Jewish Council were exempt. There was a mad rush for jobs in German factories. The scenes at the Umschlagplatz, where people were assembled for deportation by train, were frightful. The Jewish police played a particularly nasty role, in their eagerness to please the Germans and save their own lives. But on Yom Kippur, September 26, 1942, 2,000 of the Jewish police were themselves deported with their families. The same day the Ghetto's area was cut in half.

At the end of 1942, when the Notes from the Warsaw Ghetto *concludes, there were only 40,000 Jews left in the Ghetto, working for the German factories. (There had been almost half a million in 1941.) They lived shadow existences—slaves, Ringelblum calls them. His description of these slaves, in a fragmentary, elliptic style reflecting the quick gasps of their shuddering lives, is a powerful one. The sobriety with which he relates the ingenious—but unavailing—attempts at conceal-ment is overwhelming in its understatement.*

But though it seemed probable that those pathetic phan-toms left in the Ghetto would die like slaves, there were clear signs that there were some who had finally decided that they must resist—knowing the resistance must fail. Ringelblum was himself one of them, and his report of the mood of those who were preparing to resist was his own. He took part in the up-rising—after seeing to it in March, 1943, that the archives of the Oneg Sabbath group which bore his name as well were buried for future generations to discover—and his Notes with them.

26/JULY–DECEMBER, 1942

THEY ESCAPED FROM THE WAGONS!

Those who had experience.

Young men.

One [young man] escaped two times—organized eight "springers"—people who escaped extermination in Oswiecim by springing out of the railroad wagons taking them there.

RESISTANCE

The Jew from the Small Ghetto—who grabbed a German by the throat. The Other was shot—went berserk and shot thirteen Jews in the courtyard (Panska or Twarda Street).—The Jew from Nalewki Street who tore a rifle out of a Ukrainian guard's hand, and fled.

The role the youth played—the only ones who remained on the battlefield [were the] romantic phantasiasts—Samuel —couldn't survive the tragedy of the Ghetto—the decisions by the [various] factions involved in the resistance—the attempt at [setting the Ghetto on] fire—the [resisters'] appeals of the 6th of September for the populace to resist deportation regarded [in the Ghetto] as [Nazi] provocation. Attempt to assassinate Szerynski.*

The group of porters who had lost their families and dreamed of revenge—[the people who] offered money to avoid deportation—the idea of using coal gas in defense against the Jewish police—partisans—diversionary acts.

WHY? *Oct. 15*

Why didn't we resist when they began to resettle 300,000 Jews from Warsaw? Why did we allow ourselves to be led like sheep to the slaughter? Why did everything come so easy to the enemy? Why didn't the hangmen suffer a single casualty? Why could 50 S.S. men (some people say even fewer), with the help of a division of some 200 Ukrainian guards and an equal number of Letts, carry the operation out so smoothly?

The shops as traps—They took the best specialists away—"a couple of porters" laughed—they were taken away—the professionals were taken away, They looked at their hands, *clean palms.* Office employees taken away . . . only wearing work clothes—wearing slippers. Accompanied on the way [to the Umschlagplatz] by Ukrainians—they kept shooting.

Selection for deportation in the street among whole blocks —at first, on the basis of working papers, later on the basis of appearance (people dyed their gray hair).

They shaved off all the beards—tore off all the frock coats, ear locks. The street dead all day, except for after the barricade† and from five in the morning to seven—the movement from one street to another, where there had already been a barricade. But the Others kept barricading the same neigh-

---

* Head of the Jewish police in the Ghetto.

† Streets were barricaded to prevent any Jew from escaping the selection for deportation.

borhood day after day.—The Jewish agents informed the Others about the populace's mood, about the hideout methods.

The role the shop owners played in the barricades—their cooperation with the S.S.—how they fooled people, for example, [the shop owner] Toebbens at 65 Niska Street. He said he wanted to avoid a barricade, so he took away all the workers' laundry.

Jewish [work] directors helped catch the illegals,* for example at Hallman's shop.

THE UMSCHLAGPLATZ—WHAT IT LOOKED LIKE

The heroic nurses—the only ones who saved people from deportation without [asking for] money. Szmerling†—the hangman with the whip.

The scenes when the wagons were loaded—the industrious- ness of the Jewish police—the tearing of parents from their children, wives from their husbands, Rabbi Kanal, Lubliner.

The shooting on the spot of those who tried to escape through holes in the Wall at night—the exemption of people who pretended to be doctors. Nurses' headkerchiefs saved hundreds of professionals, employees of the Jewish Council.

The Great Pursuit—Szmerling currying the Others' favor.

More than once he tore the badges off policemen who had saved Jews from the Umschlag.

Faithful executor of Their orders—introduced a check of the nurses because they allowed people to escape without paying money.

Great grafter—took more than 100 zlotys per head. Most of those who were exempted—bought off the watch at the gate.—The police made enormous sums.

* Those who had no work permits.
† Commanding the Jewish police at the Umschlagplatz.

["The Thirteen"] Special Service made a lot of money exempting people too; com.[munity] institutions set up a fund to save the professionals.

The tragedy of those seized two, three, and five times—the mother who wouldn't go without her child—the husband who wouldn't go without his wife, etc.—and afterward they all went in the same wagon—hundreds of families went to the Umschlag together because of the children.

Because the quota wasn't met, the Germans seized people on the street, drove them directly into the wagons, not to the Umschlag but straight into the wagons—12,000 killed during the resettlement.

THE POT ON NISKA STREET

The 6th of September—the cruelty. In the middle of the night Lejkin was instructed to have all the Jews in the quadrangle bounded on one side by Gesia, on another by Smocza, on a third by Niska, and on the fourth by Zamenhofa to select [deportees] and round up illegals—Massacre of 25,000 people, perhaps even more. Of the barracks that were emptied out (everyone ordered out of the barracks) two or three houses set aside for each shop, most of them in the country—some shops' [workers] got back into their apartments that day— others not till the next day, or the day after.

"Ah, but we had a fine pot!" said Witasek, who directed the resettlement operation.

The tens of thousands who remained on Niska Street—the continual slaughtering—seventy people killed in one apartment on Wolynska Street—in two days, 1,000 people killed, taken to the graveyard—hundreds killed in the street during the selections, all forced to kneel on the pavement [to be killed.]

Hundreds and thousands of people lay in their hiding places

all week, without water (a water main burst), without food.

Hoffman's shop consists of two industries. One is reworking old things collected in Germany. The things are washed, mended, and then sent back.

Illegals. "Illegals" are those people who do not have [work card] numbers, people who, according to the law, should have been on the Umschlagplatz, and yet are still alive. How many there are of this kind nobody knows. There are various estimates. Many people place the number of illegals at 7,000, others estimate 10,000 and even 15,000. The fact is, they *are!*

Who are they? A large number are members of the family of "legal persons"—mostly the police, Jewish Council officials, etc.

The illegals also consist of officials of the Council, or of the YYGA, who were let go, but did not go to the Umschlagplatz; instead they went into hiding, and now they huddle close to their former colleagues for protection.

And then there is a third category—"everyday Jews," who simply hid out and are still in hiding. They pay off the Work Guard and live at home. Many of the illegals are people who worked in shops that were given up, who managed to save themselves from the Umschlagplatz. Shops of this kind were Hans Miller's, where many Jewish artists, actors, and others perished. There are houses, such as 35, 37, 41, etc., Nalewki Street, which are entirely occupied by hundreds of illegals.

The problem of offering relief to the illegals is becoming daily more pressing. The ex-officials among them receive a ration of soup and bread.

Yom Kippur, Sept. 22

The day there was a selection in the shops.—The slaughter of women, children, illegals.

The practice of torturing Jews in the cities on Yom Kippur.

The barricade of the German and Jewish householders— selection supposedly on the basis of craft,* actually on the basis of graft—the "good Germans" turned bad, e.g., Toebbens.

HOW THE SELECTION TOOK PLACE

In the Jewish Council, around 3,000 employees,† elsewhere [in other community institutions] entire departments were sent to the Umschlag.—At Hallmans' [shop] 700 were numbered off and [exempted] on the spot; the remaining thirty carpenters with their wives and children were taken away.— At the brush factory, 1,200 were numbered off [and exempted], the rest sent away, mechanically, including the shop where the *chalutzim* worked, valuable human material, the young.

Thousands of people who had managed to save their lives all the time by staying in their hiding places went to the Niska [quadrangle], because they believed they would be leaving the Ghetto for good.

The goal [of the Niska Pot]: to get the secret Jews—the ones in hiding—to come out. [It] succeeded. Tens of thousands taken in the Niska Pot.

PREHISTORY OF THE RESETTLEMENT

Letter from Lublin [warning about]—Szamek Grayer‡— about 60,000 Jews [to be left] in Warsaw, about a work Ghetto [to be set up in Warsaw]—letter from Wlodawa about the

---

* Handicraftsmen were supposed to be exempt from deportation.

† At one time, the Jewish Council had as many as 5,000 employees.

‡ Jewish Gestapo agent from Lublin sent to Warsaw to help in the extermination.

[sacrificial] "altar" being set up in the Warsaw neighborhood —the rumor about Pelcowizne—Kohn and Heller's warnings —the S.S. threat to stifle bloodily those who spread these rumors. . . .

The arrival of [Oscar] Lotisz*—the readying of special wagons to Treblinki.

HOW THE BLOCKS WERE SET UP

The slaughter at Schultz's [shop]—Nowolipie Street [the site of] the first German barricade—They took thousands of people—gave them half a day to move—the same true at Toebbens'. The activities of the "Jew boys," who proposed such plans, Hallman's humane behavior—negotiated with the House Committees for the gradual yielding of apartments.

THE BLOCKS AS SPECIAL GHETTOS

[With their] own bakeries, drug stores, grocery stores, shoe stores, barbers, even synagogues—separate towns, even to the point of local patriotism—when it came to fund raising.

The hyenas of the shops—workers had to pay money to get into a shop—money for every registration [of the shop's workers].

The work the shops were supposed to do during the barricades—[shops] sprang up quickly, had no orders, had no raw material, [workers] left the factories, except when the Germans came—the same true of the brush factories.

The shops as a means of looking after the workers' families —at first the families were taken to the shops to spend the night there [and avoid being picked up for deportation at home]—hence the idea of blocks—self-contained living and working areas—the slaughter on Nowolipie Street.

* The Lett collaborator, to help in the extermination.

Shameful document cited by the Jewish Council about the rumors that there would be a resettlement [of Jews from the Warsaw Ghetto] to the East.

[At the same time] the Council's work office knew the resettlement meant death.

The suicide of Czerniakow*—too late, a sign of weakness—should have called for resistance—a weak man.

WORK REGULATIONS IN THE SHOPS

Work period in the summer from seven to seven—O.B.W. [East German Woodworks]. The Jewish inclination to sabotage at Schultz's two shops—hard work, little food.—The only way to help yourself is to *shabrir*—i.e., to sell the possessions formerly belonging to people who have been resettled—thefts continuing to this day—commerce [in stolen goods].

Confiscation of [the workers'] possessions in the area of [?] the shops—[on the basis of a] new theory: Everything in the shop belongs to the firm—unwritten constitution.

Passes [required] for anyone living outside the shop limits to take anything out of the shop limits.

Language. Everything changed to German—all signs—the correspondence at Hallman's conducted in German.

Werkschutz (Werkschmutz)†—former policemen—smugglers—underworld characters, etc. Their chief earnings [came from blackmailing] illegals, smuggling, illegal bakeries—Gestapo agent Konrad Toebbens, fictitious shop, took money [from pretended workers] and then sent them to the Umschlag—took away the machines that Jews had set up.

---

* The head of the Jewish Council committed suicide on July 24, 1942, after a visit from two S.S. officers, who demanded that the daily quota of those resettled be raised from 5,000 to 7,000 and eventually to 10,000.

† A pun. The Werkschutz, meaning "work guard" were called Werkschmutz—*schmutz* means "filth" in Yiddish.

1. *Earnings from live merchandise*—from doing business with [work permit] numbers.

The continuous extortion of the shop workers by the German entrepreneurs, in return for the right to live—for example, Hoffman taxes all the well-to-do [workers in his shop]—the same in other shops, [the pretext for the extortion being] so that the German [entrepreneur] would be interested in protecting "his Jews."

2. *Earnings from production*—recently have—it seems—dwindled—therefore. . . .

3. *Earnings from food supply.* Means of subsistence allocated to the workers by the Food Supply Office are sold on the free market.

HEALTH SITUATION IN THE SHOPS

The ambulatory first-aid stations at the brush factories closed—almost all the the apothecaries removed, even from the shops.

APARTMENT HIDING PLACES

The horrible crowding at Schultz's, Toebbens'—better at Hallman's—the management's favoring of their relatives—at Toebbens' eight to ten workers in a room—many apartments at Schultz's without light and gas, because the former owners of the apartments didn't pay their electricity bills. *Apartments without women*—consequently filthy, neglected.

THE DISTANCE BETWEEN THE RESIDENCE BLOCK AND THE PLACE OF WORK

There are a number of shops where the distance is great. It is necessary to get up at 5:30 A.M. to go to work. Walk a long distance, and then at night, about six, walk home again without having had anything warm to eat all day. Turns people into real slaves.

WORKING FOR NOTHING

Everyone has to work for nothing: the workers in the shop, the tailor, the shoemaker, the barber, the doctor, etc.—People live by informing or *"shabriring."*—Since the resettlement, [They] have stopped paying the workers, who used to get starvation wages. The master Dallmann [?] at Hallman's, who used to earn 100 zlotys a day, nowadays pays 30 zlotys a day for food. Jews may not receive any wages, nor can officials from the Jewish Council and other public institutions.

The managers of some of the work shops, inasmuch as they have saved their workers' lives, claim the right to have them work for nothing and insist on the workers' obligation to find their own food. In general, the shop managers regard themselves as philanthropists, who can do whatever they wish, and their workers daren't raise their voices.—They are living a far better life [than they did] before the war, at the expense of the working men, who are robbed in almost every shop. In Hallman's shop, the flour distributed to the shop for feeding the workers is used to bake rolls and doughnuts for the managers and their relatives—and, at the same time, the workers are given bad bread which makes them sick. The managers don't care.

INSECURITY, UNCLARITY OF THE SITUATION

Deadline. The Damocles sword of extermination hangs constantly over the heads of the Warsaw Jews. Their fate is tied to that of the shops. So long as the shops have orders, the Jews have the right to live. But it so happens that not all of the shops have long-term orders. Not long ago (mid-October), Schultz's received orders and raw material [sufficient to last] until April—there was universal rejoicing. People drank toasts, threw parties, and the like. But an early deadline hangs over some of the shops. Included in this category is a shop that is one of the most valuable, socially speaking, the O.B.W. shop, whose deadline ended the 20th of October. Eventually, the deadline was extended another thirty days. Put yourself through an effort of the imagination in the minds of those people whose fate is linked with that of the shops. If the shops go out of existence, *they* lose the right to live. They become people without [work card] numbers, without homes, without food-supply cards.

THE SIGNS OF MODERN SLAVES

1. Numbered and stamped.

2. Live in barracks—without their wives.

3. Wives and children removed, because slaves don't require families.

4. Walk in crowds, not individually.

5. Beaten and terrorized at work.

6. Inhuman exploitation (agreement at Schultz's [?]) like coolies.

7. Ban on organization of any kind.

8. Ban on any form of protest or sign of dissatisfaction.

9. Every slave dependent for his life on his master and the [master's] Jewish assistant. At any moment a man can be sent to the Umschlagplatz.

10. The murderous discipline, and the sending of workers to forced [labor] camps because of lateness as happened at Schultz's.

11. Compulsion to work, even [when worker is sick] with temperature.

12. Worse off than slaves, because *they* must look after their own food.

13. Confiscation of property from a dead worker's family, because the right of inheritance has been abolished.

14. Locked inside the residential block.

15. Ban on leaving your apartment and walking in the street after work hours.

16. Limitation of personal freedom, of movement.

17. *Worse than slaves,* because the latter knew they would remain alive, had some hope to be set free. The Jews are *morituri*—sentenced to death—whose death sentence [has been] postponed indefinitely, or has been passed.

18. The sick and the weak are not needed, so ambulatory clinics, hospitals, and the like have been liquidated.

COMMUNICATION

Every shop is a unit in itself; by the decree of [the 29th of] October, one may not leave the shop's bounds. This is true of the Ghetto, too. Persons caught in the street without a pass are sent to the Umschlagplatz. After work hours (seven in the morning until six or five in the evening in some shops), one can move about somewhat more freely—by attaching oneself to a group that is going from work to its residence block, or to an outside work detail on its way home—but such a group is usually under close supervision, particularly if it is a small one. Individual Jews may not move about the streets.

A second way of being out in the street during the work-day hours is to ride in a carriage. They are not bothered, and this is held to be a safe method of passage.

Treblinki—The news about the gravediggers (Rabinowicz, Jacob),* the Jews from Stok who escaped from the wagons ... loaded with gold and foreign currency—the unanimous de-

---

* An escapee from Treblinki, who was the informant.

scription of the "bath," the Jewish gravediggers with yellow patches on their knees.—The method of killing: gas, steam, electricity.

The news about Treblinki brought back by the investigators sent out by the families of those deported there.°—The story about the tractors: According to one version, tractors plow under the ashes of the burned Jews. According to another version, the tractors plow the earth and bury the corpses there [by covering them over].

Treblinki as the Jewish populace sees it—they become aware of the recent extermination.

The Jews from Western Europe have no idea what Treblinki is. They believe it to be a work colony, and on the train ask how far it is to the "industrial factory" of Treblinki. If they knew that they were going to their death, they would certainly put up some resistance. They arrive carrying brandnew valises.

Women, children. Shops without women—the breaking up of families—children, whole families annihilated—[parents who] refused to leave their children; husbands who refused [to leave] their wives—the father who wraps his child in a coat to conceal his presence and takes him along to the resettlement. The little criminals who must hide in a room for months on end—the face of a child grimacing with fear at a blockade.

The tragedy of families: thousands of men without wives, men who have remained alive and don't know what they are living for—in general, the tragedy of persons who have lost some thirty members of their family—left all alone in the world—without a purpose in life.

Unhappy the women who had [work card] numbers—de-

° In July, 1942, Zygmunt (Frydryck) had been delegated to verify the news about Treblinki. He reached Malkinia, where he met Esrael Wallach, an escaped prisoner from Treblinki, who confirmed the worst reports.

pended on them [to be exempted from deportation], and stood in line—those without numbers remained [behind, but] hurried to register their children as errand boys, handwagon pullers—they were all taken away—*men* protected their wives and children.

The heroism of Dr. Korcszak, Koninski, Janowski, refused to leave the children from their home. Korcszak built up the attitude that everyone [including directors of the home] should go to the Umschlag together. There were directors of homes who knew what awaited them at the Umschlagplatz, but held that at a difficult time such as this they could not let the children go alone and must go to their death with them.

The tragedy of parents—the problem of old people—some people poisoned [their elderly] parents—others went to the Umschlagplatz with parents; the home for the aged liquidated—[its inmates] carried in rickshas to the Umschlag with their valises—children sacrificed themselves to save their parents, most of the older generation done away with—many saved in hiding places—children who didn't [?] protect their parents—in the YYGA—Jewish Self-Aid Society—there were scores of eighty-year-old cleaning women.

Most of the old people were lost at the Niska [Street Pot]— [or when their children were] moving into the new residential blocks—or are lying in hiding to this day.

Polish organizations combatted and did away with blackmail. Guard the streetcars.—Pol.[ish] professionals frightened, refuse to accept any Jew.[ish] friends [for protection] outside of the Jewish elements [belonging to their own profession].

As of the end of October, 150 Jews have been seized [who escaped to] the Other Side. Polish streetcar people's attitude to the Jews very good. Police assigned to work at the street-car platforms allowed them [Jews] to work without permits, received Jews cordially, good relations. The same true of other outside work details where Jews happened to work alongside Poles.

[Polish] professional colleagues took care of their Jewish associates: Prof. Hirszfeld, Bruno Winawer, etc. [taken care of].

Commerce—Economy. The resettlement produced a great revolution in the economy both of the Ghetto and of the Aryan side of Warsaw. Certain items became cheap. Clothing, and particularly linen, was sold at four or five times less than before the resettlement. . . . Bedding was valueless. Pillow cases were removed, and the red [comforter] covers and feather stuffing let out. Bedding lies around in every street, in every courtyard. In some courtyards they set fire to it Nor have dishes any value—they're thrown into garbage cans. This is true of glass and porcelain dishes, as well as tin ones. Beds, and furniture in general, are worthless. They chop up furniture to heat apartments with the wood. Linen has value only if it is brand new. Second-hand or mended linen is worthless and cannot be sold. A man's suit can be sold for some 300–400 zlotys, i.e., the cost of 2 kilos of ham or butter (1 kilo of butter costs more than 200 zlotys).

The graveyard is an important business center, Christian smugglers coming there. Prices are a little higher there, too. The chief middlemen between the Ghetto and the Aryan Side of Warsaw are the workers in the outside details, who take things with them to [sell on] the Other Side. But commerce with the Other Side has become more difficult lately, because every single work detail is checked, and they are not permitted to take either money or things with them. There was the case of a gendarme shooting a man in a work detail because he was wearing two pairs of pants—one of which he was going to sell on the Other Side.

Street selling is vigorously combatted by the Germans and their assistants—the Jewish police and the Work Guard. Until a short time ago, the remaining 10 per cent of Warsaw Jews were selling what they had left on Smocza and other streets; now all the selling is going on in the blocks, in homes, and the like. People are busy selling [their last possessions] after work hours.

The Polish police are the most active buyers of Jewish things. The police stations are really commercial agencies where business is transacted all day long. They also purchase gold (35 zlotys a gram as of the end of October), diamonds, foreign currency (a paper dollar is worth 40 zlotys, a gold one 200 zlotys).

WHY WERE 10 PER CENT OF THE JEWS OF WARSAW ALLOWED TO REMAIN?

Many people have attempted to answer this question, because the answer to a series of fundamental questions hangs on it. How long shall we remain in the Ghetto? How long shall we live? How long shall we survive? When shall we be done away with? The opinion of a large group of perceptive persons is that the motive behind Their allowing 10 per cent of the Jews to remain in Warsaw is not economic but political. It matters little to Them that the Jews are producing, even for the Wehrmacht. Germany, which dominates all Europe, can easily make up the [economic] loss sustained by a deportation of Jews. If They took the economic factor into account at all, They would not so casually have sent thousands of first-class craftsmen to the Umschlagplatz (incidentally, the S.S. are literally searching high and low for Jewish craftsmen now—carpenters, apprentices, and [offering] good work conditions). The same was true in the provinces, where complete cities were cleaned out of Jews, although the entire Jewish population was engaged in working for the Wehrmacht—as for example in Zamoszcz.

The fact remains that, insofar as Jews are concerned, economic criteria do not apply—only political criteria, propaganda. This being so, the question poses itself even more strongly: Why, then, has a "saving remnant" been allowed to remain in Warsaw? The answer is political. If all the Jews were to be cleared out of Warsaw and out of the Government General [of Poland] as a whole, They would lose the Jewish argument. It would be hard for Them then to attribute all their difficulties and failures to the Jews. The Jews have to remain, in keeping with the proverb: "God grant that all your teeth fall out, except one to give you a toothache!"

There is another factor that influences the Germans to allow a handful of Jews to remain in Warsaw for a while. It is world public opinion. They have not publicly acknowledged the massacre of millions of Jews. When 40,000 Lublin Jews were liquidated,* the Warsaw newspaper published a news item describing how well off the Jews were in Majdan,† how wonderfully They have turned smugglers and fences into "productive elements," living respectable lives in Majdan.

The same is true of Warsaw. They don't want to admit to the world that they have murdered all the Jews of Warsaw, so they leave a handful behind, to be liquidated when the hour strikes twelve—not just for the toothache, but also for the

* In March and April, 1942.
† The camp at Majdanek, where the Jews from Lublin province were sent for extermination.

world to see. Hitler will use every means in his power to "free" Europe of all the Jews. Only a miracle can save us from complete extermination; only a speedy and sudden downfall can bring us salvation.

Hence the bitter pessimism dominating the Jewish populace. *Morituri*, that is the best description of our mood. Most of the populace is set on resistance. It seems to me that people will no longer go to the slaughter like lambs. They want the enemy to pay dearly for their lives. They'll fling themselves at Them with knives, staves, coal gas. They'll permit no more blockades. They'll not allow themselves to be seized in the street, for they know that work camp means death these days. And they want to die at home, not in a strange place. Naturally, there will only be a resistance if it is organized, and if the enemy does not move like lightning, as [They did] in Cracow, where, at the end of October, 5,500 Jews were packed into wagons in seven hours one night. We have seen the confirmation of the psychological law that the slave who is completely repressed cannot resist. The Jews appear to have recovered somewhat from the heavy blows they have received; they have shaken off the effects of their experiences to some extent, and they calculate now that going to the slaughter peaceably has not diminished the misfortune, but increased it. Whomever you talk to, you hear the same cry: The resettlement should never have been permitted. We should have run out into the street, have set fire to everything in sight, have torn down the walls, and escaped to the Other Side. The Germans would have taken their revenge. It would have cost tens of thousands of lives, but not 300,000. Now we are ashamed of ourselves, disgraced in our own eyes, and in the eyes of the world, where our docility earned us nothing. This must not be repeated now. We must put up a resistance, defend ourselves against the enemy, man and child.

GERMAN WAR STRATEGY AS APPLIED
TO THE JEWS IN WARSAW

The German fear of approaching the large Jewish settlement [in Warsaw]. Fear of [an] uprising, with the help of Poles and paratroopers.

"Divide and rule"—[the German strategy] poisons relations between Jews and Poles and makes any help from that [Polish] quarter impossible.—[The Germans] fooled the populace about [the meaning of the] resettlement.—Chelmno* remained a secret to the greater part of the Jews.

[The Germans] set the Warsawers against the refugees. Supposedly the resettlement was to free Warsaw of its "nonproductive elements." Promised the Law and Order Service that they and the members of their family, even uncles, mothers-in-law, brothers-in-law, would be secure.

Afterward, They reassured certain shops of their priority over other trades. Afterward, one shop was promised priority over another.—Afterward, women and children in the shops themselves became dispensable—afterward, poor workers as compared with good workers. Better shops were opposed to poorer shops—red stamps—continually contracting the circle, continually deceiving, declaring that the resettlement operation was over, in order to prevent a revolt.

The Niska Street Pot.—The hermetic sealing of the Ghetto limits, to keep out help.—Hermetic sealing of communications inside and outside the country by stopping the post.

Continual blockades throughout the city. To make any kind of counteraction impossible.—Propaganda lies about the resettlement to the East, to make opposition impossible.— Supporting the Law and Order Service until the operation was over, when 1,300 Jewish policemen were rounded up and

* The death camp where the Jews of the Lodz Ghetto were exterminated.

herded into wagons for deportation*—the liquidation of the Jewish Gestapo agents.

Moral "Attrition" of the Jewish populace in the course of the three war years.

Suddenness—They denied all the rumors about resettlement, in order suddenly to surprise the Jewish Council and give it no opportunity for thought.

COMPARISON WITH WAR STRATEGY

Preparation for an offensive.—Frontal attack and knocking out the enemy.—Setting up a "pot."—The complete collapse of the enemy.—A few prisoners kept for propaganda purposes.

Winning the Warsaw community and the Jewish Council over to agree to the resettlement of the refugees and the poor people.—Convincing the shop owners to combat the illegals and the women and children.

ALLIES IN THE CAMP OF THE ENEMY

Betrayal by the Jewish Council, Law and Order Service, Work Guard, allowed to manage the work shops, with the reward of being able to save their lives and those of their families.

Closed the Ghetto borders, stopped anyone from bringing in produce, and thus starved the Jews out—created desperation, apathy—brought the Ghetto to the point where for a loaf of bread thousands reported voluntarily for resettlement. (There was one day when volunteers were sent back; there weren't enough wagons to load the "merchandise" on). Later they raised the offer of bread for volunteers to 3 kilos, to attract a larger number of volunteers.

* The middle of September, 1942.

The most important purpose of the organization of shops and residence blocks was to round up those who had no work cards for the Umschlagplatz.

Wave of fictitious marriages—sons to mothers, brothers to sisters, to protect their kinfolk. The rabbis used to issue marriage contracts without even seeing the bridal couple.

The unpreparedness of the Jewish populace. The fear of collective responsibility—the fear that the whole community might have to pay for any act of resistance.

Umschlag—There were daily executions of hundreds both at the Platz and the graveyard: of old people, sick people, weak people, and, in general, of those who were not expected to be able to survive the journey to Treblinki. This continued until the beginning of the deportation operation; afterward it was discarded. Apparently, there was fear that the executions might become known in the Polish part of the city, and might have a bad effect on the populace.

I don't have the figures for the volunteers who reported to the Umschlag. But the minimum seems to me to have been 20,000 persons who, driven by hunger, anguish, a sense of the hopelessness of their situation, had not the strength to struggle any longer, simply had no place to live, because they weren't assigned to any shop, and had no recourse but to go to their death voluntarily. In estimating the number of volunteers, it must not be forgotten. . . .

POLICE

The Jewish police had a very bad name even before the resettlement. The Polish police didn't take part in the forced-work press gangs, but the Jewish police engaged in that ugly business. Jewish policemen also distinguished themselves with their fearful corruption and immorality. But they reached the height of viciousness during the resettlement.

They said not a single word of protest against this revolting assignment to lead their own brothers to the slaughter. The police were psychologically prepared for the dirty work and executed it thoroughly. And now people are wracking their brains to understand how Jews, most of them men of culture, former lawyers (most of the police officers were lawyers before the war), could have done away with their brothers with their own hands. How could Jews have dragged women and children, the old and the sick, to the wagons—knowing they were all being driven to the slaughter? There are people who hold that every society has the police it deserves, that the disease—cooperation with the Occupying Power in the slaughter of 300,000 Jews—is a contagion affecting the whole of our society and is not limited to the police, who are merely an expression of our society. Other people argue that the police is the haven of morally weak psychological types, who do everything in their power to survive the difficult times, who believe that the end determines all means, and the end is to survive the war—even if survival is bound up with the taking of other people's lives.

In the presence of such nihilism, apparent in the whole gamut of our society, from the highest to the lowest, it is no surprise that the Jewish police executed the German resettlement orders with the greatest of zeal. And yet the fact remains that most of the time during the resettlement operation the Jewish police exceeded their daily quotas. That meant they were preparing a reserve for the next day. No sign of sorrow or pain appeared on the faces of the policemen. On the contrary, one saw satisfied and happy individuals, well-fed, loaded with the loot they carried off in company with the Ukrainian guards.

Very often, the cruelty of the Jewish police exceeded that of the Germans, Ukrainians, and Letts. They uncovered more than one hiding place, aiming to be *plus catholique que le pope* and so curry favor with the Occupying Power. Victims who succeeded in escaping the German eye were picked up by the Jewish police. I watched the procession to the wagons on the Umschlagplatz for several hours and noted that many Jews who were fortunate enough to work their way toward the spot where the exempted people were standing were forcibly dragged back to the wagons by the Jewish police. Scores, and perhaps hundreds, of Jews were doomed by the Jewish police during those two hours. The same thing happened during the blockades. Those who didn't have the money to pay off the police were dragged to the wagons, or put on the lines going to the Umschlagplatz.

A scene I witnessed at 3 Dzszika Street, opposite the Umschlagplatz, one day when every policeman had to meet a quota of four "heads" (this was several days before the end of the "operation") will remain in my mind *the* symbol for the Jewish police in Warsaw. I saw a Jewish policeman pulling an old woman by the arm to the Umschlagplatz. He had a hatchet on his shoulder. He used the hatchet to break down locked apartment doors. As he approached the Umschlagplatz where the watch was stationed, the policeman shamefacedly took the hatchet off his shoulder and transferred it to his hand. It was the general rule those days to see individual policemen dragging men, women, and children to the Umschlag. They took the sick there in rickshas.

For the most part, the Jewish police showed an incomprehensible brutality. Where did Jews get such murderous violence? When in our history did we ever before raise so many hundreds of killers, capable of snatching children off the street, throwing them on the wagons, dragging them to the Umschlag? It was literally the rule for the scoundrels to fling women on to the Kohn–Heller streetcars, or on to ordinary trucks, by grabbing them by the arms and legs and heaving. Merciless and violent, they beat those who tried to resist.

They weren't content simply to overcome the resistance, but with the utmost severity punished the "criminals" who refused to go to their death voluntarily. Every Warsaw Jew, every woman and child, can cite thousands of cases of the inhuman cruelty and violence of the Jewish police. Those cases will never be forgotten by the survivors, and they must and shall be paid for.

Beside the police, another group of [Jewish] organizations shared in the resettlement operation. Gancwajch's red-capped Special Ambulance Service was the worst. This organization of swindlers had never given a single Jew the medical aid they promised. They limited their activity to issuing authorization cards and caps, for thousands of zlotys. Possession of these, together with Gancwajch's personal assistance, exempted the owner from forced labor and was a defense against all kinds of trouble and taxes, in general. Besides, a Special Service uniform enabled its wearer to perpetrate a variety of swindles and blackmail associated with sanitation (informing on typhus cases, disinfection steam baths, and the like). It was this pretty gang that now voluntarily reported for the assignment of sending Jews to the hereafter—and they distinguished themselves with their brutality and inhumanity. Their caps were covered with the bloodstains of the Jewish people.

The officials of the Jewish Council also cooperated in the "operation," as did the Service of the K.A.M.—City Aid Committee.

Dec. 12

HATRED OF THE POLICE

So long as the "operation" was in progress (that was the name for the massacre of the Warsaw Jews), the populace was silent. They allowed themselves to be led to the slaughter like sheep. I know that porters from the CENTOS (Children's Aid Society) warehouses, who had many a time displayed courage in the face of danger, allowed themselves to be led off like lambs during the "operation." The same can be said of most of the men and women taken to the Umschlag at that time. This will be an eternal mystery—this passivity of the Jewish populace even toward its own police. Now that the populace has calmed down somewhat, and they are reviewing what took place, they are becoming ashamed of having put up no resistance at all. People remember who was responsible for the mass slaughter, and conclude that it was the Jewish police who were the chief culprits; some people go so far as to lay the whole guilt on the police's shoulders. Now people are taking their revenge. They pass up no opportunity to remind the Jewish police of their crime. Every policeman you talk to nowadays acts as innocent as a newborn babe. *He* never took part in the operation. He was assigned to this or that institution. Or else, if he *was* there, he saved people from the Umschlag. Others did the seizing, not he. From these protestations, one would gather that those who seized people for the Umschlag were themselves deported to various labor camps or to Treblinki—since none of them are around; we know the truth is exactly the opposite. It is the hoodlum and criminal element in the police that has remained among the 300 policemen who are now on guard duty in the Ghetto, while, on the contrary, the less diligent, who didn't have enough money for "protection," have gone either to Treblinki or to camps like those at Lublin.

So the time for soul-searching has come, the time for revenge. A secret hand did away with Lejkin,* the police chief in charge of the resettlement. The Jewish police are persecuted at every step. Not only by the Jews—the Poles, too,

---

* Lejkin was probably assassinated on October 20 by a member of the Jewish resistance movement.

demonstrate their hatred for the Jewish police. The ex-Jewish policemen working on the streetcar platforms are constantly persecuted by the Polish workers. In Rembertow, even German soldiers persecute them. Many shops protested against hiring policemen. One shop voted to have all former policemen dismissed. I know for a fact that ex-policemen in one outside work detail wear their caps until they reach the watch at the Ghetto Wall, because a cap is a sign of importance in the Ghetto. Once outside the Ghetto, they take their caps off, because they are afraid of the Polish populace, who hate the Jewish Law and Order Service for what they did during the resettlement. A man recognized a policeman who had taken away his parents in the street, and attacked him. In Hallman's shop the relief committee distributed dole to a sick ex-policeman. The furor against the relief committee cannot be imagined. This happens everywhere—ex-policemen are persecuted at every step.

People keep bringing up instances of the Jewish police's brutality during the resettlement. They tell this story: A Jew was killed at 50 Leszno Street. His body lay there in front of the gate. Two undertakers came along in a wagon to remove the corpse. That day, the police were scurrying around like poisoned rats, because their quota for the day was five "heads." If they didn't meet it, they and their families faced the threat of deportation. Without thinking overlong, the police took away the two undertakers, leaving the corpse to lie untended in the middle of the street. Another incident, that took place at 24 Leszno Street: A sixteen-year-old baker's boy beat up a policeman who was trying to take away the boy's mother. The boy tore the policeman's short coat. He was taken to the courtyard of the police headquarters, and there given twenty-five stripes, as a result of which he died.

Still another, no less horrible, instance: A policeman enters,

or rather, to be precise about it, breaks into an apartment.
All the tenants are hiding somewhere or other, leaving only
a three-month-old baby in his cradle. Without a moment's
thought, the policeman calls the German who is supervis-
ing the operation in from the courtyard. The German makes
a face at being offered such a victim. He beats the policeman
up badly and shoots the baby. A number of people have assured me this is true.

There are any number of horrifying stories about the conduct of the Jewish police at the Umschlag. To them, nobody
was a person, only a "head" that could be blackmailed. The
only way to escape was by buying the police off with money,
diamonds, gold, and the like. The price per head varied. At
first it was 1,000 or 2,000 zlotys. Later it went up, until it
reached 10,000 zlotys per head. The exact sum depended on
a complex of subjective and objective factors, into which the
Jewish police had sometimes to draw "Yunakes" as partners,
as well as the Letts or Ukrainians who were on service in the
Umschlagplatz. The Jewish police were without mercy. You
could be the most worthy of persons, if you didn't have ransom money, or relatives to pay the asking price, you would be
sent away. There are known cases where the police, in addition to money, demanded payment in the form of a woman's
body. My friend Kalman Zylberberg knows the badge numbers of the policemen, and the names of the women who paid
for freedom with their bodies. The police had a special room
in the hospital for this purpose. As a general rule, the police
were beside themselves during the resettlement. They were
always furious at the recalcitrants who refused to allow
themselves to be resettled. The police themselves were continually threatened with being sent to the Umschlag with
their wives and children. And then, they were demoralized
from before the resettlement. Those seized for the Umschlag,

particularly the women, put up resistance. All these things created an impossible situation for the police, who reacted like beasts.

Dec. 14

PRIESTS WISH TO RESCUE JEWISH CHILDREN

In certain circles a plan is now under discussion to rescue a certain number (several hundred) of Jewish children by placing them in monasteries in various parts of the country. Three factors have motivated the men of the cloth to propose this: first, soul-snatching. The Catholic religious leaders have always exploited such difficult moments in Jewish life as pogroms, deportations, etc., to convert adults and children. This is perhaps the most important factor motivating the proposal, although the clergy assure us they will not attempt to convert the Jewish children entrusted to the care of their institutions.

There is a second, *economic* factor. Every Jewish child will have to pay 600 zlotys a month, and for a year in advance, too. This is a very good stroke of business for the monastic orders; since they have their own fields and gardens, their food costs are very low. For the Jewish children who are unable to meet this fee, costs are to be covered by the children of the rich, who will be taxed double.

The third factor is that of prestige. Until now, the Polish Christian spiritual leaders have done very little to save Jews from massacre and "resettlement," to use Their euphemism. In view of the world-wide protest against the mass murder of Polish Jews, rescuing several hundred Jewish children may be offered as evidence that the Polish clergy did not sit with hands folded in these difficult times, that they did everything they could to help the Jews, particularly their children.

I was present at a discussion of this question by several

Jewish intellectuals. One of them categorically opposed the operation. He argued that though it was agreed that [only] children between ten and fourteen years of age were to be put in the convents (as desired by the Jewish negotiators), the children—though supposedly old enough to resist indoctrination—would fall under the priests' influence and would be converted sooner or later. The priests' promise not to convert the children would be of no avail; time and education would take their toll. He maintained that we must follow the example of our fathers and accept martyrdom in His name. We have no right to give our blessing to the conversion of our children. Jewish society has no right to engage in such an enterprise. Let it be left to every individual, to decide and act on an individual basis.

When, he concluded, 300,000 Jews have been exterminated in Warsaw, what avail is it to rescue several hundred children? Let them perish or survive together with the rest of their people.

However, others argued: We must look after the future. In time of massacre such as this, with all of European Jewry being slaughtered, the soul of each and every Jew is precious, and we must take pains to try to preserve it. After the war, the clergy will have no influence. Who knows whether they will even exist? This being so, there is no need to fear lest the children fall under the influence of the monastic orders. When one studies the pages of Jewish history closely, one discovers that martyrdom in His name was not the principle of our history. On the contrary, marranism was pseudo-Christianity.* Jews have always adapted themselves to the hardest conditions, have always known how to survive the hardest times. Sending a handful of Jewish children into monasteries

---

* At the time of the Spanish Inquisition, many Jews accepted baptism in preference to death. But they continued to observe Jewish religious practices in secret. They were always suspect to their Christian neighbors, who called them marranos, or "pigs."

will enable us to rescue those who will be the creators of a new generation of Jews. We have no right to take away the coming generation's right to live.

Those who took this position argued that one must strongly underline the difference between conversion and pseudo-Christianity. The priests themselves state that the children will not be converted, but will have to conduct themselves outwardly like Christians. True, there is some danger that if this persists for a long time some of the children will fall under the influence of the clergy—but there is a second, worse danger. If we do not carry out this child-rescue operation with the aid of the clergy, in a short time none will remain, the handful whom we are now in a position to rescue will perish as well. Numbers, some of the intellectuals said, are the most important consideration at this time. At any cost, we must rescue the largest possible number of Jews; so we must agree to the proposal to place some of our children in convents.

Still others argued that the thing had to be done, but not with the sanction of the representatives of Jewish society. Individuals were rescuing themselves in various ways—let the convent operation be a matter of individual choice.

Dec. 14

HIDING PLACES

Now, in December, 1942, hiding places are very popular. Everyone is making them. Everywhere, in all the shops and elsewhere in the Ghetto, hiding places are being built. Their construction has actually become a flourishing specialized craft. Skilled workers, engineers, etc., are making a living out of it. Hiding places go back many years. People began to hide out when the Germans entered Warsaw, in October, 1939. People hid themselves, hid their goods. On Franciszkanska and Nalewki Streets, cellars were walled up, attics, special rooms, stores of merchandise—because the Germans used to confiscate everything, removing complete truckloads of goods. Even then there were scoundrels who made it their business to knock down the walls of these hiding places. These were the professional informers, who recruited themselves for the job. The majority were porters. They used to uncover stores of goods which the Germans would otherwise never have found. The details of the removal of whole wagons full of leather worth millions from Franciszkanska Street have stuck in my memory. Days on end large military trucks removed this merchandise from the hiding places.

And then people used to hide themselves. In those days, during 1939, 1940, and part of 1941, people would be seized for forced labor almost every day—so the men hid out in the shops, under bench beds, in mezzanines, cubbies, cellars, garrets, etc. Some of the apartments were so arranged that a room could be set off for the men to hide in—usually behind a shop, credenza, or the like. The Germans knew the location of such hideouts, thanks to their Jewish informers, who accompanied them and pointed out the hiding places. Pious Jews, wearing beards and ear locks, used to hide out, too—showing yourself bearded [in the open] was perilous, because there were often Gestapo agents, or just mean Germans, who couldn't bear the sight of an "uncivilized" bearded Jew. They would shave off the offending beard, or just rip it off, skin and all.

During the time when there were blockades, the resettlement period, hideouts assumed a new importance. People took special pains to build good hiding places, because they had become a matter of life and death. Old folks, children, and women hid out there. The men were not afraid to go to all kinds of selections because they had a chance to get various work certificates and exemption papers.

In those days the hideouts were more refined, better concealed. My family, for example, used to hide out in a subroom in an old house, on the third floor. It consisted of the few steps of another house [?]. Entry was through a trap door in the floor, which the wife of a policeman, who was not afraid of any blockade—policemen were safe at the time—used to cover with a rug and a table on top of it. In another place, they used a secret tannery, specially built into a cellar, for a hideout. A third place used a clandestine grain mill, marvelously disguised. Air-raid shelters were also used as hideouts. In one courtyard the air-raid shelter was underground. Entry was through a trap door, which the men used to cover with boards. In many apartments, people set aside special rooms, masking the entry a number of ways, for example, the entry would be through the next-door kitchen. They used to lift out the tiles to enter. Entry to the sealed-off room would be through the water closet, a trap door in the next room, or in the room above, which would be connected to the hideout by a ladder. In some places the entry would be masked by a movable block of tiles, so that, in case the walls were tapped, there would be no empty hollow spaces. If the hideout was in a cellar, people made sure that it was very far away, in some distant corner, where there were no windows.

These hideouts were given away by accident, very often by a child's crying. I know of a case on Nowolipie Street where several dozen people were hiding in two walled-up rooms. The Ukrainians blockading the house threw a party in the next room. They were about to leave when they heard a child crying. They chopped down the wall and found one of the rooms, with twenty-six people in it. They shot six of them on the spot; the rest bought the Ukrainians off and went to the Umschlagplatz. The second sealed room was not discovered.

In 90 per cent of the cases it was the Jewish police who uncovered the hideouts. First they found out where the hideouts were; then they passed the information along to the Ukrainians and Germans. Hundreds and thousands of people are on those scoundrels' conscience.

After the selections—for deportation or forced work—when things calmed down a bit in the Ghetto, a new chapter in the story of hideouts began. The populace had by this time learned to distrust the Germans. It was obvious that so long as the present system continued there would be a new operation against the Jews sooner or later, and in the end the Ghetto would be liquidated. Two events contributed to the popular refusal to accept the mollifying statements of the Germans at their face value: first, the continuing massacre of Jews in Treblinki and other camps; and second, the fact that 800 people were seized in the shops and deported toward Lublin. Nothing has since been heard of them.

Consequently, the populace has begun to plan how to secure their lives in case of danger. The richer people have begun to cross over to the Other Side. Others, less fortunate, are planning hiding places. During November and December, there was a feverish activity in the construction of new hideouts, differing completely from those built during the summer, during the time of the "operation." In the first place, they had to be usable in cold weather; secondly, they had to be furnished for people to be able to live there months on end. The reasoning was that if all the Jews of Warsaw were to be liquidated, those who had hideouts would go into them and stay there until they were rescued. The new hideouts were built in one of three places: cellars, underground, or on the floor of an apartment. The present hideouts are . . . equipped with gas, electricity, water, and toilets. Some of them cost tens of thousands of zlotys. They contain food supplies sufficient to last for months (preserves, sugar, and the like). Since there is the fear that the Germans might stop the water passage, as they did in a number of the houses where the "wild people" are living, people have stocked up on supplies of distilled water, buried in barrels in the hideouts. Or else, special artesian wells are dug. Of course, only the well-to-do can afford such luxuries. I know of one case where for 3,000 zlotys a water-works man connected the water pipes of a hideout with the water pipes of an Aryan factory, so that the people in the hideout would continue to have water even if the water was shut off in the house.

The Jewish brains that are working on problems of this kind have worked out a brilliant scheme to insure against the shutting off of water. They'll creep out of their hideout at night and set fire to the next house. They say the firemen will have to open the water connections then, and those in the know will take advantage of this to put in a fresh supply of water to last for a time.

Jewish craftsmen have also thought up a way of seeing to it that there is no shortage of gas and electricity—the plan is known supposedly only to them. The idea is to steal gas and electric current from the next house. Naturally, this is only possible when the gas or electricity is cut off in one house, not in the whole street.

Some hideouts are built into apartments. They locate an alcove or room corner and wall it in so that it can't be noticed. The chief trouble with such a hideout is that windows always betray its existence. A few weeks ago, a special police division of the Property Collection Agency* came to Warsaw and used this technique: They counted the number of windows on each floor, and then sent that many policemen up to each floor and ordered them to stick out their heads. It was easy to find out whether there were any disguised rooms, and where they were.

As a general rule, walling up windows is the hardest problem. In one courtyard, the tenants concealed the walled-up

* The S.S. Werterfassung agency, which confiscated the property of Jews who had been deported from the Ghetto.

window of the basement by placing a garbage can in front of it; elsewhere, the window was concealed by steps.

As everyone knows, modern apartment houses are so constructed that all the apartments in the same line have the same layout. Walling up an alcove in one apartment does not provide an adequate hiding place, because it is quite easy to find the same alcove on a higher or lower floor in the same line of apartments. The way out of this dilemma was for all the persons living in the same line to wall up their alcoves. In one house, the residents all walled up one corner of a room, built an entry through a bakery oven, and put in a passageway from one floor to the next through a chain of ladders pushed through holes cut into the floors. An impressive hideout like that accommodates up to sixty persons.

The most important problem in any hideout is masking the entry. Every day sees the invention of new solutions, each cleverer than the previous one. What is involved is seeing to it that when the German detective taps the walls, he doesn't find any empty space. On the other side of one walled-up room, tiles were pasted into a frame, and the whole thing was pushed aside when people wanted to enter the hideout. In another place, the entry was through a water closet, in a third through a bakery oven.

Communication with the outside world is another basic problem. Arrangements are made in advance with a Christian, who looks after the needs of the Jews in the hideout on the days when they go into hiding. A few shops have hideouts so built that they have an underground connection with the Other Side. This [of course] is only possible where the shops border on the Aryan Side. Building that kind of a tunnel is one of the hardest things to do. A good deal of earth has to be dug up and removed surreptitiously. This is far from easy; consequently, the diggers make it a rule that only those who have worked on the tunnel may use the hideout.

It is said that Germans have used hounds to search houses from which Jews have been driven out, to ferret out the hidden survivors. Thus far, no way has been found to put the hounds off the trace. Lysol is said to be effective. But there is danger that, smelling lysol, the Germans will know that Jews are in hiding in that particular house.

Besides supplying Jewish craftsmen with a source of livelihood, the hideouts have become a business for gangs that sell places in them for thousands of zlotys. This includes food supply.

There is altogether too much talk about hideouts—more talk than action. The Jewish Gestapo agents know about them, so, inevitably, the Germans do, too. There was even an informer in Hallman's shop who informed on a large hideout there. The argument runs that if the Germans know about Ghetto hideouts, they have lost their value. So, a few people maintain, the best thing to do is to build a hideout on the Other Side. Find a Christian family willing to rent a large apartment, wall up a room where Jews can be concealed, and, naturally, give the Christian family proper financial satisfaction. But the populace is afraid that at the crucial terrifying moment the Germans will discover some clever way of turning to nought all our efforts at self-rescue. Whether this is true or not, only the future will tell.

Most of the Ghetto's remaining residents died in the uprising that began on April 19 and ended on May 16, 1943. The Germans bombed the Ghetto, building by building, set it on fire, and razed it to the ground. The S.S. set up a concentration camp for 2,000 Jewish and non-Jewish prisoners where the Ghetto had stood. For several months longer, we hear of a few survivors living mysterious, subterranean lives in the cellars and sewers of what had been the Warsaw Ghetto.

And the author of Notes from the Warsaw Ghetto? *In May, 1943, in the middle of the Warsaw Ghetto uprising, a radiogram from the fighters asking for help was received in London by the Polish government-in-exile. One of the three signers of the radiogram was Emmanuel Ringelblum.*

Captured by the Germans, Ringelblum was sent with some of his comrades to the slave camp at Poniatow. An armed revolt broke out there too, and many of the rebels committed suicide. But, two days before the revolt broke out, Ringelblum was smuggled out of the camp by the Jewish underground. They found a hiding place for him in the Other Side of Warsaw, where he lived with false papers, as an "Aryan."

In his underground home, Ringelblum returned to his beloved writing of the history of his time. He had directed the Oneg Sabbath group in collecting about one hundred volumes of memoirs, complete files of various official German documents, hundreds of reports. Now Ringelblum composed a history of the Jewish Combat Organization in Poland (the resistance movement). He regarded this as his life work, and he refused to leave it. In January, 1944, he had his last chance to escape. The Polish government-in-exile in London received a list from the Warsaw underground with the names of nineteen former Jewish underground leaders; the Polish government agreed to rescue these men from London, through the underground. Now only three of the nineteen on that list were still alive—one being Emmanuel Ringelblum. But all three survivors obstinately refused to leave, "because we must fulfill our duty to society."

On March 1, 1944, Ringelblum wrote an account of the rich underground intellectual life of the Warsaw Ghetto. Before it could be smuggled out of Poland, the Gestapo discovered the subterranean cellar where he was in hiding with his wife, twelve-year-old son, and thirty-five other refugees from the Ghetto. (The account was eventually received in New York, and distributed by the Jewish Labor Committee.)

There are two stories about Ringelblum's death. According to one, an attempt was made by other prisoners in the jail where he was kept to bribe the police officer to let Ringelblum go, on the pretext that he was a good shoemaker. Ringelblum would not hear of this. Pointing to his son, Uri, he said: "And what about him?" But the jailer was bribed anyway; Ringelblum's archives and notes were too important to allow him to die, whether he wished it or not. The next morning, Ringelblum's friends heard that he had been executed. When reproached, the jailer said (with a smile?), "I understand he wasn't a shoemaker, after all."

The other account of Emmanuel Ringelblum's death relates that the Gestapo knew who he was from the very first. They tortured both him and his family in an attempt to find out where the archives were hidden. But none of them would talk.

On March 7, 1944, Emmanuel Ringelblum went to his death, together with his wife, child, and the thirty-five who had shared the bunker with him, among the ruins of the Warsaw Ghetto. As he would have wished, he shares a collective grave.

CHRONOLOGY FOR NOTES FROM THE WARSAW GHETTO

Events in Warsaw			*Events outside Warsaw*
	1938	Aug. 21	Germany and the Soviet Union sign nonaggression pact, giving Germany a free hand to invade Poland.
	1939	Sept. 1	Germany invades Poland. S.S. and Wehrmacht instigate numerous pogroms in Poland.
		Sept. 17	Russians occupy Eastern Poland.
		Sept. 21	Reinhardt Heydrich, chief of German Security Police, plans ghettos in Poland.
		Sept.	Germany and the Soviet Union partition Poland into three parts: one incorporated into Reich, one to Soviet Union, and one unincorporated, under German protectorate (Government General).
Sept. 27 Warsaw surrenders to Germans.			
Oct. 4 Adam Czerniakow ordered by Gestapo to set up Jewish Council to replace Jewish Community Council within twenty-four hours.			
		Oct. 6	Hitler announces his resettlement policy for Poland, including Jewish seclusion.
		Oct. 8	Decree reincorporating provinces lost to Poland in 1918 into German Reich; also province of Lodz.

Oct. 12	First deportation of Jews from Vienna and Bohemia to Nisko in Poland.
Oct. 26	Forced labor extended to all Jews living in Government General.
Oct. 28	Jewish badge imposed at Wloclawek.
Nov.	Census shows 359,827 Jews in Warsaw.
Nov. 8	Hans Frank made Governor General of Poland. Attempt to assassinate Hitler in Munich.
Nov. 15	Germans forced to readmit Jews expelled across Russian lines.
Nov. 23	Jewish badge made compulsory throughout Government General.
Nov. 30	Russia attacks Finland.

1940

Jan. 21	Gestapo orders registration of Jewish property.
Jan. 26	Congregational worship forbidden; ritual slaughter prohibited.
March 12	Russia makes peace with Finland.
April 9	Germany invades Denmark and Norway.
April 14	Frank declares that Cracow will be "free of Jews."
April 30	First enclosed and guarded Ghetto set up—in Lodz.
May 10	Germans invade Western countries.
May 15	Holland surrenders.
May 28	British evacuate Dunkirk.

Events in Warsaw		Events outside Warsaw	
	1940 (cont.)		
June	Jewish Council reorganized; limited to carrying out orders of German authorities.	June	First issue of official "Jewish newspaper," *Gazetta Zydowska*, appears in Cracow.
		June 10	Italy enters the war.
		June 20	Hitler mentions to Mussolini plan to resettle European Jewry on French island of Madagascar.
		June 21	France signs armistice with Germany.
		July 12	Frank says he has persuaded Hitler to stop deporting Jews to the Government General.
		July 19	Hitler addresses Reichstag, offering peace to Great Britain.
Sept.	Quarantine area—later to be Ghetto —contains 240,000 Jews, 80,000 Christians.		
		Oct. 4	Vichy Jewish Statute deprives refugee Jews of their civil rights.
		Oct. 7	German troops arrive in Rumania.
Oct. 16	Decree gives Christians two weeks to move out of quarantine area, Jews to move in.		
Nov. 15	Warsaw Ghetto sealed off.		
Jan.	Jewish Council census shows 378,979 Jews in Ghetto.	**1941**	

Jan. 11		Frank obtains postponment of plans for deportation of all Jews to Government General.
Jan. 22–23		Iron Guard revolt in Rumania. First Jewish massacre of war.
Jan. 31		First attempt at creating a Jewish Council in France.
Feb.–April	72,000 Jews deported to the Warsaw Ghetto.	
Feb. 17		Rumania enters the war.
Feb. 18	Jewish Council is allowed to raise a loan from German banks on the security of blocked Jewish accounts.	
Feb. 22–23		Deportation of Jewish hostages from Amsterdam.
March 1		Bulgaria enters the war.
March 2		Hitler outlines plans for occupation of Russia.
March 4		Construction of Bunawerk factory at Oswiecim authorized.
March 30		Vichy Government appoints a Commission on Jewish Questions. British troops in Greece.
April	Schools licensed for 5,000 of the 50,000 children in the Ghetto. American Joint Distribution Committee allowed to have offices in the Ghetto.	
April 6		Germans invade Yugoslavia and Greece.

CHRONOLOGY FOR NOTES FROM THE WARSAW GHETTO

Events in Warsaw		*Events outside Warsaw*
	1941 (cont.)	
May	Census shows 430,000 Jews in the Ghetto.	
		May 14 — Germans intern 3,600 naturalized Parisian Jews.
		May 15 — Pétain broadcasts pledge of cooperation with Germany.
		End May — *Einsatzgruppen* (special extermination squads) formed.
		June 22 — Germany invades Russia.
		June 25 — Rumanian pogrom at Jassy.
		June 28 — German-inspired pogrom at Kovno, Lithuania.
July	17,800 refugees, including 3,300 children, classified as destitute.	
Aug.	3,000 Jews employed in cooperative workshops.	
		Mid-Aug. — Slovak Government disperses Bratislava Ghetto.
Sept.	Frank announces a reduction in Ghetto rations. Ghetto post office forbidden to handle foreign mail. End of parcels from neutral countries.	
		Sept. 1 — Massacre of Jews expelled by Hungarians, at Kamenets-Podolski.

Sept. 15	Slovakia adopts Nuremberg laws. Jewish badge decreed throughout Greater Reich.
Sept. 19	Liquidation of Zhitomir Ghetto in Ukraine. Germans occupy Kiev.
Sept. 23	Experimental gassing at Oswiecim.
Sept. 28–29	Massacre of 34,000 Jews from Kiev.
Oct. 2	Paris synagogues blown up by secret action of Gestapo.
Oct. 12	Moscow partly evacuated.
Oct. 20	First deportation from Reich decreed (to Lodz).
Oct.	Vast massacres at Riga, Vilna, Kovno, and Dvinsk.
Nov. 4	Lodz deportations completed.
Nov. 6	15,000 massacred at Rovno. First Reich Jews arrive in Riga, Minsk, and Kovno.
End Nov.	First massacre at Rostov. Threat to Moscow over.
Dec. 7	Riga massacres concluded (27,000).
Dec. 11	Germany declares war on United States.

Oct. 5	Death edict for leaving Ghetto without permission.
Oct. 23	Liquidation of the Small Ghetto.
Oct.	Streetcar lines abolished.
Dec. 1	Receipt of food packages forbidden, under pretext of danger of epidemics.
Dec. 7	Pearl Harbor leads to withdrawal of American relief organizations (JDC).

CHRONOLOGY FOR NOTES FROM THE WARSAW GHETTO

Events in Warsaw		*Events outside Warsaw*
1941 (cont.)		
Dec. 16	Frank reports about 2,500,000 Jews in Government General. Must be "gotten rid of."	
Dec. 17	German post office refuses to accept mail out of the Ghetto—excuse of epidemics, again.	
Dec. 22		Vilna massacre completed (32,000).
Dec. 30		Simferopol massacres completed (10,000).
Dec. 31		First permanent gassing camp opened at Chelmno, near Posen.
Dec.	Jewish cemetery walled off—coffins used for smuggling. Free soup kitchens supporting 100,000 people.	
1942		
Jan.	Visits and tours of Ghetto abolished for soldiers on leave. Continues, nevertheless.	
Jan. 15		Resettlement operation begins in Lodz.
Jan. 31		229,052 Jews reported killed in Baltic states and White Russia. First deportation to Theresienstadt.
Feb. 15		Singapore falls.
March 15		Hitler promises Russia will be annihilated in the summer.

	March 16 — Belzec death camp opens.
	March 17–April 21 — Most of Lublin Ghetto resettled.
	April–July — Resettlement extends to whole of Poland.
April 12 — Rumored arrival of extermination brigade.	
April 18 — Bloody Friday—execution of printers and distributors of Ghetto undercover press. (Ringelblum blames Kohn and Heller.)	April 14 — News of massacre of Lublin Ghetto. News of pogroms in provinces.
	April 26 — Reichstag approves Hitler's abrogation of German law.
May — "The Thirteen" gang killed.	May 31 — First of big air raids on Germany (Cologne).
June — News of massacres in Pabianice and Biala Podloska.	June 1 — Jewish badge decreed in France and Holland.
	June 23 — First gas-chamber selection at train for Oswiecim (Paris).
	July — Massacres extended to Minsk, Lida, Slonim, and Rovno.
	July 1 — Germans reach El Alamein (Egypt), and the Don river (Russia).

CHRONOLOGY FOR NOTES FROM THE WARSAW GHETTO

1942 (cont.)

Events in Warsaw	Events outside Warsaw
July 22 — 380,000 in Warsaw Ghetto. Jewish Council publishes notice of deportation to East regardless of sex or age. Czerniakow commits suicide. By Oct. 3, 310,000 resettled.	
July 29 — Meeting of Zionist youth organizations decides to combine a unified striking force.	
July — Zygmunt comes back with verified news of extermination camp at Treblinki.	
	Aug. 4 — First deportation train from Belgium to Oswiecim.
Aug. 5 — Extermination squad descends on Ghetto. Operation lasts a week.	
Aug. 7 — Blockade of every street and house begins.	
	Aug. 10–22 — 40,000 Jews resettled from Lwow (20,000 left).
	Mid-Aug. — Germans in north Caucasus.
	Aug. 19 — Allies raid Dieppe.
Aug. 20 — Josef Szerynski, head of Jewish police, badly wounded by assassin.	
	Aug. 26–28 — Roundup of 7,000 stateless Jews in Vichy Free Zone.
	Aug. — Hans Frank: "1.2 million Jews will no longer be provided with food."

Sept. 21   Yom Kippur—Ghetto area reduced by more than half. More than three-quarters of population already evacuated. 2,000 Jewish policemen deported.

Sept. 22   S.S. and S.D. take over formal administration of Jewish affairs in Warsaw.

Oct. 3   First Warsaw resettlement ends.

Oct. 20   Coordinating Committee of resistance movement formed.

Oct. 29   Jacob Lejkin, police officer, shot.

Sept. 16   Lodz resettlement ends. Germans enter Stalingrad.

Sept. 30   Hitler repeats prophecy of destruction of world Jewry.

Oct. 4   All Jews in concentration camps doomed to extermination at Oswiecim.

Oct. 10   Ordinance lists thirteen ghettos and forty-two Jewish quarters in Government General.

Oct. 14   Jews virtually outlawed from Holland.

Oct. 18   Jews and "Easterners" in Reich given by Ministry of Justice to Gestapo.

Oct. 28   End of first phase of Polish resettlement. More than fifty ghettos recognized.

Oct. 29   16,000 Jews killed at Pinsk.

Nov. 7   Allies land in North Africa.

Nov. 11   Germans occupy Vichy France. Italians occupy Nice.

CHRONOLOGY FOR NOTES FROM THE WARSAW GHETTO

Events in Warsaw		*Events outside Warsaw*
	1942 (cont.)	
	Nov. 22	Russian counteroffensive begins.
	Nov. 26	Jewish munitions workers in Reich to be replaced by Poles.
	Dec. 17	United Nations declaration pledging punishment for extermination of Jewry.
	1943	
Jan. Only 40,000 Jews left in the Ghetto.		
	Jan. 14	Allies agree on unconditional surrender at Casablanca meeting.
Jan. 18 Second extermination operation begins. First resistance.		
	Feb. 2	German 6th army surrenders at Stalingrad.
	Feb. 5–12	First resettlement from Bialystok.
	Feb. 15	Russians take Kharkov.
	Feb. 27	Roundup of Jewish munitions workers in Berlin for Oswiecim.
	March 13	Cracow Ghetto liquidated. First of new crematoria opens at Oswiecim.
	March 15	Deportations begin from Salonika and Thrace.
	March	Deportation trains from Holland to Sobibor death camp—those from Vienna, Luxembourg, Prague, and Macedonia to Treblinki.

April 19–May 16		Liquidation of the Warsaw Ghetto. Ghetto uprising in force. Ghetto bombed, set afire, razed. A concentration camp for 2,000 Jewish and Christian prisoners established on site by S.S.
1944	Aug.	Russians advance. Lodz's Ghetto survivors transferred to Oswiecim.
1946	March 7	Emmanuel Ringelblum executed on ruins of the Ghetto, together with wife and child.
	Sept.	Ten cases of Ringelblum Archives dug up.
1950	Dec. 1	Two rubber-sealed milk cans of Ringelblum Archives dug up—documents up to March 1943.

INDEX

Adalberg, Samuel, 126
Addis Ababa, 148
Africa, 112
Against the Stream, 151
Agudas Israel, 129, 243
Allies, 10, 157, 183, 260
Alsace, 71
Alter, 124, 148
America, 9, 10, 15, 17, 49, 68, 221, 291
American-Jewish Joint Distribution Committee, 24n., 63, 219
Anders, 232, 233, 277, 281
Anin, 30
Archbishop of Canterbury, 297
Arensztajn, Mark, 199
Asch factory, 16
Asch, Sholem, 192
Asher, Rabbi, 52
Ashkenazy, 190
Auerbach, Rachel, 201
Auerdow, 54
Auerswald, 229, 236, 237, 255, 256, 276, 285
Austria, 23
Azef, 280, 280n.

Bach, 151
Balaban, Majer, 126, 150, 174, 250
Balkans, 173
Baltic Canal, 14
Bank Marion, 71
Bank of Poland, 30
Bank of Remittances, 30
Baranowice, 227, 228
Bardia, 166, 166n.

Baruch, 105
Barykada Wolnosci, 269
Batuly, 21
Bauch, 264
Bedzin, 33, 121, 134, 156
Belgium, 10, 40n., 71, 141
Belzec, 47, 67, 85, 140, 292, 295, 298
Berel the Pig, 224
Berenson, Ludwig, 162, 176, 177
Berlin, 31, 47, 47n., 63n., 65, 78, 92, 213, 254, 258
Berlin Illustrated Daily, 12
Berlinski, 50
Biala Podloska, 25, 293
Bialystok, 122, 200, 214, 216, 258, 259, 273
Bizet, 125
Black Sea, 14
Blajman, 271
Blond Solomon, 183
Blumenfeld, Rabbi, 192
Bobruisk, 284
Border Patrol, 302
Bordeaux, 71
Borkowski, 128
Bratislava, 156
Braude, Shea, 77
Bregman, H., 242
Brenner, 75, 75n.
Brenner Pass, 53n.
British Royal Air Force, 150n., 290n.
Bulgaria, 145n.
Bydgoszcz, 12, 126, 136
Bzszeszinska, 137
Bzszesziny, 49
Bzura River, 162

CENTOS, (Children's Welfare Society), 202, 219, 234, 255, 283, 333
Calmann, 125
Camp Guards, 163, 170, 176, 181
Cap, 16
Caritas, 113, 119, 140, 214
Catholics, 170, 226, 336
Cesler, 259
Chajke, 273, 274
Chanukkah (1940), 113
Chasidim (see Pietists)
Chelm, 30, 197
Chelmno, 295, 296, 298, 327
Children's Month (1941), 234, 246
Christian, King of Denmark, 37
Christians, 16, 19–22, 24–28, 41, 46, 52, 63–70, 72–80, 90–93, 111–113, 117, 118, 137–139, 166, 168, 170, 199, 217, 252, 267, 336, 344
Churchill, Winston, 265
Ciano, 75
Ciechanow, 191
Citizens' Committee, 162, 177
City Cleaning Company, 147
Cologne, 301
Communists, 262
Converts, 39, 105, 109, 118, 127, 129, 130, 133, 138, 140, 147, 190, 213, 214, 215, 226, 229
Cooperman, 8
Council of the Four Lands, 23
Cracow, 24, 25, 28, 28n., 29, 30, 31, 33, 36, 37, 38, 41, 42, 44, 45, 52, 55, 61, 63, 68, 70, 105, 106, 124, 140, 150, 172, 182, 262, 326
Cracow, Rabbis from, 127
Czebynya, 33
Czechoslovakia, 69
Czerniakow, Adam, 29, 53, 68, 74, 88, 88n., 110, 129, 133n., 144, 146, 147, 148, 149, 152, 156, 164, 190, 212, 224, 234, 245, 247, 254, 255, 282, 303, 316
Czerwiec, 261
Czestochowa, 42, 74, 112, 262, 273, 274
Czyzew, 12

Dallmann (?), 318
Damascus pogrom, 16
Danzig, 31, 136, 139, 140, 141
Death's Head Corps (see Totenkopf)
Denmark, 35n., 37, 55
Diamond, 262
Dickstein, 250, 251
Dobrowice, 181
Drewnica, 121
Dunkirk, 40n.

Egypt, 54n.
Ehrlich, Josek (Yussele) 106, 106n., 145, 231, 232, 280, 281
Ehrmann, 147
Elijah, 150
Eljowicz, 26
England, 17, 35n., 47n., 91, 125, 153, 153n., 157, 166, 174, 183, 216, 221, 270, 301
Epstein, 130
Esterowicz, 281
Ethiopia, 148, 148n.,
Ethnic Germans, 8, 13, 43, 116, 131, 147, 185, 198, 203, 279
Etingon, 91

Falenti, 175
Feist, 266
Feuchtwanger, Lion, 244
Finland, 12n.
Fischer, Governor, 74
Flame, 56
Fonari, 296
Food Supply Agency, 286, 317
France, 19, 21, 55, 71, 216
"Frankenstein," 283, 293
Frank, Hans, 28n., 40, 40n., 55, 65, 68, 125, 171, 218, 229, 239
Fridlajn, 64
Friedman, 79
Friedman, Philip (Felix), 26
Frumke, 273, 274

Gajewski, 169
Galicia, 124, 296
Gall, Archbishop, 30

Gancwajch, Abraham, 113, 120, 131, 185, 188, 193, 200, 212, 243, 246, 250, 271, 272, 277, 280, 284, 332
Gattenhafen, 30
Gazetta Zhitowska, 172
Gdynia, 30n.
Gebetner, 137
Gefen, 191
Gellman, 54
George II, King of Greece, 250n.
George V, King of England, 10
Gepner, Abraham, 19n., 82, 117, 117n., 150, 150n., 214, 286, 287
Ger, 111
Ger, Rabbi of, 247, 265
Gerling (Gerlich?), 178
German Army, 173, 173n., 262, 268
Germany, 10, 15, 22, 23, 33, 34, 35n., 39, 40n., 56n., 71n., 92, 137, 139, 147n., 153, 153n., 165n., 168, 174, 180, 183, 183n., 191, 201, 216, 221, 222, 225. 246, 288
Gertner's Restaurant, 16, 37, 38, 121
Gestapo, 11, 24, 28, 31, 49, 53, 66, 67, 71, 78, 90, 114, 145, 151, 152, 153, 158, 171, 175, 179, 182, 188, 201, 211, 212, 215, 225, 247, 259, 261, 271, 272, 275, 277, 278, 280, 281, 314n., 328, 339, 344
Gilbert, 128
Ginsberg, 155
Giterman, Isaac, 24n., 28, 150, 152, 152n., 153, 157, 157n., 168, 170, 224, 242
Glajchweksler, 248
Glowno, 137
Goebbels, Josef, 45, 175
Goering, 178, 178n., 179, 183
Goldfajl, 41
Government General of Poland, 10, 34, 48, 63, 122, 149n., 180, 212, 251, 262, 273, 303, 325
Gradek, 111
Grayer, Szamek, 314
Greece, 88, 88n.
Grochow, 44, 76, 143, 144
Grodno, 18, 122
Grodzinsk, 129
Gruber's Postal Savings Bank, 13

Gryce, 70
Gurman, 280
Guzik, 24n.
Gypsy, 276

Haberbusz, 78
Hagen, 149, 211
Hallman, 311, 314, 316, 317, 318, 334, 344
Hammer, 198
Hammer and Cross, 153
Hanemann, 164
Hartwig, 111
Hasensprung, 150
Hashomer Hatzair, 12, 56, 151
Hebrew Immigrant and Sheltering Aid Society, 214, 215
Heller, 158, 178, 189, 192, 211, 212, 215, 216, 243, 270, 280, 315, 331
Helsinki, 12n.
Heneberg, 80
Henrikow, 76
Herring, 258
Herrschaft, Adam, 21
Hertz, Joseph, 297, 297n.
Herzl, Theodor, 64, 259
Hess, Rudolf, 183, 183n., 184, 190
Himmler, Heinrich, 112, 262
Hirszfeld, 21, 129, 195, 225, 323
Hitler, Adolf, 9, 22, 40, 50, 51, 52, 53, 53n., 54, 55, 64, 75, 75n., 88, 139, 140, 150, 173, 200, 216, 244, 251, 260, 261, 264, 266, 288, 289, 291, 294, 299, 300, 301, 326
Hochmann, 144
Hoffmann, 183, 313, 317
Holland, 40n., 55, 141
Hoshana Raba (1941), 225
House Committees, 34, 118, 125, 138, 160, 161, 162, 163, 176, 177, 187, 195, 206, 207, 223, 230, 231, 234, 240, 247, 249, 253, 284, 294, 315
Hungary, 12
Hurwic, 277

Institute of Judaic Studies, 282
Iraq, 182, 182n.
Italy, 10, 13, 56n., 71n., 88, 88n., 92, 112, 112n., 114, 148, 260, 288
Indelmann, 35

Jabotinsky, Vladimir, 64
Jalowecki, 230
Janowski, 322
Japan, 56n., 92
Jaracz, 137
Jaszunski, 259
Jewish Community Council (Warsaw), 17, 23n., 129
Jewish Council (Cracow), 37, 42, 45
Jewish Council (Czestochowa), 112
Jewish Council (Konskie), 149
Jewish Council (Lodz), 121, 158, 167
Jewish Council (Lublin), 224
Jewish Council (Paradyz), 149
Jewish Council (Radom), 40, 41, 67, 227, 228, 262
Jewish Council (Warsaw), 9, 17, 25–29, 41, 49, 67, 68, 72–81, 87, 106–110, 117, 118, 122, 133, 140–167, 171, 177, 177n., 182, 190, 191, 195, 209, 234, 235, 238, 245, 255, 270, 314, 314n., 328
Jewish Council (Wartegoj), 73
Jewish Council (Zgierz), 37
Jewish Council (Zofjowka), 121
Jewish Councils, 30
Jewish Culture Organization, 242
Jewish District Aid Committee, 70n.
Jewish Gazette, 52
Jewish Law and Order Service (Lodz), 89
Jewish Law and Order Service (Warsaw), 75, 87, 90, 125, 128, 129, 139, 140, 145, 154, 155, 156, 159, 160, 162, 171, 176, 181, 190, 197, 207, 208, 214, 232, 236, 259, 266, 302, 327, 328, 329, 330, 331, 333, 334, 340
Jewish Special Court, 176
Josefow, 47
Jud Suess, 152
Judaic Library, 109
Judtowa, 282, 284

K.A.M.—City Aid Committee, 332
Kalisz, 8, 10, 12, 43, 115, 175, 212, 213

Kaluszyn, 177
Kamersztajn, 248
Kaminar, 110
Kaminski, 84
Kampinos, 162, 171, 186
Kanal, 311
Kant, Immanuel, 175
Kargel, 164
Karolkowa, 45
Kastaniecki, 21
Katzenelson, Isaac, 120
Kautsky, Karl, 244
Kercelak's Trading Place, 38
Kharkov, 260
Kholm, 252, 254
Kiel, 150n.
Kielce, 30, 124, 129, 141, 248, 262
Kiev, 198, 296, 301
Kirshbojm, Menachem Mendel, 156
Knepel, 121
Kobieszin, 158
Kohn, 158, 178, 179, 189, 192, 211, 212, 215, 216, 243, 248, 270, 280, 315, 331
Kohn, Menachem, 215
Konarski's high school, 68, 72
Koninski, 322
Konskie, 149
Koral, 79
Korczak, Janusz, 77, 80, 185, 247, 322
Kosciusco, 39n.
Kot, Andrej, 21
Kovno, 258
Kowel, 273
Kozak, 250
Kozienice, Rabbi from, 55, 66
Kramszczik, 235
Krasne, 182
Krasnik, 28
Kremensohn, 248
Kundt, 68, 69
Kupcziker, 144, 155
Kutno, 64, 80, 106, 115, 116
Kutzik, 208

Lag B'Omer (1942), 287
Lajfuner, 175
Lajpunger, 250

Lake Ilmen, 260
Lassalle, Ferdinand, 16
Laughter through Tears, 152
Lehmann, 229
Lehmann, Samuel, 224
Lehrmann, 237
Leist, 65, 83, 188
Lejkin, 237, 302, 312, 333, 333n.
Lemberg, 200, 212, 219, 273, 295
Lenczic, 23
Lenin, Vladimir, 244
Leningrad, 12
Letts, 310, 315n., 330, 335
Levin, 29, 277
Lewandowski, 10
Lewartow, 8
Liberty, 151, 152
Lichtenbojm, 133, 133n., 140, 147, 190
Linarski, 90, 90n.
Lithuania, 258, 273
Lithuanians, 257
Lloyd George, David, 299
Lodz, 8, 9, 18, 26, 39, 39n., 43, 45, 91, 118, 120, 144, 166, 168, 180, 180n., 230, 248, 327n.
Lodz News, 8
Lojwicz, 18
Lomsza, 214
London, 49, 65, 249, 296, 297, 298
Lotisz, Oscar, 315
Lowicz, 137, 158, 162, 163, 166
Lubawicz, Rabbi of, 133
Lubelski, Szymke, 121, 121n.
Lublin, 10, 21, 23, 25, 37, 39, 52, 124, 126, 140, 148, 161, 174, 182, 243, 248, 264, 273, 314n., 325, 325n., 333, 341
Lubliner, 311
Lubowicz, 127
Luft, 207
Luxembourg, 40n.

Maccabee sports organization, 22, 232
Madagascar, 70, 71
Majdanek, 325, 325n.
Malicka, 137
Malkin, 42

Malkinia, 321n.
Mandel, 277
Mandeltort, 120
Mannes, 123, 161, 171
Marpa, 12
Marranos, 337, 337n.
Marseilles, 71
Marx, Karl, 175, 244
Maximilian II, Emperor of Germany, 140
Maza, 11n.
Mazow, 247
Mazowiecki, 41
Meissner, 179
Memorial Song, 117
Mendel, 34, 176
Mendele, Rabbi, 150
Mendele Mocher Seforim, 130, 130n.
Mendelssohn, Felix Bartholdy-, 125
Merin, 32, 33, 44, 155, 156, 247, 262
Merysz, 33
Mesz, 278
Meyerbeer, 125
Michalowicz, 137
Mickiewicz, 36
Milajkowski, 15n., 194
Milch, 183
Miller, Hans, 313
Minsk, 247, 254, 258
Mirele Efros, 199
Mirkow, 147
Mlawa, 107, 175, 180
Mlinarski, 156, 156n.
Modlin, 15
Molotov, 177n.
Moltke, 183
Mordi, 174
Morgenstern, 214, 215
Mosciecki, 55
Moscow, 221
Mozhaisk, 252, 254
Murmansk, 260
Mussolini, Benito, 53n., 54, 75, 75n., 88, 260
Myszkow, 34

Nagoszow, 25
Najsanc, 156
Naleczow, 11

Napoleon, 216, 252, 299, 300
Nathanson, 129
National Democratic Party (Poland), 27, 45, 138, 164, 244
Nazi Party, 178
Nazi Party Winter Aid, 132, 222
New Warsaw Courier, 76
Nisko, 33
North Africa, 173, 173n.
Norway, 34, 34n., 37, 55, 150
Nowodworski, 36
Nowy Kurier Warszawski, 172

O.B.W. (East German Woodworks), 316, 319
Oderberg, 33
Okencia, 76
Oneg Sabbath, 275, 295
Opoczno, 175
Opole, 127, 129
Oranienburg, 63
Orleska, 11
Osowa, 197
Ostrow, 8, 11, 33
Ostrowiec, 226, 262, 298
Oswiecim, 105, 108, 127, 129, 145, 156, 204, 211, 215, 231, 232, 233, 248, 271
Oswiecki, 198
Otwock, 12, 35, 48, 49, 55, 56, 74, 90, 112, 118, 176, 228, 257

P.O.W. (Polish Military Organization), 226
Paderewski, Ignacy, 10
Pakolski, 137
Palestine, 26, 44n., 80, 122, 137, 156, 168, 173, 173n., 179, 257
Parczew, 25, 140
Parszawiak, 113
Partisans, 30
Passover (1941), 146, 150, 151, 152, 154, 155, 158, 167, 170, 173, 174, 176
Passover (1942), 272
Pelcowizne, 315
Pétain, 148, 148n.
Peter, King of Yugoslavia, 145n., 250n.

Pfefferman, 233
Pfeiffer, 80
Piaseczna, 132
Pietists, 21, 125, 127, 128, 264
Pinczow, 144
Pinkiert, 138, 180, 197, 210
Piotrkow, 24
Pius, Pope, 47
Plawski, 36
Plock, 139, 149
Plonsk, 127
Plutos, 65
Polaw, 76
Polesia, 212
Polish Central Welfare Council (RNA), 29
Polish government-in-exile, 297
Polish Self-Aid Society, 230
Polish Workers Party (PPS), 49, 71
Pomerania, 132, 136, 152
Pomiechowek, 213
Poniatowski, 236
Popower, 83
Portugal, 210
Posen, 8, 11, 12, 13, 45
Powonzk, 170
Powanzki, 218
Poznanski, 167
Praga, 8, 18, 47, 63, 72, 73, 74, 78, 79, 87, 91, 267
Praga, Rabbi of, 111
Prague, 303
Prog, 33
Property Collection Agency, 342, 342n.
Prussia, 38
Pruszkow, 75
Pruzhany, 259
Przhewarski, 236
Prszibilko-Potocka, 137
Puls, Frederik, 217
Pultusk, 132
Purim (1941), 139, 152

Rabinowicz, Jacob, 320
Rabska, Susanna, 138
Radlinski, 137
Radogoszcze, 61

Radom, 8, 40, 105, 117, 124, 131, 140, 148, 227, 228, 248, 262, 270, 273
Radomsk, 76, 123, 139
Rajsze, 8, 63
Rajtnemer, 143
Rawamazowiecka, 174
Rawicki, 158
Red Cross, 19, 131
Rejowiec, 140
Rembertow, 173, 177, 334
Ribbentrop, Joachim von, 30, 53, 53n., 75
Riga, 258
Ringelblum, Emmanuel, 88, 88n.
Ringelblum, Uri, 15
Riviera, 71
Rivnik, 33
Rome, 53, 53n.
Ronikier, Count, 29, 68, 127, 133
Roosevelt, Franklin D., 148, 260
Rosen, Councilman, 161
Rosen, P., 52
Rosenberg, Alfred, 179, 179n.
Rosh Hashana (1940), 61, 62, 64, 65, 66
Rosh Hashana (1941), 224
Rostov, 242, 296, 301
Rovno, 263
Rubinstein, (the mad jester), 138, 148, 173, 177, 177n., 208
Rubinsztajn, Dr., 248
Rumania, 13, 263, 276
Rumkowski, Chaim, 26, 43, 47, 50, 53, 62, 89, 118, 120, 126, 180
Runda, 240
Russia, 12n., 91, 122, 124, 125, 138, 147, 147n., 165, 165n., 175, 183, 195, 198, 199, 201, 216, 221, 227, 242, 252, 262, 267, 300
Russian Army, 198, 260
Ruzyn, Rabbi of, 264
Rydz, 55
Rypin, 106
Rzeszow, 14
Rzhanowski, 21

S.A. (Sturm Abteilung), 131
Sachsenhaus, 82, 83, 144

St. Petersburg, 208
Samuel, 309
Sapieha, Metropolitan, 127
Schipper, Isaac, 69
Schamme, 204
Schraempf, 44
Schubert, 131, 247
Schultz ("the infamous"), 48
Schultz (shop), 315, 316, 317, 319
Sejm, 26, 28, 150
Seraphim, Joachim, 126
Serbia, 195
Shapiro, 161
Shavli, 258
Shramek, Abraham, 71
Shevuot (1941), 190
Shur, 175
Siedlce, 66, 148, 184
Siegfried Line, 167, 167n.
Silesia, 8, 32, 33, 41
Simon, 151
Sirota, 179
Skierniewice, 30, 181
Sklar, 266
Slonim, 295
Slovakia, 71
Smolensk, 254, 260
Socha, 33
Sochaszew, 45, 166
Sokolov, 257
Sosnowiec, 32, 33, 34, 106, 121, 134, 156, 246
South America, 267
Spain, 53
Spanish Inquisition, 131, 337n.
Spartacus, 71
Special Ambulance Service, 332
Special Court, 239, 253, 276
Spiss, 137
S.S. (Schutz Staffel), 36n., 51, 52, 74, 93, 110, 114, 121, 131, 132, 162, 197, 310, 311, 315, 316n.
Staczszek, 12
Stanislaw, Simeon, 121
Stalin, Josef, 177, 177n., 254
Starachowice, 226
Starogard, 153
Starogrod, 170
Stempowski, 137

Stok, 320
Strasbourg, 71
Straszum Library, 259
Strength through Joy, 252n.
Strength through Malicious Joy Society, 252
Studenicki, 36
Der Stuermer, 68, 135
Stuka, 136
Stupnicki, Samuel, 120
Surov, 267
Sweden, 9, 47
Swieca, 141, 281
Switzerland, 10, 52, 267
Sym, Igo, 137, 139
Szczecin, 23
Szeniszer, 142
Szerynski, 176, 229, 236, 237, 310
Szmerling, 311
Szternfeld, 156, 199, 248, 277, 284
Szymek, 11, 15
Szymke, 123
Szymonowicz, 277

TOZ, 189, 219
Tabernacles, Feast of (1939), 70
Talyn, 168
Tarnow, 262
Tarnowski, Count, 68
Tass, 175
Tczew, 136
Tenenbaum, 266
Thirteen Leszno Street, 107, 110, 113, 115, 147, 149, 157, 158, 166, 171, 174, 178, 179, 185, 186, 188, 189, 192, 193, 199, 200, 203, 211, 225, 231, 250, 251, 277, 278, 284, 312
Timoshenko, 221
Tine, Milek, 232, 233, 277, 280, 281
Tisovec, 66, 67
Todt, 284, 284n.,
Toebbens, 263, 311, 314, 315, 316, 317
Tolstoy, Leon, 300
Tomoszow, 41
Toporol, 165, 187, 191, 287, 287n.
Torun, 8, 11, 72, 241

Totenkopf, 13, 115
Treblinki, 257, 315, 320, 321, 321n., 329, 333, 341
Turkey, 10, 201
Turkow, Jonas, 289
Tworki, 158
Tykoczynski, 79
Tzipke Fayer, 125

Ukraine, 176
Ukrainians, 163, 170, 171, 207, 208, 257, 296, 310, 330, 335, 340
Umschlagplatz, 182, 310, 311, 313, 314, 316, 319, 320, 322, 325, 329, 331, 333, 335
Ulrich, 77
United Nations, 297

Van der Meersch, Maxence, 299
Velvele, Rabbi, 24
Vichy, 71
Vienna, 15, 39, 44, 127, 129, 141
Vilna, 11, 67, 73, 90, 187, 254, 258, 263, 273, 295, 296
Vistula, 55, 150, 190
Vitebsk, 254
Voelkisher Beobachter, 152

Wajc, Emil, 241
Wajgel, 219
Wajnberg, 237
Warsaw Courier, 23, 24, 122, 250
Warsaw News, 17, 69
Warszawiak, J., 246, 247, 250
Wartegoj, 25, 73
Wehrmacht, 13, 324
Welles, Sumner, 30
Wengrow, Rabbi of, 89, 167
Werfel, Franz, 244
Werthajm, 142
Wielcza, 45
Wielikowski, 162, 234
Wigder, 175
Wilner, 284
Winawer, Bruno, 323
Winter Relief, 223, 238
Witasek, 312
Witos, 71
Wloclawek, 17, 22

Wlodawa, 30, 40, 314
Wloszczowa, 12
Wolhynia, 273
Wolnosc, 146
Work Guard (*Werkschutz*), 313, 316, 316*n.*, 324, 328
Worms, 144
Wower, 7
Wroclaw, 125
Wyszkow, 12

YIVO—Yiddish Scientific Institute, 259
YYGA (Jewish Social Self-Aid Organization), 55, 89, 188, 206, 227, 235, 238, 313, 322
Yom Kippur (1940), 72, 167
Yom Kippur (1942), 314
Your Freedom and Ours, 144
Yugoslavia, 125, 145, 145*n.*, 154, 157, 183, 183*n.*

Zabludowski, Benjamin, 67, 190, 254, 255,
Zachariajch, 284

Zagan, Shachna, 152
Zajdler, 248
Zaks, 266
Zalman "The Bourgeois," 12
Zamoszcz, 161, 325
Zarnow, 175
Zawierczie, 33
Zeglembia, 32
Zembrow, 274
Zevi, Sabbatai, 179
Zgierz, 37, 63
Zholibozh, 90, 190
Ziambo, 250
Ziegler, 210, 211
Zilberstajn, Jacob, 241
Zinnenberg, 111
Znicz, Michale, 231
Zofjowka, 51, 92, 121, 158
Zog, King of Albania, 250*n.*
Zubatov, 192
Zucker, Mietek, 35
Zukerman, H., 80
Zwajbojm, 225
Zweig, Stefan, 244
Zygelbojm, 297, 297*n.*
Zylberberg, Kalman, 335